THE NEW POLITICIANS
OF FIFTH-CENTURY ATHENS

THE NEW POLITICIANS
OF FIFTH-CENTURY
ATHENS

W. ROBERT CONNOR

PRINCETON UNIVERSITY PRESS

PRINCETON, NEW JERSEY

1971

This book has been composed in linotype Granjon
Printed in the United States of America
by Princeton University Press, Princeton, New Jersey

For
Edward Christopher

Contents

Preface

PREFACES are for warning and for thanking and I have a good deal of each to do. The reader should be warned that this title does not promise a narrative history of the years of the fifth century nor biographies of the major politicians of the period, nor a discussion of the role of ideology in Athenian politics, nor an attempt to assess the morality or wisdom of the Athenian people or of their leaders during these years. Still less is it an attempt to draw analogies between fifth-century Athens and twentieth-century America. My intention is a much more modest one which I can perhaps best clarify by briefly describing the origin and growth of this book.

Some years ago, largely as the result of historiographic investigations of the ancient traditions concerning fifth-century Athens, I began to become skeptical about many widely held notions about the nature of Athenian political life. I was struck by the discrepancy between the politicians known to us from literary sources and those mentioned in inscriptions —decrees and ostraca. In a study of the influential fourth-century historian Theopompus of Chios, I found reason to suspect that he, and others, had imposed an excessively narrow and rigid schematization upon fifth-century history. As I continued my work I began to see that the writers of later antiquity concentrated on the major or romantic figures, Pericles, Aristides, Alcibiades, to the neglect of men of only slightly less significance or of those whose careers were slightly less colorful. Further, the ethical interests of many of these writers kept them from considering some questions that seem to us vital for an understanding of the period, and even from preserving material that would enable us to make those inquiries for ourselves.

All these considerations convinced me that there was a great danger that the domestic history of Athens during these crucial years would be misunderstood or oversimplified. And indeed in modern literature on the period there were occasional signs that facile moralizing, careless terminology, anachronistic categorizations, and tendentious partisanship were compounding the difficulties inherent in the study of a remote and sometimes insufficiently documented period. A thoroughgoing reexamination of the domestic history of Athens seemed imperative. But I could also foresee a major difficulty: if the ancient documentation had such large lacunae and if so many eminent scholars of recent years had inadvertently been misled, was it reasonable to hope that one more try in the same direction would produce better results? Undeterred, brashly, arrogantly, I set out, hoping two guides might help me. One was the principle, set forth by Arthur Bentley in his *Process of Government,* and others, that the study of political groups is the best way to understand how the government of a state operates. This approach seemed to me to have produced valuable results when applied to other eras and places; perhaps it was time to attempt a more extensive use of it in Athenian history. My second guide was a philologist's prejudice: that a word, properly understood, can reveal that to which it refers. The first of these turned me to studies of political and social organizations in Athens and to prosopography; the second to the vocabulary of Greek politics. I wanted to know how the Greeks talked about political leaders, groups, and the ideals and objectives of politics. I wanted to see if their terminology developed, and I wanted to study carefully the differences between their way of speaking and ours, to see if they contained any clue to the distinctiveness of that civilization.

My two lines of inquiry gradually converged. On leave in the fall of 1966 I went to Innsbruck to try to think out—or rather walk out—the problems and questions that surrounded this study. I left Austria clutching a huge amorphous typescript which attempted to cover the expectations and attitudes the Athenians had about politics, the groups they formed, changes in the pattern of politics, the role of ideology in the life of the city, and much else. This monstrous incoherence was soon trimmed to an investigation of a single change in the structure of politics. Even this, I found to my dismay, was complicated enough to demand book-length treatment, and extensive revision. I spent autumn 1968 in Oxford, reading, rethinking, and revising.

Moreover an awkward problem arose that I had not foreseen at the start. The change with which I was concerned was what is commonly called the rise of the demagogues. But "demagogy" and all its cognates seemed to me, despite their ancient origin and inoffensive etymology, to have become hopelessly emotional. I tried to avoid them by entitling my draft "The New Politics in Ancient Athens" only to find that the phrase "New Politics" rapidly became more emotional than the words I had abandoned. Since I do not wish to monger facile historical parallels, I have tried to expunge that phrase, while retaining references to "new politicians," by which I mean Cleon, Cleophon and Hyperbolus, and some rather shadowy imitators. I do not deny that there are analogies between Athens in the 420's and Europe and America of today, but the perceptive reader will find them for himself without my sloganeering.

Finally, one more warning. I have not attempted exhaustively to document my debts to my predecessors nor to supply a complete bibliography on every problem, nor to revise the notes to call attention to works that came into my hands after early 1969. I have instead tried to refer fairly completely to the ancient evidence and to mention those modern works that seem to me stimulating or fundamental, or, that rare combination, both. The scholar will be able to fill in the gaps for himself, I am sure; the beginner in the field—to whom this book is addressed—will gradually be led to a more detailed knowledge of the scholarship as he works through what may seem to him an already ponderous accumulation of footnotes.

Thus far warnings to the unsuspecting. If I were to name all those to whom I owe thanks for help in the preparation of this book, the list would be long, and I fear I could not make it complete. Several secretaries and assistants, my colleagues, my wife and other *philoi* will be content, I hope, with a *praeteritio*. But I am anxious to thank my university for two term leaves, Harry Avery for permission to quote his unpublished doctoral dissertation *Prosopographical Studies in the Oligarchy of the Four Hundred*, and John Davies for letting me see galley proofs of parts of his *Athenian Propertied Families*. Finally the friendliness and assistance of Erich and Maria Thummer contributed more to this book than I can readily say and deserve greater thanks than I can readily express.

Princeton
August 1969

1. Political Groups in Fifth-Century Athens

Introductory

Political "Parties"

Family Ties

The Extension of Family Ties
Marriage Ties—The Politics of Largess—Is a More Elaborate Model Necessary?

The Political Club: The *Hetaireia*

Conclusion: Political Friendship

ABBREVIATIONS

AJP	*American Journal of Philology*
AthPol	*Aristotelis* ΑΘΗΝΑΙΩΝ ΠΟΛΙΤΕΙΑ, ed. H. Oppermann (Stuttgart 1961)
B-S	G. Busolt, *Griechische Staatskunde*, dritte Auflage . . . bearbeitet von H. Swoboda, 2 vols. (Munich 1920 and 1926)
BSA	*Annual of the British School in Athens*
CP	*Classical Philology*
CQ	*Classical Quarterly*
CR	*Classical Review*
Edmonds	J. M. Edmonds, *Fragments of Attic Comedy*, Vol. I (Leiden 1957)
FGrH	F. Jacoby, *Die Fragmente der Griechischen Historiker* (Berlin 1923-1930; Leiden 1940—)
HSCP	*Harvard Studies in Classical Philology*
IG²	*Inscriptiones Graecae*, Editio minor (Berlin 1913—)
JHS	*Journal of Hellenic Studies*
LSJ	H. G. Liddell and R. Scott, *Greek-English Lexicon*, revised by H. S. Jones (Oxford 1940)
PA	J. Kirchner, *Prosopographia Attica*, 2 vols. (Berlin 1901 and 1903)
RE	Pauly-Wissowa, *Real Encyclopädie der classischen Altertumswissenschaft* (Stuttgart 1894—)
SEG	*Supplementum Epigraphicum Graecum*
TAPA	*Transactions of the American Philological Association*
Theopompus	W. R. Connor, *Theopompus and Fifth-Century Athens* (Washington D.C. 1968)
TGF	A. Nauck, *Tragicorum Graecorum Fragmenta*, with a supplement by B. Snell (Hildesheim 1964)
VS	H. Diels, *Die Fragmente der Vorsokratiker*, neunte Auflage herausgegeben von W. Kranz (Berlin 1960)

1. Political Groups in Fifth-Century Athens

Introductory

POLITICS as we know it came into being, we are told, in Athens during the fifth century B.C. Though hackneyed, this assertion reminds us that many of the terms we use and their connotations, many of the categories for our analyses of political events, have their origin in this period. When we speak of politics, we cannot avoid language and patterns of thought that are ultimately Attic. Yet the fact that in some respects we are very near to the city may deceive us in other respects. Athens attracts us because we feel that she is in some sense ours. Remote and yet familiar, she fascinates the observer and leads him on. Her politics resembles our politics just enough to provoke a facile assurance; her ways are enough our ways to obscure the great differences which separate us. But the origin and dynamic of these ways are as foreign to us as the masks and music of ancient tragedy or the rites of the Mysteries.

The present investigation concerns only a small portion of the history of this obsessive century. Our topic is the development in this period of a pattern of political life which both in ancient and in modern times has often been called *demagogy* —literally the leadership of the people. But the word can readily deceive us. It need not inevitably refer to specious or corrupt ways of appealing to the masses; indeed the early uses of the word are far more neutral and much less emotional.[1] Today, however, the word has become unavoidably pejorative. Its use calls to mind images of irresponsible and self-seeking politicians and provokes the most intense feelings of political zeal; in effect, it prejudges the situation. It has become so charged with emotion that neither apology nor ety-

---

[1] Cf. M. I. Finley, "The Athenian Demagogues," *Past and Present* 21 (1962) 6. On the early uses of the word *demagogos* and *demagogia* see chapter 3 below, *Demagogos*.

3

mology can render it useful. I shall thus avoid "demagogy" and its cognates and simply refer to a new pattern of politics and to "new politicians."

The new form of politics grew and matured with the rapidity of a child's progress to adulthood. A boy born near the middle of the fifth century would have grown to maturity amid the as yet incomplete emergence of this fashion of politics. As an adult he would have seen it flourish and dominate his city. And if in his middle and later years he witnessed its eclipse, he might have guessed that its vitality would nonetheless outlast his own.

The lifetime of this imaginary Athenian youth defines the period of this investigation. The pattern with which we are concerned could only be found once the Athenian assembly, the *ecclesia,* had obtained its full powers, that is after the restriction of the Areopagus council in 462 B.C. By the commencement of the revolutionary period around 412 the new form of politics had fully developed.

To understand the emergence and growth of the new type of democracy which became clear especially in the last third of the century, we must know something of the way the life of the city had been carried on in earlier decades. The organization of civic machinery, the ways of selecting archons and generals, the relations between assembly and council, all the apparatus which we somewhat misleadingly called the "Constitution" of Athens cannot be neglected, and I shall presume that the reader has some familiarity with it.[2] But, as historians have come increasingly to recognize in recent years, the formal structure of the state is but the skeleton of her politics. The nerves, the tendons, the musculature of the body politic

[2] The most convenient modern treatment of Athenian Constitutional history is C. Hignett, *A History of the Athenian Constitution* (Oxford 1952). The most useful ancient source is the Aristotelian *Athenaion Politeia,* hereafter *AthPol.* Comprehensive bibliography and discussions can be found in G. Busolt and H. Swoboda, *Griechische Staatskunde,* 2 vols., hereafter B-S.

is to be found in the organization of forces and often of interest groups within it. It is this structure, rather than the bare bones of the "Constitution," which gives vitality to a city and makes her history come alive.

If, then, we are really to comprehend the changes of which we have already spoken, we must go beyond constitutional history to a study of the ways in which individuals combine to influence the policies of their city. We must investigate political groups and find ways of talking about them that are both clear to the modern reader and accurate descriptions of ancient ways of life.

Political "Parties"

Historians, of course, have not been silent about political groups. They have long recognized that different factions existed in Athens and that the history of the city is in large measure the story of their interaction. But the ways of characterizing and describing these groups are far from satisfactory—consider, for example, the commonly used term "party." Books and essays on fifth century Athens are filled with "parties" of various sorts. One hears of "the party of Cimon," "the oligarchic party," "the radical party," "the peace party," even the "pro-Persian party," and one wonders exactly what the word denotes. The various "parties" mentioned are surely not entities like The Republican Party or The Labour Party. Nor are the phrases close translations of ancient idioms or of official titles. The word is vague and quite often used with some embarrassment or apology. Leonard Whibley, for example, who developed what would today be called a "model" for Athenian politics during the Peloponnesian War, admitted that the three parties which he identified as "democrats," "moderates," and "oligarchs" were "more or less in solution and had a tendency to merge in one another."[3]

---

[3] L. Whibley *Political Parties in Athens during the Peloponnesian War*, Cambridge Historical Essays, no. 1 (Cambridge 1889) 38, and note the com-

The warning was intended to remind the reader that ancient "parties" did not much resemble modern political parties. For the modern party is a rather elaborate organization, operating primarily for the election of candidates; often it professes some ideology or doctrine; surely it outlines some program. The modern party is often a long-lived creature, adapting to new circumstances, and often outlasting any one campaign or any one issue. In ancient Athens where most state offices were filled by lot, where political affiliations were subject to rapid change, where political organization was often thought synonymous with conspiracy, such institutions simply did not exist.[4]

Yet Whibley and other writers persisted in using the term "party" for ancient Athens, perhaps because its vagueness was so convenient. And they had some justification. As long as the historian's primary concern was narrative or "constitutional" history the word was useful. It spared the writer long and often fruitless investigations of exactly who was supporting a particular measure or which groups felt threatened. It enabled the writer to get on with his work as he saw it—recounting the events that actually took place. To speak of "a victory of the peace party" was an acceptable way to indicate that a group of generals willing to compromise in order to obtain peace had been elected in a given year. Among professional historians "party" was a kind of shorthand that was

---

ments of A. B. West in *CP* 19 (1924) 137 n. 1. West's comments in the footnotes seem to me to undercut much of what he says in the text.

[4] Athenian writers did, of course, talk about democrats and oligarchs, and even about a group in the middle, but they did not suggest that these groups were highly organized or had any structure which we might compare to that of a modern political party. If one searches the ancient sources for some sign of parties, *AthPol*, chapter 28, perhaps comes closest. But while it implies a continuity of two groups over generations, it stops short of suggesting that these groups formed any self-sustaining organization. And the passage, moreover, has long been recognized as an inadequate characterization of Athenian politics. See U. von Wilamowitz, *Aristoteles und Athen* I (Berlin 1893) 184. A passage in the scholia to Aelius Aristeides (Dindorf III 446; an improved text can be found in *Theopompus* 36) which speaks of two *politeiai* of the Athenians is equally oversimplified and inadequate.

likely to deceive no one. Anyone familiar with the ancient sources knew that ancient political "parties" lacked close similarity to the organization and continuity of modern parties. As for the layman, less familiar with the primary material, ignorance inevitably breeds more ignorance; the professional could not really be troubled about him.

Gradually, however, a change has taken place in the use of the word. The greater degree of caution detectable in recent allusions to Greek "parties" is probably not due to some sudden blossoming of concern for the lay reader. It is more likely to be the result of developments among professional historians: more sophisticated conceptions of historical cause, a greater demand for precise language and, perhaps most important, a shift in interest from the question "What actually happened?" to the question "How did it happen?" As attention moved from the sequence of events to the way Athenian politics operated, a different and more exact terminology became essential. The term "party" was increasingly recognized as unsuitable, particularly after the publication of a carefully reasoned attack by Olivier Reverdin, in which he contended: "Many historians . . . were victims of their misusage of the terms 'party' and 'political party' to distinguish generalized trends of Athenian political opinion. These words, which are inappropriate, turn out in effect to create that thing in the minds of those who employ them, and thus falsify their vision of historical reality."[5]

It is difficult to measure the full harm which the casual use of this word has brought about, both in contributing to misconceptions of classical antiquity among the general public and in misleading classicists and ancient historians them-

[5] O. Reverdin, "Remarques sur la vie politique d'Athènes au Ve siècle," *Museum Helveticum* 2 (1945) 201-202. Reverdin follows the path pointed out by V. Martin in the *Bulletin* of the Budé Society for July 1933, 28-37. Note also the very general but very perceptive article of L. Pearson, "Party Politics and Free Speech in Democratic Athens," *Greece and Rome* 7 (1937) 41-50. And T. Walek-Czerneck, "Les partis politiques de l'antiquité et dans les temps modernes," *Eos* 32 (1929) 199-214.

selves. Perhaps its most pernicious effect was that, by suggesting to the student of the period that he already had some grasp of the way political forces were organized, it discouraged careful analysis of the structure of Athenian politics. The terminology was facile and, as a result, both political and social history suffered. From time to time, for example, it is apparent in the scholarship concerning this period that social classes and political groups have been confused. The tacit assumption is often made that the "parties" of ancient Athens— "oligarchs," "moderates," and "democrats,"—corresponded closely with social or economic classes, "rich," "middle class," and "poor."[6] That this is at best a half-truth will emerge as our investigation progresses. But the potential gravity of the misconception should be appreciated at the outset. Neither political nor social history can properly be understood if the constituent groups are misidentified.

It is not surprising, considering the cogency of Reverdin's attack and the dangers in the abuse of words such as "party," that the term has been used with much greater caution in recent years. Yet, deplorably, only occasionally have the full implications of his argument been taken seriously.[7] For the most part scholarship has avoided the word but retained the concept. Its efforts have been bent on constructing more elaborate apologies and more skillful evasions of the term "party" rather than on a thorough reconsideration of the question: "What were the political groups in fifth-century Athens?"

Thus studies of the city's domestic politics are confronted with a difficulty. The old schematization into two or three "parties" is transparently inadequate, but no new model has been developed. Some of the reasons are easy to find, for ex-

[6] The introduction to A. Meder's useful dissertation, *Der athenische Demos zur Zeit des pelopon. Krieges* (diss. Munich 1938) xxviii n. 52, makes this confusion especially clear.

[7] In rather different ways both A. H. M. Jones, *Athenian Democracy* (Oxford 1957) 130-131, and Raphael Sealey, "The Entry of Pericles into History," *Hermes* 84 (1956) 234-247, have pointed the way to an analysis of Greek politics that is not based on any of the conventional "party" schematizations.

ample the problem of documentation. The record of Athenian foreign policy during the fifth century is impressive and relatively full, but domestic politics are much harder to study. The epigraphical record seems less helpful; literary sources seem to fail at all the crucial points. Thucydides' record of his city's war with Sparta is an eloquent one, but only rarely does he include details about the processes by which the city made its decisions. He normally speaks of the "The Athenians," not of individual groups or factions within the city. The decrees preserved on stone, for all their interest, were often proposed by men otherwise unknown to us. Even the rich finds of ostraca that recent excavations have turned up, and which might be expected to yield valuable information about the rivalries and coalitions of Athenian politics, are difficult to date and too scattered to be of much help. Thus the task of developing a better description of Athenian political life is not an easy one; indeed, a detailed picture of the membership, organization, and policies of the constituent groups in Athenian politics probably cannot be drawn. But if precision is impossible, a general schema describing the principal types of association and the outline of the operation of these groups is not beyond our reach. Indeed, in some respects it is already well known.

Family Ties

Let us follow the career of an imaginary Athenian politician. Imagine him a young man in the 450's or 440's eager to serve his city and to win prestige for himself. In his day a political career no longer meant what it had a generation or two earlier. Then an aspiring leader might seek to win various public offices, eventually become eponymous archon, and thereafter serve for life in the council that met on Ares' hill. But by the middle of the century this Council of the Areopagus had lost most of its former powers and the archon, like so many other state officials, was little more than a figurehead chosen annually by lot. The generalship, of course, was still an elected office and a very important one. If he wished to hold it, there were minor offices, *phylarchies* and *hipparchies*, that might lead to that higher honor, and he would need to win the respect of other citizen warriors over several campaigns. Good family connections, a handsome appearance, and wealth would help. But a political career, as distinguished from a purely military one, would require influence in the various assemblies of the city—in the law courts, in the *boulē*, that is, the council which first thrashed out most matters of public concern, and finally in the meetings of the *ecclesia*, the frequent convocations of all free adult Athenian males. He would need some sort of power base, men that would listen to him and men he could rely upon. To win the support he needed he would turn to citizens whose interests and attitudes he shared, to men of the same economic and social class, and above all to those he had known longest and most intimately, his own family.

Many of the politicians of this period belonged to what might be called "political families," families that had a tradition of involvement in public affairs and whose scions were encouraged or expected to take part in politics. Cimon, for example, was the son of the famous Miltiades and Hegesypile, a Thracian princess. His father had been a ruler of a huge fief in the Thracian Chersonese, a fighter, a general, a commander at Marathon, and a man deeply involved in the affairs of Athens throughout his life. Miltiades' father, Cimon's grandfather, was reputed to have been a less than brilliant intellect, but he enjoyed the great prestige which Greeks accorded to three-time winners in the Olympic Games. We know little of his political career, but his assassination one night before the Council house, reputedly at the instance of the tyrant Peisistratus' sons (Herodotus 6.103), might lead us to suspect that he was an important man in the city and considered dangerous. One of Cimon's own sons, Lacedaemonius, became a *hipparch*, a cavalry commander, and later, just as the Peloponnesian war broke out, a general. Thus for four generations this family played an important role in the city and had members who rose to positions of great prominence.

It would be natural, then, for an ambitious Athenian to seek the support of his brothers and the other members of his immediate family, the *oikia*.[8] Greek society was far more conscious than most modern ones of the ties which linked the small family to more remote kin, thus providing a further source of political support. Many Greek *oikiai* belonged to larger organizations, *genē*. All the families of a *genos* claimed descent from a common ancestor and were closely held together by six ties conveniently summarized by George Grote:

1. Common religious ceremonies. . . .
2. By a common burial-place.
3. By mutual rights of succession to property.
4. By reciprocal obligations of help, defense, and redress of injuries.
5. By mutual right and obligation to marry in certain determinate cases, especially when there was an orphan daughter or heiress.
6. By possession, in some cases at least, of common property, an archon and a treasurer of their own.[9]

Although the *genē* claimed a common descent, the ancestor on whom they based their genealogy was usually a mythical figure. Thus they cannot strictly be called a form of "blood" relationship. Rather they were groups formed to look after common interests, in effect privilege groups.[10] As such, their

---

[8] For a general discussion of the family in ancient Greece see W. K. Lacey, *The Family in Classical Greece* (London 1968).

[9] G. Grote, *A History of Greece* (London 1884) III 54-55. Cf. G. Glotz, *La Solidarité de la famille dans le droit criminel en Grèce* (Paris 1904) 17-18.

[10] See W. S. Ferguson, *CP* 5 (1910) 257-284, and compare his later comments in *Classical Studies Presented to E. Capps* (Princeton 1936) esp. 151ff.

membership was largely drawn from those who had privileges to defend, that is, from the better-off citizens, and their dependents. There were perhaps a hundred of these *genē*.[11] It is most improbable that all citizens of Athens were *gennetai;* perhaps only a quarter of them were, but it was an important and influential quarter and included most of the families which were prominent in politics during the early and middle parts of the fifth century.[12]

In his important study of the *genos* of the Salaminioi, *Hesperia* 7 (1938) 1-74, Ferguson was able to show that the origin of this *genos* is to be dated in the sixth or possibly very late in the seventh century B.C.

[11] Any exact estimate is impossible. A *genos* sometimes divided into two as the Salaminioi did. Sometimes it is difficult to distinguish a *genos* from an *oikia*, as in the case of the Alcmaeonids where all known members belong to one family. Cf. the next footnote. But we know the names of roughly 60 *genē* for sure: 58 are listed in J. Toepffer, *Attische Genealogie* (Berlin 1889); G. Colin, in *Bulletin de Correspondance Hellenique* 30 (1906) 194-215, adds the Pyrracidae and the Erysichthonidae; and D. M. Robinson, in *AJP* 28 (1907) 430-432, adds the Epicleidae and Glaucidae. The Medontidae are a problem, see Crosby, *Hesperia* 10 (1941) 21. On the Demontionidae see most recently W. E. Thompson, *Symbolae Osloenses* 42 (1968) 51-68; on Democleidae see *SEG* x 362. There is no recent comprehensive study of the *genē*, hence the difficulty of estimating their number.

(Ferguson, *CP* 5 [1910] 277, says 91 *genē* are known, but he obtains that figure by adding to the known *genē* those demes whose names resemble those of *genē* [i.e. end in -*idae*]. This is perhaps the best explanation of these names, but it is not certain.)

[12] Twenty-five per cent is only a rough approximation, for we cannot be sure of the average size of the *genos*. The Alcmaeonidae are said to have comprised 700 households at one time (Herodotus 5.72) but this figure cannot be typical; perhaps it includes households in which the wife was an Alcmaeonid who had married outside her *genos*. (H. T. Wade-Gery has denied that the Alcmaeonidae were a *genos* at all; for the debate see W. S. Ferguson, *Hesperia* 7 [1938] 43 n. 3.) Perhaps 100 adult males would be a reasonable estimate of average size; cf. W. S. Ferguson, *CP* 5 (1910) 279. If we calculate 100 *genē* with 100 members each, we reach a total of 10,000 *gennetai* out of a citizen population of roughly 40,000 just before the Peloponnesian war broke out. (For the population figure see B-S II 764). Thus only 25 percent of the population would be members of *genē*. The third fragment of the *AthPol* (fr. 385 Rose) gives rather different figures for the *genē* which presumably apply to a very early period of Attic history: "Four tribes of them were separated, in imitation of the seasons of the year, and each of the tribes was divided into three portions, so that there should be twelve portions in all, just like months in the year, and these were called trittyes and phratries. In the phratry thirty *genē* were arranged, just like days in the month, and the *genos* was composed of thirty men." This fragment seems to me of little

12

In the later periods of Greek history, from which most of our information about the *genē* comes, they rarely have any political character and have become purely religious and social fellowships. It is commonly assumed that they "had already ceased to play much part as such in Athenian politics, well before the reform of Cleisthenes in 507."[13] But this inference is far from certain. Plato and Lysias hint that *syngeneia* still had political significance in their day,[14] and we occasionally hear of members of the same *genos* helping one another.[15] A further indication of their importance is afforded by the extraordinary solidarity of these *genē* in Greek law and custom. Finally, historical example suggests that there was often too much at stake for a *genos* to neglect politics. The action of one member could affect the whole group, for better or for worse. Consider one instance of the latter: in the seventh century Megacles, an eponymous archon of the city and a member of the famous Alcmaeonid *genos*, committed

---

value and several arguments speak against basing any calculations upon it— not least the suspicious synchronism with the calendar that permeates it. Yet, if its figures are accepted, it would point to a total number of *gennetai* only slightly larger than the 10,000 which I have estimated.

[13] A. Andrewes, *The Greeks* (Cleveland 1962) 82.

[14] Plato, *Republic* 491 c; [Lysias] 6.53. Both use *syngenes* and cognates, a vague word that can be contrasted either with the immediate family (*oikia*), see Plato, *Gorgias* 472 b, *Isaeus* 8.33; or with the wide, mythic family, the *genos*, Plato, *Laws* 878 d. It usually denotes some unspecified or intermediary stage of relationship. Thus these passages in Plato and Lysias are not *proof* that the *gennetai* still had political importance, but they do suggest that relationships beyond the immediate family were still significant. See also P. Mac-Kendrick, *The Athenian Aristocracy 399-31 B.C.* (Cambridge, Mass. 1969).

[15] Note, for example, Euryptolemus' proposal in Xenophon, *Hellenica* 1.7.21, for the trial of his kinsman, Pericles (the son of the famous statesman), for alleged misconduct after the battle of Arginusae. The proposal is really a clever effort to give Pericles a better chance of acquittal.

Thucydides 3.82.6 suggests that the ties of kinship became weaker in the revolutionary period at the end of the century. Thus I presume that before 411, *a fortiori* before 431, kinship ties were stronger than in the better documented period of the fourth century which often colors our view of earlier times. We are more likely, in short, to underestimate the importance of the *genē* than overestimate it. There are occasional signs of intra-genos rivalry. One of these is Theodorus Metochites, *Miscellanea*, eds. Müller and Kiessling (Leipzig 1821) 608.

a religious offense while trying to suppress a conspiracy (Plutarch, *Solon* 12). The penalty fell not on him alone, nor only on his immediate family, but on the whole *genos* (Herodotus 5. 70-71). Generations later the alleged wrath of the gods against the Alcmaeonidae was still a matter of political propaganda, and the Lacedaemonians attempted to use it as a weapon against Pericles, whose mother was an Alcmaeonid (Thucydides 1. 126). Behind the actions of the Spartans is the notion that in Athens the actions of one member of a *genos* might affect all his descendants and relatives, even many years later. That this type of thinking was not foreign to Athenians of the fifth century is suggested not only by the strong interest in genealogy evidenced in the works of Pherecydes (*FGrH* 3) and to a lesser extent in Herodotus, but also by occasional hints in the art works of the period. The presence of a statue of Philaios, the legendary founder of the Philaid clan, in the dedication commemorating Marathon and honoring Miltiades at Delphi indicates a belief in the unity and coherence of a *genos*.[16] When attitudes such as these prevailed, a *genos* would be anxious to maintain and increase its prestige. It might be very cautious about encouraging a member to seek a political career, but once that career was started it was clearly important to see that it was as successful as possible. Thus the *genos* must be considered, I believe, not just as a social unit of some significance but as a vital political unit as well. It was a natural source of support for a member who aspired to a political career, for, as Gustav Glotz remarked, "the *gennetai* were always under a common discipline, and in their relations with other *genē* were obligated always to aid and protect one another with all means in their power."[17]

[16] Pausanias 10.10.1ff. The manuscripts are corrupt at the crucial point but, as P. Vidal-Naquet shows in *Revue Historique* 238 (1967) 281-302, *Philaios* is the necessary correction. This is a valuable contribution, for it compels us to reject certain important portions of the stimulating discussion of religious propaganda in the Delian League by J. P. Barron in *JHS* 84 (1964) 35ff. The rest of Vidal-Naquet's argument, however, seems to me less probable.

[17] G. Glotz, *La Solidarité de la famille*, 18. Possibly all Athenians, whether

14

The Extension of Family Ties

Yet, however helpful the support of *gennetai* might be, and however important family groupings were in the politics of Athens, the politician who sought real power would have to look beyond his own *genos*.[18] No one family, even if very large, could hope to dominate the city. Even the Peisistratids, during their tyranny in Athens, apparently found it advisable to enlist the aid of other prominent families and shared important positions with them.[19] A politician would have to find some way of extending the influence of the *genos*. One method was obvious.

Marriage Ties

Greek *genē* were regularly, though not inevitably, exogamous. Their members could seek brides from other *genē*, at least under most circumstances. When such a marriage was contracted a tie of *kedeia* resulted, a marriage alliance was formed.[20] The effect of such a tie was to bind the two households closely together.[21]

---

members of a *genos* or not, were, theoretically at least, members of a phratry, or "brotherhood." But I am reluctant to assign any great political significance to them. On the phratries see B-S I 250-256 and II 958-964; the comments of W. S. Ferguson in *CP* 5 (1910) 257-284; *Classical Studies Presented to E. Capps* 144-158; and A. Andrewes, "Philochorus on Phratries," *JHS* 81 (1961) 1-15.

[18] For an attempt to trace the role of family groups in the Periclean period see R. Sealey, *Hermes* 84 (1956) 234-247, reprinted in Sealey, *Essays in Greek Politics* (New York 1967) 59-74.

[19] See *SEG* x 352 (B. D. Meritt, *Hesperia* 8 [1939] 59ff.) and the comments of A. Andrewes, *The Greek Tyrants* (London 1956), 109.

[20] The word *kedeia* can mean either "care for the dead" (mourning, funeral rites, etc.) or "connection by marriage." Perhaps it properly refers to the obligation to participate in the funeral which in-laws undertook. In the fourth and fifth centuries B.C. the word and its cognates are commonly used to contrast marriage ties with blood ties, e.g. Aristophanes, *Wasps* 731, Aristotle, *Politics* 1262 a 11, and Lysias 19.48.

[21] One would like to know more precisely just how far the tie of *kedeia* extended. Eustathius on *Iliad* p. 779.43 is explicit but not very helpful. But M. Broadbent, *Studies in Greek Genealogy* (Leiden 1968) 131, is more useful. The connection is likely to be as wide as the *pentheroi* and *gambroi* in Draco's

The value of these ties, as well as their necessity, was demonstrated for any who might doubt their importance in the early days of Peisistratus' tyranny. According to Herodotus (1.59ff.), Peisistratus, in exile after his first seizure of power, made an agreement with the leader of one of the rival factions, Megacles, an Alcmaeonid. The arrangement was that Megacles would help restore him to power and that he would marry Megacles' daughter. Peisistratus returned, but when he refused normal intercourse with the girl the agreement collapsed and he was again driven out (Herodotus 1.61). The story is paradeigmatic: a successful marriage alliance leads to supreme power.[22] But it also contains the hint that a marriage alliance might be less stable than support from other members of the same *genos*. Members of the same family had little alternative but to support the group into which they were born.[23] A marriage tie between two families could be very strong and very lasting, but death, divorce, or adultery could destroy it. A marriage could bind two families closely together, but it was not irrevocable.

The family of Cimon provides a case study in the fifth century operation of marriage alliances. The family enriched itself when Elpinice, Cimon's half-sister, married Callias, the wealthiest Athenian of the time. He was an Olympic victor, a relative of the politician Aristides the Just, and the *proxenos* of Sparta in Athens, that is, the Athenian citizen officially

---

law and these Broadbent defines for us, ". . . the *gambroi* of the victim in Drakon's law are those who marry into his household, the husbands of his sisters and daughters and the members of his parental household. The *pentheroi* are the males of the households into which he and his brothers and sons have married." When families are large, this could be quite an extensive group.

[22] There are signs of the political significance of *kedeia* ties in Xenophon, *Memorabilia* 1.1.8; cf. Plato, *Politicus* 310 b. The speaker in Lysias 19.12ff. describes an unfortunate marriage alliance which his family made.

[23] Note the assertion in Plato Comicus fr. 192 that "no dear one is more reliable than some one of the same blood, even if the relationship is remote.":

οὐδεὶς ὁμαίμου συμπαθέστερος φίλος
κἂν ᾖ . . . τοῦ γένους μακράν.

16

charged with attending to Spartan interests in Athens. Another member of Cimon's family, we are not sure just who, married into the family of Melesias, a prominent wrestling master mentioned by Pindar. Thucydides, this Melesias' son, was an important politician and opponent of Pericles in the 440's and is referred to as a *kedestes*, an in-law, of Cimon.[24]

Cimon himself, probably in the later part of his life, married Isodice, a descendent of the Alcmaeonid Megacles who had been prominent in Peisistratus' day. That marriage may well have sealed the agreement between Pericles and Cimon which Plutarch reports. Some time in the 450's Cimon, on motion of Pericles, was recalled from his ostracism and was privately assured of command of a naval expedition against Persia, on the condition that Pericles be given a free hand in the internal affairs of the city.[25] The parties involved, perhaps agreeing with the barbarians in Herodotus' account (1.74) who knew that "without strong ties agreements don't stay strong for long," may have felt that a marriage alliance was the surest way to guarantee some permanence for the agreement. It did last a few years, but the untimely death of Isodice, followed by the death of Cimon on his expedition to Cyprus, put an end to it. In the 440's the struggle between Thucydides the son of Melesias and Pericles suggests that the two families had relapsed into the rivalry that had formerly characterized their relations.

We need not think that such marriages were inevitably the result of cynical plotting by the power-hungry. But we can readily recognize that a well-chosen bride would bring a valuable dowry with her: the means for a family to strengthen itself, to look after its interests and to advance its prestige. An ambitious suitor cannot be blamed if his heart is captivated

[24] On the family of Thucydides see H. T. Wade-Gery, *JHS* 52 (1932) 210, reprinted in *Essays in Greek History* (Blackwell, Oxford 1958) 246.

[25] Plutarch, *Pericles* 10; *Cimon* 17; *Moralia* 812f. For a fuller discussion of the evidence and the chronology see *TAPA* 98 (1967) 67-76, and cf. chapter 2 below, The Alliance of Pericles and Cimon.

by a woman who happens to belong to a wealthy and influential family. Nor, he might think, would it be proper for him to reject the expressions of mutual respect implicit in the support and encouragement of his new in-laws. Though political aggrandizement was not always the object of the marriage, it might yet be a useful by-product.

The Politics of Largess

In Republican Rome a relatively small number of prominent families seem often to have dominated the city's political life, in part by using marriage alliances to extend their influence. The power which they enjoyed, however, was based as well on the support of numerous retainers, *clientelae*. The conventions of Roman life encouraged, even obligated, a client to support his patron in political as well as in other ways. The relationship between them thus provided a valuable foundation for a political career.[26] Were there not similar means for an Athenian politician to extend his sway? Perhaps, but we know of no exact Greek equivalent of the Roman client-patron relationship. The nearest parallel is the tie between the resident alien, the metic, and his Athenian protector, the *prostates*. But this is not a relationship between citizens and thus not likely to be politically significant. The Greek equivalent of the Latin *cliens* is *pelates*, a very unusual word in the fifth century.[27] Thus it seems improbable that a Roman analogy can be applied to Athens.

But, scholars have asked, may there not have been other ways of winning support, for example by economic pressure? "There were tenant-farmers in Attica and apartments to let in Athens. Perhaps a wealthy family could influence the po-

[26] On the *clientelae* see C. Meier, *Res Publica Amissa* (Wiesbaden 1966) 34-41; R. Syme, *Roman Revolution* (paperback reprint, Oxford 1966) passim, esp. 15, 70-77.

[27] The only example which can be applied to fifth century Athens is Plato, *Euthyphro* 4 a. But the *pelates* is a Naxian. See also O. Schultheiss, s.v. *Pelatai*, *RE* 19 261-264. *Hektemoroi* is sometimes used as a synonym of *pelates*, see *AthPol* 2.2.

18

litical behavior of its dependents by economic pressure."[28] The question is an important one and the suggestion is welcome. But the "perhaps" in its wording represents great uncertainty. We hear little of compulsion and pressure. And although this may simply be the result of an upper-class bias in our sources, the proud and independent Athenian might be expected to resist intimidation. It is true that in sixth-century Athens economic pressure may have been used, and that the geographic arrangement of politics which can sometimes be detected in the history of this period may reflect the domination of wealthy families over the residents of the small farms in the vicinity of their estates.[29] But in the fifth century regional groupings which often indicate the presence of such pressure seem to disappear, or at least significantly to diminish. The reforms which Cleisthenes made after the tyranny was overthrown seem to have destroyed this system, even though he perhaps arranged some judicious gerrymandering to protect Alcmaeonid interests.[30] If economic intimidation was being extensively used by the second half of the century, when our documentation becomes relatively abundant, we might expect some clearer traces of the animosity which such pressure would provoke. The silence of Old Comedy on this matter warns us not to assume that there was any wide use of compulsion.

But where intimidation fails, largess sometimes succeeds.[31] Many of the great politicians of the middle years of the century were great benefactors, donors of parks, dedicators and contributors to the festivals of the city. Private philanthropy

---

[28] R. Sealey, *Hermes* 84 (1956) 241.

[29] On regionalism in early Athenian politics see R. Sealey, *Historia* 9 (1960) 155-180 in answer to A. French, *JHS* 77 (1957) 238-246, reprinted in Sealey, *Essays in Greek Politics* 9-38; and R. J. Hopper, "'Plain,' 'Shore' and 'Hill' in Early Athens," *BSA* 56 (1961) 189-219.

[30] See D. M. Lewis, "Cleisthenes and Attica," *Historia* 12 (1963) 22-40.

[31] Compare the standard of judging a politician set forth in Lysias 17.10. And see J. K. Davies, "La storia di Atene e il metodo del Münzer," *Rivista Storia Italiana* 80 (1968) esp. 213.

was not neglected, as the following fourth century account of Cimon's generosity indicates. Note especially the last sentence with the hint that the purpose of this generosity was political aggrandizement:

> Cimon the Athenian stationed no guard over the produce in his fields or gardens so that any citizen who wished might go in and harvest and help himself if he needed anything on the estate. Furthermore, he threw his house open to all so that he regularly supplied an inexpensive meal to many men and the poor Athenians approached him and dined. And he tended also to those who day by day asked something of him. And they say that he always took around with him two or three youths who had some small change and ordered them to make a contribution whenever someone approached him and asked him. And they say that he helped out with burial expenses. Many times he also did this: whenever he saw one of the citizens ill-clothed, he would order one of the youths who accompanied him to change clothes with him. From all these things he won his reputation and was first of the citizens.[32]

What Gorgias said of Cimon (*VS* 82 B 20), that he "made money to use it and used it to be honored," is more a tribute to his skill in winning the support of citizens too numerous, too poor, and too ill-born to be tied to him in other ways. This is the politics of largess, wherein generosity to city and to citizen wins the gratitude of its beneficiaries and is converted into political support. According to Plutarch, Nicias was one of the great masters of this technique, though the recipients of his generosity were the citizens as a whole, rather than some needy individuals:

> Pericles, whose leadership of the city was based on real merit (*aretē*) and his power as a speaker, could avoid in

[32] Theopompus, *FGrH* 115 F 89. For a fuller discussion see *Theopompus* 30-37.

his relation with the masses hypocrisy and specious eloquence. Nicias lacked Pericles' qualities but was very wealthy, and he used that wealth to become leader of the people. And since he lacked confidence in his ability to beat Cleon at his stratagems of pleasure pandering and slick vulgarity by which he manipulated the Athenians, he tried to control them by financing choral and gymnastic and other displays. In extravagance and favor he surpassed all his predecessors and contemporaries.[33]

The story attests Nicias' skill in this technique. But the theory behind it was most frankly stated by Alcibiades:

Athenians, I have a better right to command than others. . . . The Hellenes, after expecting to see our city ruined by the war, concluded it to be even greater than it really is, by reason of the magnificence with which I represented it at the Olympic games [416 B.C.], when I sent into the lists seven chariots, a number never before entered by any private person, and won the first prize, and was second and fourth, and took care to have everything else in a style worthy of my victory. Custom regards such displays as honourable, and they cannot be made without leaving behind them an impression of power.[34]

The success of Cimon and Nicias is an indicator of how effective the politics of largess could be, both in creating a sense

---

[33] Plutarch, *Nicias* 3. Plutarch goes on to mention the Palladium which he dedicated on the acropolis, and the temple in the precinct of Dionysus, which was surmounted by tripods commemorating Nicias' frequent victories in choregic contests. Compare Plato, *Gorgias* 472 a. His dedications on Delos were also famous, especially the great bronze palm tree mentioned later in the same chapter of Plutarch's *Nicias*.

[34] Thucydides 6.16.1-2, trans. Crawley. Alcibiades goes on to note that his *choregiai* and other expenditures provoke envy among his fellow citizens, but he does not seem to expect that the envy will hurt his political career. On such expenditures see also the introduction to J. Davies, *Athenian Propertied Families* (Oxford, forthcoming), who appositely compares this passage with Lysias 25.12-13, and comments on the importance of such liturgies in Athenian politics.

of obligation in those who benefited from the politician's generosity and in attracting favorable attention to him. But it was a voluntary and casual system, both for the donor and, more significantly, for the recipient. Largess could produce votes in an assembly, prevent envy or annoyance from resulting in an ostracism, secure election to a generalship. But the beneficiaries were not organized, and would probably have resented any hint that they were obligated to reciprocate by supporting Cimon. Thus the politics of largess could not result in the formation of any proper political group nor guarantee any truly reliable support.[35]

Is a More Elaborate Model Necessary?

In our investigation of various kinds of political groups we have in effect been following an imaginary politician through several stages of preparation for his career. He has won the support of his immediate family and of his *genos*, he has made a judicious marriage with the daughter of another respected and influential family; he has wisely abstained from any threats and intimidation of his neighbors and dependents, but rather has cast himself as the friendly and generous benefactor of those who need his help. Given time, ability, and luck, he is likely to rise in the favor of his fellows. Is it really necessary to assume that he must also become a member of some rather highly organized political groups in order eventually to be considered one of the first men of the city? Is it not, in other words, sufficient to explain Athenian politics by positing the existence of a fair number of leaders at any given point in time, backed by their relatives, *gennetai*, and in-laws, and perhaps by a few dependents? Majorities would

[35] Much the same might be said of the tendency of members of the same deme to support one another. Since through the period we are dealing with demesmen would tend to live near each other, they would naturally tend to share some interests and attitudes. It is not surprising to find them supporting each other, and sometimes even unanimous on an issue. See W. K. Lacey, *The Family in Classical Greece*, 278 n. 42; N. M. Pusey, *HSCP* 51 (1940) 218-219; and note Blass' emendation in Lysias 6.53.

be formed by persuasion, through appeals to interest, emotion, patriotism, prejudice, or by the operation of charm, bribery, charisma, and the other familiar weapons in the politician's arsenal. Such a model would be flexible, simple, obviate the need for any discussion of "parties," and have the merit of focusing attention on individual debates and issues rather than on vast overriding historicist trends and tendencies.

Such an approach to Athenian politics has much to commend it. Indeed, for some parts of the century it is perhaps as close an approximation as can be obtained. When in 427 B.C. Diodotus rises in the assembly to challenge the vindictive treatment of the Mytileneans which Cleon has advocated, neither Thucydides nor any other source suggests that he is the leader of a party or of some other organized group. Neither before nor after this is he known to have stepped upon the political stage. We detect no party creed or factional motive in his speech. Perhaps the most reasonable presumption is that he was a private citizen whose outrage at the policy made him stand and oppose it. He became a *temporary* politician and won his case by the cogency of his cause and the cleverness of his speech. The highly flexible, extremely simple model for Athenian politics just described works well in such a case. Furthermore, it has the great merit of focusing our attention on what is known of the debate, the issues and appeals involved, rather than on what can only be guessed: Diodotus' stand on other issues, his background and political associations.

But does the model work equally well for the day-to-day routine business, the tedious hours that some politicians must have spent on matters of detail, personal privilege, amendments and surrejoinders? More important, does the model account adequately for men who, unlike Diodotus, had influence in Athenian politics for long periods of time? And finally, will the model work for the full period we are concerned with, for Cimon and Pericles and Thucydides the son of Melesias, as well as for that obscure son of Eucrates who rose one day in 427 B.C., caught Thucydides' attention and thereby won immortality?

It is here that some changes become necessary in this attractive and useful schema. Our sources, moreover, tell us that some politicians enjoyed rather more organized support. Pericles' most formidable rival during the 440's, Thucydides the son of Melesias, is said to have formed at least some rudimentary organization of his supporters: "He did not allow the so-called *kaloi kagathoi* (gentlemen) to be dispersed in and mingled among the populace, as had been the case, dulling their prestige amidst the masses. Instead he separated them off and assembled them together and made their collective influence count, as if it were a weight in the balance.[36]

Alcibiades would seem to have done something similar, though it is not clear just how large a group he assembled or how they were organized.[37] It would be premature then to

---

[36] Plutarch, *Pericles* 11. The simile used in this passage, καὶ συναγαγὼν εἰς ταὐτὸ τὴν πάντων δύναμιν ἐμβριθῆ γενομένην, ὥσπερ ἐπὶ ζυγοῦ ῥοπὴν ἐποίησεν, might be used to support views which I regard as excessively simplistic: that two groups, or even "parties," dominated Athenian politics—wealthy conservatives and radical proletarians (though the latter seem until Pericles' day to have been able to attract well-born aristocrats as leaders). The view derives some support from *AthPol* 28, on whose inadequacies see note 4 above. But, as I understand the simile, we are not asked to assume that there were two neatly divided and well-organized groups. The implication is rather simpler: there may have been many groups but Thucydides' was prestigious and its attitude made readily visible by the seating arrangements. Thus, opinions of men who might otherwise have remained unnoticed won prestige. In some cases where political groups were divided roughly evenly this unit of support, even if small, might prove valuable, even decisive. For this sense of *ropē* see LSJ s.v. II A.

The passage continues with a further metaphor and the assertion that the strife between Pericles and Thucydides made the old division between demotic and aristocratic preferences deeper, and caused one part of the city to be called the "demos" and the other "oligoi." But even this falls short of stating that Pericles and Thucydides were the leaders of two large and sharply defined "parties." See also chapter 2 below, The Alliance of Pericles and Cimon.

[37] Note Nicias' attack in Thucydides 6.13.1, and compare Aristophanes, *Ecclesiazousae* 297-298, and R. Sealey, *Hermes* 84 (1956) 241.

propose any model at this stage of our analysis. At least one major type of association which from time to time had political effects remains to be discussed. Until this form of organization, the *hetaireia*, is understood, any generalization about Athenian political groups is likely to be inadequate.

The Political Club: The *Hetaireia*

In 1937 American excavators working on the North Slope of the Acropolis in Athens came across an exceptional and revealing find. Roughly 40 feet below the surface, in a deep well shaft, they discovered 190 pottery fragments bearing the name of Themistocles. They quickly recognized that these were ballots probably for an ostracism of the early fifth century, but the most interesting discovery was made when the pieces were more closely analyzed. It turned out that the ostraca were not by 190 different Athenians but rather were prepared by some small group. Fourteen different hands can be detected by anyone who chooses to go to the Agora Museum in Athens and carefully examine these ostraca.[38]

The excavators conjecture that the ostraca were part of a group prepared by enemies of Themistocles for distribution to citizens who were illiterate, or who simply preferred to save themselves the inconvenience of scratching Themistocles' name on a broken pot. When the ostracism was over, the unused supply was dumped into an abandoned well where it remained relatively undisturbed until the recent excavation. Chance, and the skill of modern archaeology, has thus produced an indication of organized activity in this ostracism. The crucial question—who were these fourteen Athenians?—remains unanswered, but it is possible that what the archaeologists discovered was the result of the operation of a *hetai-*

[38] The excavation report by O. Broneer is in *Hesperia* 7 (1938) 228-243. There are also signs of the activities of scribes in ostracisms, that is literate individuals who wrote down the names requested by illiterate citizens. But this group of 191 ostraca—all but one for Themistocles—is too concentrated to admit this explanation.

reia, one of the political clubs of ancient Athens which often had a perceptible effect on the life of the city.

These clubs have been surveyed in several works, notably the exceptional doctoral dissertation of G. M. Calhoun, *Athenian Clubs in Politics and Litigation.*[39] The evidence collected by Calhoun indicates that the *hetaireiai* were dining or drinking clubs of congenial men, usually of roughly the same age and social standing. The clubs are not indisputably attested before the fifth century, but their origin may well go back to Homeric times. Herodotus (5.71) seems to refer to their importance in the seventh century in his account of the conspiracy of Cylon, an Athenian Olympic victor who fancied himself a tyrant and, "winning over a *hetaireia* of men of the same age, tried to seize the acropolis."

It is important not to overinterpret the evidence concerning these clubs. They were perhaps very informal gatherings, often largely social. Surely they were not essentially or inevitably political, still less conspiratorial.[40] Their activities were as varied as the disposition of the members—some of whom were content, no doubt, to dally in the amiable company of flute girls. Others helped each other out financially or supported members who were in trouble in the courts.

---

[39] The dissertation was submitted to the University of Chicago, then printed in the Bulletin of the University of Texas (no. 262, Austin 1913). It is supplemented, especially in the study of the *synomosiai,* by F. Sartori, *Le eterie nella vita politica ateniese del VI e V secolo a.c.* (Rome 1957), but Calhoun's work remains fundamental.

[40] Thucydides' suggestion, 3.82.6, that as the Peloponnesian war went on the *hetaireiai* came to be conspiratorial seems to me probable, though, of course, some of them undertook political activities in pre-Peloponnesian war days. Plato, a generation younger than Thucydides, grew up in a time of their increasing and virulent activity and naturally assumed that *hetaireiai* were formed "to get away with something" (*Republic* 365 d; cf. *Epistle VII* 325 c-d). Thus I would agree with Sealey, *Essays in Greek Politics* 119, that most *hetaireiai* of the early and middle parts of the century cannot be properly called "oligarchic." They normally worked within the democracy, and probably professed loyalty to it. Under exceptional circumstances, when feelings were especially bitter or when there seemed to be a possibility of bringing in aid from outside, some of them—not necessarily *all* of them—began to plan ways of establishing the rule of the *oligoi.*

Others talked politics and argued about which measures and which individuals they would support. And under circumstances which encouraged the politicization of all action, and bred in some men frenzy and fanaticism, certain *hetaireiai* might be led to sedition, assassination, and conspiracy to overthrow the government.

Even under less extreme circumstances the potential value of these clubs would be clear to any clever politician. And Pericles, Cimon, and most successful politicians of the pre-Peloponnesian war days were probably members of *hetaireiai* and beneficiaries of their support; they gained thereby, as Plutarch says of Themistocles, "no little protection and influence (*dynamin*)."[41] Aristides' alleged avoidance of membership in such clubs would seem to be exceptional for his day.[42] Since the *hetaireiai* provided a ready way to extend a politician's influence to a group outside the immediate circle of family and in-laws, one would expect most politicians to take advantage of them. At the same time, the clubs were normally small enough to plan and act in confidence. The author of the speech against Alcibiades preserved with the works of Andocides knew how useful they could be when ostracisms were held: "In situations of this sort those who have *hetairoi* and confederates come out better than the rest . . ." (pseudo-Andocides 4.4).

The groups met in private houses for dinner, drinking, entertainment and talk, and thus were probably only rarely larger than a moderate-sized dinner party. The group of fourteen men who wrote the 190 ostraca against Themistocles

[41] Plutarch, *Aristides* 2. The evidence for various politicians' membership in *hetaireiai* is collected in Calhoun's monograph, see especially p. 18.

[42] I am skeptical of the tradition that Aristides did not belong to a *hetaireia* (Plutarch, *Aristides* 2). It is so much a part of the rhetorical, highly antithetical contrast between Aristides and Themistocles that it must be treated with great caution. At the beginning of the same chapter of his biography, Plutarch says that Aristides was a *hetairos* of Cleisthenes. The word need not imply club membership, but Plutarch's desire for antithesis may have led him to discount a tradition that Aristides was a club member.

was perhaps not far from the average size of a *hetaireia*.[43] But a man might belong to more than one. Thus a politician might win the support of several *hetaireiai* and add them to the alliances he had already forged. Proper coordination would be extremely important for the effective political functioning of these groups.[44]

How many citizens were members of *hetaireiai* during the period of our study? Surely not all, for club membership demanded leisure time and some prosperity. But was it even a large majority of the citizens? This has sometimes been argued, but caution is needed.[45] Our sources tend to inform us

[43] There is no explicit reliable evidence on the size of *hetaireiai*. But there are a number of suggestions and hints in the literature which point to relatively small numbers. For example, Agathon's victory celebration, the setting of the Platonic *Symposium*, seems a small gathering, more than seven, but not *much* more. Andocides' speech, On the Mysteries, is also suggestive. Andromachus (sec. 13) denounced ten citizens who, he alleged, were present with slaves at a parody of the mysteries. Teucrus (sec. 15) named twelve. And Diocleides (sec. 38) reported that on the night the Herms were mutilated he saw some 300 men in groups of five, ten and even up to twenty in the theatre of Dionysus. He was lying, and he does not say that they were *hetaireiai*. But his lie was a plausible one, and the most likely reason for adding the detail that the men were standing in small groups is, I believe, to add verisimilitude and make the large number of 300 seem more acceptable. He implies, in effect, that the mutilation was the coordinated work of many small groups.

Plutarch, *Cimon* 17, mentions a hundred *hetairoi* of Cimon who fell at the battle of Tanagra. If the number is not a mere exaggeration, these may have been, as Calhoun, *Athenian Clubs* 30, suggested, the members of the various *hetaireiai* which supported Cimon, or simply a rather more loosely organized group of friends. The word *hetairos* never seems to be a strictly technical term in Greek and can usually be freely interchanged with *philos*, friend. Thus it is hard to draw a clear distinction between the narrower "clubman" relationship and the more inclusive "friend" relationship discussed in chapter 2 below.

[44] See Lysias 12.43-47 on the coordination of the *hetaireiai* in the revolution of the Thirty.

[45] See G. Calhoun, *Athenian Clubs*, 23. He adduces a passage in Plato's *Apology* 36 b to show that "political clubs [were] one of the things to which the majority of citizens customarily gave their attention." But the passage does not mention *hetairoi* or *hetaireiai*; it does allude to *synomosiai*, but surely Socrates was not attempting to assert that a majority of the citizens were normally *synomotai*. His contention is much simpler. He lists such activities as moneymaking, household management, and the various forms of politics as the sort of things that interested most people but failed to attract him. The passage does not help determine the percentage of club members at all.

most fully about upper-class life in Athens, far less adequately about the poorer citizens. About the latter we can often only conjecture. But it is hard to imagine some of the coarser types of Athenian society—the sausage-seller and other figures familiar to us from Aristophanes, or whatever real life model Euripides may have had for the peasant in his *Electra*—as club members. Poverty and club membership seem normally to have been mutually exclusive.[46] The clubs were, after all, a part of dinner-party and banquet society, and not casual entertainment for everyman. Like the *genē*, they probably included only a minority of citizens, but again a prosperous and articulate minority.

The paths to political power in ancient Athens seem to run in much the same direction. They lead us to small groups whose membership seems regularly to be drawn from the relatively well-to-do. It is not surprising that most of the well-known names of Athenian politics, the Cimons and the Pericles, were wealthy and belonged to distinguished families. Democracy professed to guarantee even the poorest citizen a voice in his city's affairs, but to make that voice heard, coordination, prestige, and influence were very important.[47]

[46] Ephialtes is an apparent exception, see Chapter 2 below, Ephialtes, but "poor" is here perhaps only a relative term. Ephialtes was a general, and thus presumably a man of some leisure.

[47] Thus it is not surprising that many politicians of the later part of the century were not members of *hetaireiai*. Cleon, Hyperbolus, and others perhaps found that there were advantages in avoiding the clubs and instead building up a following among the unorganized citizenry. Admittedly neither Cleon nor Hyperbolus provides an indisputable example, but the evidence points against their membership in any club. It has been suggested that Cleon had a *hetaireia* (see R. Sealey, *Hermes* 84 [1956] 241), but the proof is not convincing. His associate Theorus is addressed as a *hetairos* in Aristophanes' *Wasps* 1238, but, as the scholiast points out, the line is a parody of Alcaeus. The title, *hetairos*, is perhaps ironic, like the description of Aeschines as *aner sophos kai mousikos* a few lines later (1244). The whole tone of the *Wasps* seems to me to point away from any suggestion that Cleon was a member of a *hetaireia*. The case of Hyperbolus is largely an *argumentum e silentio*, but the wording of Plutarch, *Nicias* 11, is interesting, possibly significant. The passage discusses the *staseis* of Nicias and Alcibiades (cf. Plutarch, *Alcibiades* 13) but gives no hint of such a group for Hyperbolus. Instead it states that

Conclusion: Political Friendship

We have attempted in this brief chapter only a sketch of some of the main forms of Athenian political organization. But if our approach has been correct, we can begin to see the main outline of political power in this society. The man who sought political prominence would probably be, during much of the period, a member of a well-established family. And he would recognize that the support of that family was important for his success in politics. Generous offerings and dedications might help secure the good will of the *genos* to which he probably belonged. He would choose his wife carefully. The next logical step would be to join a *hetaireia* or two, and in the company of his fellows show himself affable, sensible, and reliable. When the conversation turned to politics, his ideas would have an audience and, if all went well, it would be easy to put forth the suggestion that his colleagues, and their friends and allies, appear at the next assembly to back him, or that they render some other service in the council or in the law courts. With good luck and a persuasive manner he would be on the way to a political career.

This may seem to a modern reader rather diverse backing —family, members of the same *genos*, drinking companions. But to a Greek this was a coherent unit. All these were *philoi,* a word which in ancient usage normally included both friend

---

he got his influence (*dynamis*) from his boldness, not his boldness from his influence. (In Plutarch, *Aristides* 2, this word for influence, *dynamis*, describes the power Themistocles obtained from his membership in his *hetaireia*.) Plutarch may be hinting, in other words, that Hyperbolus reversed the usual pattern in politics—he lacked organized support, but acted boldly nonetheless.

Thucydides 8.54.4 seems to suggest that Peisander was not a member of the political clubs he approached. Cf. A. E. Raubitschek's review of F. Sartori, *AJP* 80 (1959) 87.

For many other politicians of the period, especially the *demagogoi*, the sources mention no *hetaireiai*, though, of course we cannot be sure that their silence is not mere accident. As will appear later, however, there is some basis for thinking that these politicians adopted a rather different technique for acquiring political support.

30

and relative, all those who were really close to a man.[48] Beginning Greek books tell one to translate it "friend"; "one's own people" might be more exact. But we need not quibble over the word, provided the inclusiveness of the Greek term is kept in mind.[49]

Thus, in effect, we have been studying throughout this chapter what might be called the kinds of *philia* that have political implications, "political friendship" for short. And from even this brief study it emerges that the groups which operated in Athenian politics were largely "friendship" groups of various sorts. The normal way to influence was to acquire the right friends and to see to it that they were active in rendering support. And, *per contra*, one of the best ways to destroy a politician was to win away or drive away his *philoi*. Hence the politically motivated trials of associates of famous politicians.

Athenian politics, thus, were often what we would call highly personal. But this is not to say that considerations of economic interest, class loyalty, or patriotic concern did not operate in ancient Athens. It would be a strange world indeed where these were entirely eliminated. They were surely present in Athens, but in a way that differs significantly from what we moderns expect. These considerations found expression through friendship groups. Then, as now, a citizen's social class, economic status and his conception of what was good for the city influenced his choice of friends. "Like attracts like" says the Greek proverb, and in the Greek city likeminded men formed groups and the groups gave voice to the economic and social concerns of their members. Modern analogies are easy to find, but they may deceive us in some important respects. In today's world political parties are the commonest vehicle for the attainment of political goals. Pressure

---

[48] One exception: Euripides, *Orestes* 80.

[49] Cf. A.W.H. Adkins, " 'Friendship' and 'Self-sufficiency' in Homer and Aristotle," *CQ* 13 (1963) 30-45.

groups and lobbyists work through them; the aspiring politician will probably join one early in his life; even radical and revolutionary groups must plan their activities with an eye to the probable reactions of major parties. But in a society where no political parties exist, smaller groups, even less consciously political groups, can have a great importance in political life. They take on many of the functions which we would ascribe to parties.

Thus he who would understand Athenian politics must understand Athenian friendship. He must inform himself not only about the meetings of the assembly and the council, but about the gatherings of families and friends as well. If he will understand what happens in the bouleuterion or on the Pynx, let him study the clubs and the symposia and the genealogical charts of families. And he must not stop there. He must ask what conventions and attitudes governed relations among *philoi*; he must ask what friends expected of one another and what they considered to be their duty to the city. Only when he understands political friendship will he properly comprehend Athenian politics.

2. Political Friendship and Civic Loyalty

Introductory

The Operation of Political Friendship
Anecdotes concerning Political Friendship—Friendship as a Motive for a Political Career—The Obligations of Friendship

Some Ethical Problems in Friendship
Friends and the City—Reflections of the Problem in Tragic Poetry: The *Antigone*

The Responses of the Politicians
Themistocles—Aristides—Ephialtes—Pericles

The Effects of Political Friendship
The Alliance of Pericles and Cimon—The Political Function of Friendship

Toward a New Model
Many Small Groups—Coalitions—Personal Ties—Were the Poor Included? —A Test Case: The Ostracism of Hyperbolus

2. Political Friendship and Civic Loyalty

Introductory

IN THE second book of his *Reminiscences of Socrates* Xenophon recalls a day when Crito complained to Socrates that it was difficult for a man to live in Athens if he wanted to mind his own business. He added, "Right now . . . certain people are bringing actions against me, not because I did them any wrong, but because they suspect that I'd rather pay them off than have trouble" (*Memorabilia* 2.9.1). Socrates then suggested that Crito find himself someone who would serve as a good watch dog and protect him from these intrusions. "You can be sure," he told Crito, "that there are men here in Athens who would be quite honoured to count you as a friend." Following this advice, Crito found one Archedemus, "an excellent speaker and man of affairs, but poor," whom he won over by gifts and courtesies. Crito soon found himself enjoying the advantages which the friendship of even an impoverished and relatively obscure politician could bring. When, for example, cases were brought against Crito, Archedemus in turn brought suit against those who had filed them, and would not withdraw until Crito was out of trouble.[1]

We have no way of knowing how often episodes similar to this took place in the fifth century, but Xenophon's story of Crito and Archedemus points in the same direction as the investigation in Chapter 1. It once again suggests the impor-

---

[1] Archedemus (*PA* 2326) elsewhere receives a rather bad press. The comic poets christen him "Bleary eyes" (Aristophanes, *Frogs* 588, cf. Eupolis fr. 9), impute foreign birth to him (Eupolis fr. 71), and ascribe to him "primacy in the abominations of the upper world" (Aristophanes, *Frogs* 425). Prose writers are more subdued: Xenophon, *Hellenica* 1.7.2, says he was a leader of the *demos* in 406 B.C. and active in the prosecution of the generals after the defeat at Arginusae; Lysias 14.25 suggests he was a bad influence on the younger Alcibiades; Aeschines 2.139 and Plutarch, *Moralia* 575 d, say he pursued a pro-Theban policy. The period of his greatest political influence was probably in the last years of the Peloponnesian war, though the allusions to him in Eupolis would suggest some prominence a decade or so earlier.

tance of *philia*, both in politics and in daily life. We have already noted the principal types of friendship groups in ancient Athens; but we must take a wider approach to political friendship, initially by looking at the ways in which it operated and then by examining an ethical problem which it raised and which few Greek politicians could avoid.

The Operation of Political Friendship

Some of the ways in which friendship could affect the operation of politics have already been pointed out; Archedemus' support of Crito in the law courts indicates that it was not only in the assembly and the council that friends could be important. But of course it was in the legislative process that friends could be most crucial—they could supply a claque and the support needed to form a majority.[2] They could heckle other speakers and sometimes provide the politician with a spokesman in the Council (the *boulē*) when he himself was not a member.[3] And even outside the city walls friends could be useful. Friends of Pericles, for example, are said to have kept the ostracized Cimon from joining the Athenian ranks just before the battle of Tanagra.[4] Furthermore, a friend who was a politician could help a citizen gain office, put into his hands an administrative or military task that would bring him repute, arrange some ambassadorial junket or intercede on his behalf in a law court.[5] The pattern is familiar enough today and was no less common in antiquity.

[2] On claques see G. Calhoun, *Athenian Clubs*, 121-123.

[3] Lot was used to select the members of the *boulē*, thus a politician could not be sure that he would be included. Further, there was a restriction on the number of times a man could serve: a second nonconsecutive term was permitted but no more. See C. Hignett, *A History of the Athenian Constitution*, 226-228. Unless a man was a general, and thus regularly sat with the *boulē*, he would have to rely on his influence with its members if he wished to have a say in its proceedings. For this reason, if for no other, friendship would be likely to have considerable importance in the politics of ancient Athens.

[4] Plutarch, *Pericles* 10; cf. *Cimon* 17.

[5] Compare the discussion of friendship in Plutarch's *Precepts of Statecraft*, esp. 808 b-c; and note the useful article by S. Perlman, "The Politicians in the Athenian Democracy of the Fourth Century," *Athenaeum* 41 (1963) esp. 343 n. 82.

Anecdotes Concerning Political Friendship

Scattered through Plutarch and other writers, mostly of Hellenistic and Roman times, are anecdotes which convey some idea of the varied ways in which friends might assist a politician. The stories are not invariably accurate and they are perhaps of greater value as indications of the kinds of activities which friends undertook than as exact descriptions of what historical figures actually did. Yet as illustrations they are useful and interesting, and in some cases there is no reason to doubt them.

For example, in the 25th chapter of his life of Themistocles Plutarch repeats an old story: that friends of the exiled Themistocles transferred some of his wealth, quite illegally, from Athens to his retreat in Asia. Another story which also goes back to at least the fourth century B.C. has already been mentioned in Chapter 1, The Politics of Largess; young men who accompanied Cimon gave small donations to those who asked for his help. And Nicias' friends, we are told in Plutarch, *Nicias* 5, gathered around his door and turned away casual callers who might otherwise disturb his leisure and privacy. Old comedy also mentions a friend of Nicias, as anonymous speaker in a fragment of one of Telecleides' plays, who proclaims at embarrassing length that he will not tell the details of an embarrassing episode in which Nicias paid off an informer:

> Nicias, Niceratus' son,
> gave him three *mnas,* and then an extra one.
> The reason why I know full well—
> but I won't tell;
> the man's a friend of mine;
> his qualities are extra-fine.[6]

---

[6] Telecleides fr. 41 quoted *apud* Plutarch, *Nicias* 4:
τέσσαρας δὲ μνᾶς ἔδωκε Νίκιας Νικηράτου·
ὧν δ'ἕκατι τοῦτ' ἔδωκε, καίπερ εὖ εἰδὼς ἐγὼ
οὐκ ἐρῶ, φίλος γὰρ ἀνήρ, σωφρονεῖν δέ μοι δοκεῖ.

In real life friends were perhaps more discreet and their services more concrete. Ephialtes, who is said not to have been a rich man, was offered ten talents by some friends of his, but thought it better to turn down this ancient equivalent of a campaign fund contribution.[7]

But it was Pericles who made the most extensive use of friends, if we are to believe the ancient anecdotes. They mention changes made in the Council of the Areopagus, colonies founded, a Megarean decree introduced for him; they even supply the names of some of these friends: Ephialtes, Lampon, Charinus, and the ubiquitous Metiochus:

> Metiochus is our general;
> Metiochus checks our roads;
> Metiochus certifies our cereal
> And approves our daily loaves.
> YES—Metiochus tends to all.
> BUT—Metiochus is in for a fall.[8]

Some of the details of these stories can, and should, be doubted, but the types of activities which they report were probably not unusual ones for the friends of politicians in ancient

[7] Aelian, *Varia Historia* 11.9 and cf. 2.43 and Plutarch, *Cimon* 10. It was recognized in antiquity that accepting money from someone could so obligate a person that the relationship with the donor became practically that of a slave to a master. See Xenophon, *Memorabilia* 1.5.6, and cf. L. Pearson, *Popular Ethics in Ancient Greece* (Stanford 1962) 17 and 145-148, and nn. 11-12 on p. 248.

[8] The doggerel on Metiochus is found in Plutarch, *Moralia* 811f. Compare Archilochus fr. 122 (Lasserre-Bonnard) and below, The Alliance of Pericles and Cimon. Menippus, Ephialtes, Charinus, and Lampon are mentioned a few pages later in the same essay: 812 d. Compare Chapter 7 of Plutarch's life in Pericles. Both this chapter and *Moralia* 811 c ff. mention the second century B.C. philosopher Critolaus, and his advice that the statesman should reserve himself for important occasions, just as the Athenians used their two state galleys, the Paralus and the Salaminia, only on important missions. Critolaus *may* have cited Pericles as one who followed this practice; if so, he would be the likely source for some or all of the information which Plutarch gives. This would suggest that what I believe to be an error in Plutarch's dating of Charinus' Megarean decree (see the following note) was not first made by Plutarch but was inherited by him from earlier sources.

Greece.[9] The implication of these stories is very similar to what Xenophon has Socrates say about the value of friends:

> The good friend puts himself at the disposal of any need of his friend, whether it's his personal finances or his public career. If there's occasion for generosity, he joins in helping; if it's the torment of anxiety, he contributes his financial resources and his energy. He'll speak in his favor; he'll even use force. He shares his friends' joys when they are doing well, and backs them up when they're in trouble. In whatever service hands can render, whatever foresight eyes attain, whatever ears can hear or feet traverse, the friend does not fail in his assistance.
>
> Xenophon, *Memorabilia* 2.4.6-7

The friend, in other words, was the *allos autos*, the extension of the self.[10] In the same passage Socrates points out that many people failed to cultivate their friendships properly. But he is not trying to suggest that no one was aware of the political utility of friends. To the Greeks, that idea was no piece of arcane wisdom, but a lesson easily observed and often expressed. In the argument between Creon and Oedipus, Sophocles alludes to the political importance of friends in these lines: "Isn't this plot of yours sheer folly, to hunt a

---

[9] Doubts might particularly be felt about the implication that Ephialtes was merely the agent of Pericles in the reform of the Areopagus. See C. Hignett, *History of the Athenian Constitution*, 197; R. Sealey, *Hermes* 84 (1956) 245. Despite the confidence of K. J. Dover, *AJP* 87 (1966) 203-209, I continue to feel that the case for a fifth century date for Charinus' Megarean decree is uncomfortably weak. See *AJP* 83 (1962) 225-246. Dover's argument seems to me to depend on the unproved assumption that "The Megareans" in *Pericles* 30.4 means Megarean historians, and then on further inferences from the miserable remains of these perhaps deservedly ill-remembered writers to show that they must all have worked at a relatively early date. When Dover has finally dated every one of them before the end of the third century B.C., he optimistically concludes that "it is not credible that this historian back-dated an event of ca. 351 by eighty years." I find this chain of reasoning tenuous and retain my previous skepticism about Charinus and his decree.

[10] Aristotle, *Nicomachean Ethics* 1169 b 6. This became a common characterization of friendship in antiquity. See G. Bohnenblust, *Beiträge zum Topos* ΠΕΡΙ ΦΙΛΙΑΣ (Berlin 1905).

tyranny without the support of the people and of friends—for that's a beast which is caught with the people and with money" (Sophocles, *Oedipus Tyrannos* 540-542).

To a Greek audience these lines would probably not seem a fantasy about some never-never land of poetic imagination but rather a link between the kind of reality they knew and the kind which was confronting the figures in Sophocles' tragedy. For the poet alludes to something that must have been clear to any clever politician. The complaint of a later writer that the more he looked at politics the more he despaired of ever following that career, "for it was impossible to accomplish anything without true friends and trusted *hetairoi*," simply translates the lines of Sophocles into the hard prose of political reality.[11]

Friendship as a Motive for a Political Career

There is one further political implication of friendship that must be mentioned, not only for its inherent interest but also because it symbolizes the central position of friendship in Athenian political life.

From time to time the ancient sources suggest that the desire to help friends may have encouraged a citizen to go into politics. According to Xenophon, for example, when Socrates was trying to convince Plato's relative Charmides to go into politics he used, among others, the following argument to persuade the reluctant youth: "Don't neglect the city's affairs, if you can do something to improve them. For if they go well not just the other citizens but also your friends and not least yourself will profit" (*Memorabilia* 3.7.9).[12]

---

[11] Plato, *Epistle VII*, 325 c-d. The letter is sometimes thought a forgery, but its author, whether or not he understands Plato's philosophy, writes with conviction about Greek politics. Aristotle's inclusion of *polyphilia* as one of the bases of political power (*Politics* 1284 a 21) confirms what the writer of the letter has to say about political friendship.

[12] Socrates does not seem to have been successful in persuading Charmides to enter democratic politics, but under the Thirty Tyrants he became one of the ten rulers of the Piraeus and died in the same battle as his cousin Critias, Xenophon, *Hellenica* 2.4.19.

The suggestion in this passage that a man might be led into politics in part to help his friends is confirmed in another section of the same work. Once when Critoboulus and Socrates were discussing friendship, the philosopher drew a distinction between those who go into politics "to embezzle, to treat others with violence, to live in luxury," and the man who "seeks to be honoured in a state that he may not be the victim of injustice himself and may help his friends in a just cause, and when he takes office may try to do some good to his country."[18] The former might find that his selfish motives interfered with friendship. But why, Socrates asks, should the latter be incapable of cooperating with other similarly-minded men? "Will his connection with other gentlemen (*kaloi kagathoi*) render him less capable of serving his friends? Will he be less able to benefit his city with the help of other gentlemen?"

Thus Socrates, at least as Xenophon recollected him, assumed that one possible reason for going into politics was the desire to help one's friends. The idea does not seem to be an esoteric notion restricted to the circle of Socrates and his admirers, but rather is expressed in a way suggesting that it was widely and perhaps uncritically, held.

The Obligations of Friendship

It is possible to go one step further. It can be seen, I believe, that political groups in fifth century Athens were largely groups of *philoi*; it can be shown that the Greeks themselves were aware of the importance of friends in politics; and finally it can be added that Greek ethical thought was much concerned with the extent and nature of the obligations which a man had to his friends. This concern is clear in the ethical treatises of later antiquity, in Cicero and in Plutarch, but is also present in some of the passages we have already seen in Xenophon, and in Platonic dialogues such as the

---

[18] Xenophon, *Memorabilia* 2.6.25, trans. E. C. Marchant in the Loeb Classical Library.

Euthyphro. But it is in the *Meno* that this topic is treated in a way that is most relevant to our inquiry. Socrates asks Meno what he thinks *aretē* (excellence) is, and Meno, brashly and confidently, assures Socrates that the answer is easy. He then proceeds to commit the inevitable and expected error: he gives examples of several kinds of *aretē* rather than a comprehensive definition. He mentions the *aretē* of a man, the *aretē* of a woman, the *aretē* of a child, the *aretē* of a free man, the *aretē* of the slave. He does not discuss each one, but he explains what he thinks *aretē* is for a man: "to be able to attend to the affairs of the city, and in attending to them to see that he helps his friends and hurts his enemies, while taking care that he himself is not harmed" (Plato, *Meno* 71 e).

Meno, like Xenophon, is no brilliant intellect, and his opinions are often quite conventional. But therein is the great value of the passage for us. For the sentiment that he expresses is likely to be one that was widely held by the Athenian "man in the street," and thus by the Athenian voter.[14] Polemarchus' position in the *Republic* is based on a similar notion,[15] and the same idea is expressed without embarrassment by Solon when he prays that he might be a joy to his friends and bitterness to his enemies.[16]

Euripides draws a Heracles of a similar disposition in the *Heracles Driven Mad*. Just after Heracles' nick-of-time arrival his father Amphitryon says to him: "It's your nature to befriend your friends and to hate your enemies, but don't go too far" (Euripides, *Heracles Driven Mad* 585-586).[17] Amphitryon knows that his son will want to act on the basis of this widely-held principle: help your friends and hurt your

---

[14] Note A.W.H. Adkins' exegesis of *Meno* 71 e in *Merit and Responsibility* (Oxford 1960) 229-231. Callicles in Plato's *Gorgias* represents an extremist version of the same attitude; See *Gorgias* 492 b-c.

[15] *Republic* 332 d. See Adkins' explication in *Merit and Responsibility*, 279 n. 6.

[16] Fr. 13, line 5. Cf. Archilochus fr. 120 (Lasserre-Bonnard).

[17] For the interpretation of the opening words, *pros sou*, see Wiliamowitz' note on this line in his edition. Note the similar sentiment in fr. 1092 (Nauck).

enemies. But he fears that Heracles may do something excessive, and he vaguely foresees the possibility that in fact materializes a little later when Heracles is driven mad and wildly kills his own children.[18]

In the three examples cited—Solon's prayer, Meno's conversation with Socrates, and Amphitryon's comments to Heracles—a single principle emerges which is the crystallization of much of what we have been studying. Friends were obligated to help one another and were so strongly bound to mutual assistance that a man might undertake a political career, file law suits, contribute time or money, even on occasion risk his life for the well-being of friends. It is this friendship ideal which ultimately gave strength and cohesion to the various political groups that we have investigated. Any man who values his own friends will find much to admire in this ideal, but at the same time he will recognize that loyalty to friends is rarely an untroubled matter. He will perhaps foresee some of the conflicts which might beset a man whose view of human excellence was, like Meno's, "to be able to attend to the affairs of the city, and in attending to them to see that he helps his friends and hurts his enemies, while taking care that he himself is not harmed."

[18] As Aristotle recognized, the pitiable and horrible acts which tragedy depicts are most likely to take place "when the painful deed is done in the context of close family relationships (*philian*)" (*The Poetics* 1453 b 14ff, trans. G. F. Else in *Aristotle's Poetics: The Argument* [Cambridge, Mass. 1957]). Thus in the *Heracles Driven Mad* Heracles' insanity results in the murders of his own children; in Sophocles' *Trachiniae*, Deianeira is deceived by Nessus and poisons her husband Heracles. Or consider the *Medea*. Medea quite deliberately destroys her own children in an attempt to harm Jason and his new bride. Although she is a barbarian princess, Medea acts on the Greek idea of hurting her enemies; but in her intense desire to be "a burden to my enemies and well disposed to my *philoi*" (line 809) she fails to recognize who her true *philoi* are. Thus, though the motivation is quite different, both Medea and Heracles misconceive their situations, act excessively, and destroy their own children. They suffer because of a *hamartia*, which is to be understood not as some "tragic flaw" but, as G. F. Else has shown, as "the doer's ignorance of the close blood relationships between the doer and sufferer of the *pathos*" (*Aristotle's Poetics: The Argument*, 414, cf. 379-385). For further comments on the role of *philia* in Greek tragedy see below, Reflections of the Problem in Tragic Poetry. . . .

Some Ethical Problems in Friendship

οἱ μὲν γὰρ οὐδὲν διὰ φιλίαν παρὰ τὸν λόγον ποιοῦσιν, ἀλλ'
ἄρνυνται τὸν μισθὸν τοὺς κάμνοντας ὑγιάσαντας· οἱ δ' ἐν
ταῖς ἀρχαῖς πολλὰ πρὸς ἐπήρειαν καὶ χάριν πράττειν. . . .

For physicians never neglect reason for friendship's sake.
They earn their fee by healing the sick. But those in political office often do many things for spite or favor.

Aristotle, *Politics* 3. 1287 a 35-38

Favoritism in politics is an old and persistent story, familiar
to Aristotle and familiar to us. Modern politics, too, relies
heavily on "connections," "influence," personal ties and ac-
quaintances, some of which claim and perhaps even deserve
to be called "friendship." But the differences which separate
classical and modern attitudes toward political friendship are
even more important than the similarities.

The contrast takes many forms but can perhaps best be
understood by a comparison of two rather arbitrarily selected
statements by two famous politicians, one a recent president
of the United States, the other an Athenian leader of the fifth
century. Arthur Schlesinger's account of the presidency of
John F. Kennedy contains the following notes made by the
president on the subject of private and public morality: "We
consider it graft to make sure a park or road, etc., be placed
near property of friends—but what do we think of admitting
friends to the favored list for securities about to be offered to
the less favored at a higher price? . . . Private enterprise system . . . makes OK private action which would be considered
dishonest if public action"

(Schlesinger, *A Thousand Days*, p. 101).

Plutarch records the anecdote that Themistocles once
looked upon the archon's seat and remarked, "May I never sit
on such a throne without seeing to it that my friends get bet-

ter treatment than my enemies."[19] The comment sounds odd to modern ears, not because we are surprised to find a politician favoring his friends, but because of the openness with which this favoritism is expressed. It fails to acknowledge that curious but important line we draw between what is permitted in private life and in public life. A modern politician may find the line peculiar and indicative of weaknesses in our private morality, but he would be very cautious about any public statement that seemed to promise preferential treatment for his friends. Themistocles' comment, on the other hand, though by no means the only attitude adopted by Greek politicians toward their friends, had strong support in ancient Greece. It is, after all, nothing other than the practical application of the definition of *aretē* given by Meno, or an attempt to realize in the here-and-now of political life the prayer which Theognis tells Cyrnus that he addressed to the king of the gods: "Cyrnus, I pray Zeus will grant me an even score both with my friends who love me—and an even greater power over my enemies. This way I'd seem to be a god among men, if only fate catches up with me when I've evened up all scores" (Theognis A 337-340).

Every Greek knew one was expected to reciprocate a friend's help. The man who failed to do so was a *deilos* just as much as the man who was too cowardly to stand up against an enemy. In Theognis' view both would be both physically and morally repulsive: "Don't let anyone persuade you, Cyrnus, to make a repulsive (*kakos*) man your friend. What good is it to have a *deilos* for a friend? If you're caught in grievous toil and destruction, he won't rescue you, and if he's had some good luck, he won't want to share it with you.

---

[19] Plutarch, *Moralia* 807 b; cf. *Aristides* 2. The anecdote may be apocryphal, though it is interesting that it seems to suggest a time when the archon still had considerable powers, i.e. the early fifth century, probably before the introduction of sortition in 487/6. In any event, it is based on an attitude towards friends that was widespread in Greek antiquity.

You're wasting your time doing favors to *deiloi*, you might as well try to sow the gray salt sea. You won't harvest waves of grain from the sea, nor get back your favors from the ugly" (Theognis A 101-108).[20] No politician once in office would be anxious to have the men who had supported him up to this point brand him a *deilos* for refusing to repay their assistance. Greek poetry and song, indeed the whole apparatus of Greek *paideia*, emphasized the importance of loyalty to a friend:

> To me it would make
> No difference when or how my life should finish
> If through continuing it, saving it,
> I brought disaster on a friend and knew
> No honor left in me, no faith, no love.[21]

For the man concerned with honor, *timē*, the treatment of friends could be crucial: "Whoever avoids betraying his friend, has great honor both among mortals and among gods, to my way of thinking."[22] In these passages loyalty to a friend approaches an absolute value and is praised without restriction or qualification. The authors and poets are primarily thinking, to be sure, of situations in which a man is tempted to abandon a friend in battle or other dangerous circum-

[20] This is the friendship of utility. Aristotle was well aware of its existence and prominence, even if he preferred to stress what he regarded as the higher types, friendship based on virtue or pleasure. (Aristotle, *Nichomachean Ethics* 1156 a 6ff.) In the *Lysis* of Plato Socrates takes a different tack and convinces his interlocutor that utility is a prerequisite to friendship. The higher types are of course well represented in Greek civilization and have received suitably laudatory treatment in literature ancient and modern. But for the understanding of Greek politics it is the more mundane variety, friendship based on mutual advantage, that must be examined and understood.

[21] Orestes in Euripides, *Iphigenia in Tauris* 605-607, trans. Witter Bynner in the Chicago Greek Tragedies. Bynner's translation is rather free: what Orestes says is that it would be most shameful, *aischiston*, to fail to consider his friend's interests, *ta ton philon*, in this situation. He invokes the "shame" standard, the antiquity and continued force of which are well set forth in Adkins, *Merit and Responsibility*, 48f. and 154-156.

[22] Part of a banquet song. D. Page, *Poetae Melici Graeci* (Oxford 1962) no. 908.

stances. But in a culture which accords such unreserved praise to loyal friendship, it would not be surprising to find the claims of the friend and the claims of the city in perplexing conflict. That is why Socrates' confidence that the good Athenian gentleman, the *kalos kagathos*, would have no difficulty in serving simultaneously his friends and his city seems surprisingly uncritical; it is also easy to foresee in Meno's definition of a man's *aretē* more than methodological difficulties.

Friends and the City

Any politician, ancient or modern, may find himself caught between the conflicting demands of friend and of country. The situation is universal, but the ways of responding to it vary with place and time. The culture in which the politician lives may suggest to him the way to resolve the problem. It may make very clear that the claims of the friend are to be subordinated to those of the city; it may lead him to attempt some reconciliation or compromise, or the politician may conceivably find that his culture is willing to tolerate the subordination of some civic interests to those of his friends. What the culture deems acceptable will not always be what is acceptable to the politician, but it will be hard for him to escape being influenced by widely-felt attitudes.

Here the contrast between President Kennedy's comments and those ascribed to Themistocles is again relevant. The modern American politician, however he may decide to act, operates in a society which makes fairly clear the priority of the state's claims over those of a friend. He knows what is expected of him and so does his friend. They may choose to violate the implicit standard, the *nomos*, of their society, but if they do so they are aware of the risk.

The conflict was not resolved with equal clarity in fifth century Athens. Loyalty to the city was, of course, expected. But the literature of the age is surprisingly silent about what we would call patriotic obligation, and surprisingly inexplicit about the priority of the city's claims over those of the friend or relative.[23] The contrast between Athenian and modern politics is a sharp one, so much so that one recent student of Greek ethics could describe the commonest Greek attitude towards the problem in these terms: "The city's claims *may* override others in times of stress; but where the city's interests are not threatened, or seem irrelevant to the case in hand, there is nothing in these standards of value to prevent the *agathos polites* (good citizen) from attempting to thwart the laws of the city on behalf of his family and friends, with whom he has closer ties."[24]

Thus it is no surprise to find Crito pleading with Socrates to let him arrange an escape from prison and a refuge in Thessaly or elsewhere for the condemned philosopher. To a Greek what *is* surprising is Socrates' insistence that even in this case the laws demand obedience and that they require that "he care neither for children nor for life nor for anything else more than for what is just" (*Crito* 54 b).

Socrates and his contractual theory of government support a view that has enjoyed great popularity in modern times. But in his own age Socrates was an all but isolated innovator, in this as in so many things.[25] Earlier Greek literature pro-

---

[23] Cf. A. H. Chroust, "Treason and Patriotism in Ancient Greece," *Journal of the History of Ideas* 15 (1954) 280-288, esp. 280-281. "The city . . . was neither the first nor the only institution which made demands on the allegiance or loyalty of the Athenian. . . . The loyalty and attachments which . . . friendship groups elicited from the members were extremely strong." Indeed, as Chroust points out, they could lead from time to time to what we would deem cases of indisputable and indefensible treason.

[24] Adkins, *Merit and Responsibility*, 231. Cf. N. M. Pusey, "Alcibiades and to *philopoli*," *HSCP* 15 (1940) 215-231.

[25] In 406 B.C. Euryptolemus is said to have argued before the Athenian assembly that it would be *aischron* for him to put the interests of his relative, Pericles (the son of Pericles and Aspasia), ahead of those of the whole city (Xenophon, *Hellenica* 1.7.21). The passage marks an interesting development in Greek ideas of what is shameful, especially when contrasted with passages like Euripides, *Iphigenia in Tauris* 605-607, discussed above; cf. n. 21. Euryptolemus' attitude in many ways parallels that of Socrates.

vides only partial parallels to his views on the supremacy of the laws. Even in later antiquity the semiphilosophical discussions of friendship indicate, if only by the disproportionate space they devote to its political implications, that a citizen might still decide to support a friend over his own city.[26] Nor was the speculation idle, as an episode reported by Thucydides shows. At the time of the first invasion of Attica in the Peloponnesian war Pericles offered to give his farm to the city, suspecting that his old friend, Archidamus, king of Sparta, might spare it, "either from a personal wish to do him a favour, or as the result of instructions given by the Spartans in order to stir up prejudice against him" (Thucydides 2.13.1, trans. Rex Warner). Pericles' gesture and Thucydides' comment on it reveal the power that friendship could have in those days. An old friend who was the head of one of the rival cities might possibly do a favor to the leader of the other, even in time of war, even when that other leader was the man whose determination made that war unavoidable, even when the strategy of his city in that war was to ravage and destroy the crops of the Attic countryside.[27] And if that farm were spared purely through malicious intent, to weaken Pericles' standing in the city, Thucydides is sure that the idea would not be Archidamus', but the idea of those who gave him instructions.

Reflections of the Problem in Tragic Poetry: The Antigone

Athenians of the fifth century could thus conceive of a King of Sparta who, at some risk to himself and possibly even to his city, might follow part of Meno's idea of human *aretē* "in attending to the affairs of the city to see that he helps his friends. . . ." On the tragic stage they could sometimes see actions exemplifying parts of this definition. One could re-

[26] Note Cicero's *de amicitia*; Aulus Gellius' *Attic Nights* 1.3; and cf. below, The Responses of the Politicians, and n. 33.
[27] Cf, the exchange between Glaucus and Diomedes in *Iliad* 6.119ff.

gard Euripides' *Orestes*, for example, as a dramatic representation of that section of Meno's definition of *aretē* which encourages a man "to see that he hurts his enemies." Orestes, like Archilochus, knows "one great thing: to pay back with dreadful miseries anyone who makes you miserable" (Archilochus, fr. 120. Lasserre–Bonnard).

> . . . above all else I want my death
> to hurt the man I hate. He betrayed me,
> he made me suffer, so let him suffer now
> for what he did to me.
>
> Euripides, *Orestes* 1164-1166,
> trans. W. Arrowsmith

Greek tragedy was never far from the central problems of the society which gave it birth. It spoke through myth, it utilized grand and famous princes as its characters, it masked and stylized what it had to say, but its remoteness lay only in externals, not in inner concerns. Those concerns were often fully contemporary, as in the *Orestes*, whose theme is not the misfortune of some far-off prince, but a problem which could be detected in the Athens of Euripides' own day—"the disease of demented loyalty that pervades the play."[28] Blinded by his hate for Menelaus, Orestes kills his aunt, Helen, and is preparing to murder his cousin, Hermione, when, at the moment of ultimate horror, Apollo *ex machina* stops the action of the play.[29] The *Orestes* in effect is an adaptation of

[28] The phrase is W. Arrowsmith's in his introduction to the Chicago translation of the play.

[29] Thus the *Orestes* resembles the tragedies discussed above, The Obligations of Friendship. Orestes' intense desire to hurt his enemies blinds him to the obligations of *philia*. (*Philia* ". . . is not 'friendship' or 'love' or any other feeling, but the objective state of being φίλοι, 'dear ones' by virtue of blood ties," Else, *Aristotle's Poetics*, 349). Orestes misconceives the situation and fails to recognize who his *philoi* really are; on the view adopted above, n. 18, that is his *hamartia*. Note that at the moment he decides to murder Helen he turns to his companion Pylades and says, "There's nothing better than a real *philos*" (line 1155); the irony of the language brings out the peculiar state of his mind. He is about to kill a woman who is closely related to him (his

Meno's approach to *aretē*, carried to its extreme and turned to madness.

The actions on which Greek tragedy focuses normally involve some disordering of the proper relationships among *philoi*—adultery, incest, murder, or the involuntary spilling of kindred blood. Manslaughter for the Greeks was horrible, but it was not a tragic subject unless it took place among *philoi*.[30] Most frequently, then, the circle within which Greek tragedy takes place is the family and a few close associates—not the *polis*. Sometimes, however, the circle widens to include the whole city. When this happens—consider the *Antigone*—new possibilities become available to the playwright: new problems among the *philoi* and the potential conflict between *philoi* and *polis*. The very first lines of Sophocles' play emphasize the dislocation of the Greek conventions of *philia*, wrought by Creon's proclamation that Polyneices should not be buried. Although it is the duty of the *philos* to see that his friend receives burial, Antigone is prevented from doing so by what she regards as an unnatural order from Creon. She tells her sister Ismene, "the evils proper for our enemies are coming upon our *philoi*" (line 10). It would be perfectly all right to leave an enemy unburied, but kin, Polyneices, must not be treated in this horrible way. Antigone is determined to correct this violation of *nomos*, of convention, and will bury her brother even if it

---

mother's sister) and who is thus *philē*, but he seems not to recognize or care what their relationship is. Instead Pylades, the proposer of this horrible deed, seems to him his true *philos*.

[30] Cf. Else, *Aristotle's Poetics*, 353, "In the *Oedipus* the tragic fact is not that Oedipus has killed a man, but that that man was his father." Note Plato, *Euthyphro* 4ff. Euthyphro is prosecuting his father for having caused the death of a dependent (*pelates*) of theirs on Naxos. Socrates expresses surprise, the normal reaction, I believe, of a Greek seeing a man take a *philos* to law on such a matter. Euthyphro replies with what to our way of thinking is a sensible statement: what makes a murder horrible is not the spilling of kindred blood but rather the injustice of killing any man. But Euthyphro himself does not fully understand the implications of this statement and just how radically it diverges from conventional Greek notions, as Socrates points out in the ensuing dialogue. See also above, The Obligations of Friendship.

means death: "Why, it would be a fine thing to die doing this. I will lie at his side, dear one of the side of dear one, having dared a holy crime."[31]

Creon, as has often been pointed out, has a different conception of *nomos*.[32] He believes that his proclamation is just and must be obeyed; it is, after all, a law, a *nomos*. But he also has a different conception of friendship (*philia*): "I'd never take a man who was hostile to his country for a friend, for I know this: the country is our source of security, and only if the ship of state sails well can we make our friendships. My aim is to improve our city by such *nomoi* as these" (lines 187-191).

In effect, he asserts that loyalty to the city is an essential qualification for being a *philos*: a radical idea for a Greek. Thus the play involves two conflicting conceptions of *nomos* and two ideas of what constitutes a *philos*. Antigone maintains the conventional notions with more than conventional determination. Yet Creon also has a case, and a strong one, as any patriot would recognize. He asserts the priority of the interests of the city over those of the friend: "I have no respect for the man who prefers friend to fatherland" (lines 182-183). And he, like Antigone, is fully determined to act on the basis of his convictions. Both Creon and Antigone are idealistic and stubborn; both argue with other relatives—Antigone with her sister, Creon with his son. Both refuse to yield, and both finally lose that which should have been dearest, *philtaton*, to each of them: Haemon, Antigone's betrothed and Creon's son.

---

[31] *Antigone* lines 72-74:

καλόν μοι τοῦτο ποιούσῃ θανεῖν.
φίλη μετ' αὐτοῦ κείσομαι, φίλου μέτα,
ὅσια πανουργήσασ'·

[32] Note especially line 449 and lines 480-481. I have avoided discussing the secondary literature on this play, but the most recent article on the subject is particularly apposite and is also a good introduction to some wider questions of interpretation which I have deliberately excluded: W. M. Calder III, "Sophokles' Political Tragedy, *Antigone*," *Greek, Roman, and Byzantine Studies* 9 (1968) 389-407, note esp. 404-405.

It is a very thin line which separates this play from melodrama. What saves it is not only the careful characterization of Antigone and of Creon, but also the fundamental, perhaps irreconcilable, conflict between their two ideas of law and of friendship.

The Responses of the Politicians

The conflict which underlies the *Antigone* can also be seen in the political life of the period. Friends and city could and did come into conflict, and, as in the *Antigone*, there was no ready resolution. A politician might enter upon his career for the reasons which Socrates approvingly listed for Critoboulos, "that he may not be the victim of injustice himself and may help his friends in a just cause, and when he takes office may try to do some good to his country" (Xenophon, *Memorabilia* 2.6.25, trans. E. C. Marchant), but find later that his objectives were not readily compatible with each other. To be sure, Socrates had added the useful qualification that may have escaped many less sharp-minded Athenians, "in a just cause." But, as Socrates must have known better than anyone, men might disagree about what "just cause" meant. The desire to help his friends might blind a man to the needs of the city or he might find himself caught when the interest of a friend clashed with the civic interest.

While it is easy to conjecture that these clashes took place, it is far more difficult at this remove to discover the specific forms they took. But once again a group of anecdotes in Plutarch and other authors are suggestive, though again we have no guarantee that the stories are correct in every detail. Skepticism is imperative, even if it could positively be shown that many of them derive from a good fourth century source.[33] But even if apocryphal, they serve to illustrate some

[33] There were a great many treatises on friendship in antiquity; Speusippus, Xenocrates, Clearchus, Cleanthes, and Chrysippus are all said to have written such works. Among the Peripatetics the question εἰ δεῖ βοηθεῖν τῷ φίλῳ παρὰ τὸ δίκαιον καὶ μέχρι πόσου καὶ ποῖα was often considered in these treatises; cf. Aulus Gellius, *Attic Nights* 1.3.10-12. It would seem that the story of

types of responses available to politicians when they found themselves in these uncomfortable straits.

Themistocles

One of these anecdotes has already been mentioned. Themistocles' comment that he hoped he would never sit on the archon's throne without seeing to it that his friends got better treatment than his enemies (see above, Some Ethical Problems in Friendship) exemplifies one extreme in dealing with the problem. But the solution is simplistic and not likely to have been satisfactory as a general principle, either to the politician or to the city. The politician would have to decide how much better treatment his friends were to get than ordinary citizens, and how far he would depart from just and legal standards to assist them. The city would have to consider whether it could tolerate anyone so openly committed to favoring one group over others. Like many electoral promises, such a comment might win support, but prove difficult to fulfill. Indeed, another anecdote suggests that when he was elected general Themistocles adopted a different approach to the same problem. We are told that the poet Simonides approached him with an improper request. Themistocles' reply is said to have been: "You would not be a good poet if you got out of rhythm; I would not be an urbane magistrate if by repaying favors I got out of harmony with the law."[34] The answer was worthy of Themistocles and his

---

Pericles' answer to an importuning friend came from Theophrastus' work on friendship. Perhaps the others have the same source. See G. Heylbut, *De Theophrasti libris* ΠΕΡΙ ΦΙΛΙΑΣ (Diss. Bonn 1876), and O. Regenbogen, *RE* Suppl. Band 7, 1485-1486.

[34] οὔτ' ἐκεῖνος ἂν γένοιτο ποιητὴς ἀγαθὸς ᾄδων παρὰ μέλος, οὔτ' αὐτὸς ἀστεῖος ἄρχων παρὰ νόμον χαριζόμενος, Plutarch, *Themistocles* 5, cf. *Moralia* 807 b. The comment is an elaborate series of word plays, largely untranslatable. The most obvious and important is the pun on *nomos*, which can mean either "law/convention" or "musical tune." *Asteios* is literally "of the inner-city," hence sophisticated, here perhaps with a hint that he has the interest of the city at heart. *Charizomenos* is "giving pleasure," "creating *charis*," either by doing a favor or through the skilled use of language (cf. Plato, *Gorgias* 462 c).

renowned cleverness. It does not repudiate the claims of friendship, but it does impose a limit on them and affirm his intention of obeying the laws of the city.

Aristides

The ancient traditions which delighted in contrasting Themistocles with his contemporary Aristides allege, as we might expect, that the two men took drastically different approaches in their treatment of friends. Themistocles, we are told, did his best to gratify his friends, but Aristides noted that the power which came from friends encouraged many men to do wrong, and adopted a much more cautious policy. He is said to have avoided the *hetaireiai* altogether because he wished neither to be joined in wrongdoing with clubmates, nor to offend them by refusing to go along with their undertakings.[35]

The story, like many anecdotes, is suspect; its presumption that the *hetaireiai* were inevitably engaged in wrongdoing seems to point to an origin in the late fifth century, after the gradual conversion of these clubs to revolutionary cells.[36] If true, it would be an interesting anticipation of developments later in the century, the significance of which we shall have occasion to study later. If we can overcome our skepticism about the stories of the just and virtuous Aristides, his career may provide one of the first fifth century examples of a politician struggling to avoid excessive dependence on political friendship. Yet the approach ascribed to Aristides is not likely to have been widely followed. In a society where friends were protection and security and power itself, where advancement and influence often depended upon alliances, no one could lightly dispense with friends. Unless some alternative form of support could be found, or unless one's prestige was so great that it seemed unshakable, friends were essen-

[35] Plutarch, *Aristides* 2, *ad fin.*
[36] On the development of *hetaireiai* see Chapter 1 above, The Political Club. Note also the criticism of the traditions about Aristides and Themistocles in the same section.

55

tial. One might avoid the *hetaireiai*; one might experience some temporary ascendancy without the support of *philoi*, but Aristides' own ostracism indicates how slippery this path could be. The ostracized and impoverished Aristides would have been a forceful example to any who might have contemplated following in his footsteps.

Ephialtes

The next response we hear of concerning the problem of political friendship represents a compromise between the approaches of Themistocles and of Aristides. Ephialtes, the man more than any other responsible for the reform of the Areopagus Council, had a reputation for incorruptibility in antiquity: "Ephialtes, Sophonides' son, was very poor. When his *hetairoi* offered him ten talents, he did not accept, saying, 'If I respect your generosity, I would be compelled to abandon justice in returning the favor; if I didn't respect it, and didn't reciprocate, you'd think me a man of no favor.' "[37] His decision to turn down the money is very similar to what is said of Eteocles in Euripides' *Suppliants*: "Though his friends kept offering him money, he never accepted it, and he never let them yoke his character into the slave-like harness of their gold" (Euripides, *Suppliants* 875-877).

Not that the *Suppliants* is some allegory of Greek politics in which Eteocles is a covert Ephialtes; rather Ephialtes, if the anecdote is correct, was simply acknowledging what was often thought, if rarely so fastidiously put into practice. "It's easier to protect yourself from an enemy than from a friend," said Alcmaeon the philosopher from Croton (*VS* 24 B 5). Later, well after Ephialtes' death, an aristocratic politician who also wrote tragic poetry set down some lines which, like

[37] Aelian, *Varia Historia* 11.9. The anecdote is again a play on words. *Acharistos*, here translated "a man of no favor," means properly someone who doesn't return favors, an ingrate, therefore someone unpleasant, possibly hostile. Cf. *charizomenos* in Themistocles' reply to Simonides, esp. n. 34 above.

this anecdote, could apply to the difficult situation in which a friend finds himself when entreated to repay a favor by doing something illegal or improper: "Whoever in his association with his friends does everything to gratify them, converts immediate pleasure into a subsequent animosity" (Critias, VS 88 B 27). Ephialtes' policy, to judge from the anecdote, was to attempt to avoid any obligation by refusing the gift or favor at the outset. It was a far-seeing policy, and an admirable one, especially for a poor politician. Yet for these very reasons it was perhaps not much more likely than Aristides' solution to be universally followed.

Pericles

Just as the ancient writers provide rather full information about Pericles' use of friends in his political career (above, Anecdotes Concerning Political Friendship) they also discuss his response to some of the ethical problems arising from friendship. The story is widely told, for example, that when a friend wanted him to bear false witness on a matter which included an oath, Pericles replied that he was a friend "right up to the altar"—that is, that he would help his friends so long as he was not forced to violate some religious obligation such as an oath.[38] It is not clear whether or not this is a stronger restriction on friendship than Themistocles' refusal to do anything contrary to *nomos*, but it once again indicates an attempt to find some balance between the demands of friends and other moral obligations. Nor, as we shall see, should this anecdote be taken as a full description of Pericles' manner of treating his friends. It nevertheless reveals one more way of handling the possible difficulties.[39]

[38] The story is mentioned three times by Plutarch, *Moralia* 186 c, 531 c, 808 a. Note also Aulus Gellius, *Attic Nights* 1.3.20, Arsenius, *Violetum* p. 417, ed. C. Walz (Stuttgart 1832) and cf. Apostolius, *Centuria* 11.31 a in *Paroemiographi Graeci* II 523 (ed. E. L. von Leutsch, Göttingen 1851).

[39] The neat phrase and the nimble escape from embarrassment suggest the same source as the Themistocles anecdote (above, Themistocles) but, of

The Effects of Political Friendship

"Now when the *demos* rules, there is no escape from trouble, and when this trouble comes, it takes the form not of animosities among the troublesome, but of strong friendships. For the troublemakers put their heads together and arrange public business in a cabal" (Herodotus 3.82.4).

The speaker is Darius; the time, shortly before his accession to the throne of Persia; the setting, Persia in the sixth century B.C. But these comments from Herodotus' *History* could apply equally well to Athens of the fifth century.[40] They speak of a democratic society in which friendship plays an important, even essential, part. And they hint at one of the dangers of such a system—that groups of friends acting in concert might impose their narrow interests upon the whole city. Whether this often happened in fifth century Athens may be doubted, but that it was a danger is amply clear. We are not usually informed in sufficient detail to speak with precision about the successes won by coteries of friends in Athens, but from time to time we have signs that political friendship could be a powerful instrument in controlling the operation of the state. Perhaps the most famous example is the friendship formed between two old rivals, each prominent in his own right, Pericles and Cimon.

The Alliance of Pericles and Cimon

There were grounds for bitterness between the two men. Pericles' father Xanthippus had once indicted Cimon's father (Herodotus 6.136.1) and had rivaled him in military fame. When Cimon himself was on trial, Pericles had appeared, al-

course, it may simply be an echo of Pericles' own verbal dexterity. Note, for example, his justly admired phrases quoted in Plutarch, *Moralia* 186 c and d, and in Aristotle, *Rhetoric* 1411 a ff.

[40] Later in this work and especially in Appendix I, I treat the peculiar debate in which Darius makes this comment, and attempt to ascertain the relationship between the ideas expressed by him and the other speakers to developments in Athenian politics.

though only perfunctorily, as one of the accusers.[41] A few years later, under suspicion for favoring Sparta, Cimon was ostracized. Pericles is not likely to have been upset at the prospect that his rival would be in exile for ten years. But events took a different turn. In 457 a Lacedaemonian force moved into Northern Greece, ostensibly to help fellow Dorians, but from the Athenian viewpoint to interfere in an area of considerable interest to her. She now found herself in an awkward position both with Sparta and at home, as rumors of Spartan correspondence with traitors filled the city.[42] When the Athenian generals decided to block the Spartans' return to the Peloponnese, the two armies clashed at Tanagra in Boeotia. Before the battle Cimon arrived and asked to be allowed to take his regular place in the battle order. Pericles saw to it that the Athenians refused permission.[43] But the gesture was an effective confirmation of Cimon's loyalty, and of his innocence of the charge of favoring the Spartans, *Lacedaemonophilia*, that had been made against him at the ostracism. When he was turned away from the battlefield he asked "Euthippus of Anaphlystus and his other *hetairoi*, all of whom were implicated in the charge of laconizing, to contend

[41] Plutarch, *Cimon* 14; *Pericles* 10. The ultimate source would seem to be Stesimbrotus, *FGrH* 107 F 5.

[42] Thucydides 1.107.2ff. and A. W. Gomme *A Historical Commentary on Thucydides* (Oxford 1945) I 314.

[43] Beloch found the whole account of Cimon's appearance "eine Haüfung von Absurditäten" (*Griechische Geschichte* II² 210-211). See, however, Gomme's *Commentary*, I 326 n. 2. There are difficulties, e.g. the accounts in Plutarch, *Pericles* 10 and *Cimon* 17, differ slightly. *Cimon* 17 indicates the *boulē* met and rejected Cimon's request to be allowed to fight. *Pericles* 10 speaks only of events on the battlefield—friends of Pericles keep Cimon from taking his place. The latter account is the more compressed and dramatic; the former requires us to assume either that the *boulē* met on the battlefield or that Cimon's request was relayed to Athens for a decision. If the second assumption is correct, Cimon must have appeared well before the battle, for some time would have been required for the exchange with Athens. This makes a less dramatic story but not a less credible one; the matter was one of great delicacy and potentially of great consequence for the generals, especially if they lost the battle after turning away Cimon's help. Their wisest course would have been to involve the *boulē* in the decision, thus combining self-protection with constitutional nicety.

with all their strength against the enemy and to let their deeds be the proof of their innocence. They took Cimon's armour and set it in the midst of their company. There they made their stand and breathed their last—one hundred of them. Great was the legacy of repentance at the false charges made against them and of grief which they left among the Athenians."[44] When the battle was over and the Lacedaemonians had cut their way back to the Peloponnese, and when a little later the Athenians had once again restored the *status quo ante*,[45] a motion was made to recall Cimon. The proposer, significantly, was Pericles.[46] "Some say that Pericles did not move the decree restoring Cimon until he had negotiated with Elpinice, Cimon's sister, a secret agreement

[44] Plutarch, *Cimon* 17; cf. *Pericles* 10. B. Perrin in the notes to this passage in his translation of the *Cimon* (New York 1910) says: "Thucydides gives us none of these details of the behaviour of Cimon and his friends at Tanagra, but they have the air of authenticity, and probably came to Plutarch ultimately from Stesimbrotus or Ion, who are contemporary witnesses." Granted that the circumstantiality of the account speaks for its authenticity, there is yet a peculiarity. The implication of the story is that the friends fought together in a group. Normally this would mean that they were all from the same tribe as Cimon, Oineis. But the one man whose name and demotic are given, Euthippus of Anaphlystus, would have been a member of the tribe Antiochis, and thus normally would have fought in a different part of the battle line. Did the friends then assemble from different tribes and parts of the line and form a group, once Cimon had been denied permission to take his place among the members of the Oineis contingent? Or is this part of the story a later accretion?

[45] Sixty-two days later under the leadership of Myronides, the Athenians won a victory at Oenophyta that gave them a strong say in the affairs of Boeotia and those of the Opuntian Locrians (Thucydides 1.108). The chronology of Cimon's return and of the Five Years' Truce is disputed. See Gomme's *Commentary*, 1 326-327. I believe that Cimon was recalled soon after Oenophyta and that the Five Years' Peace was considerably later; see *Theopompus* 24-30.

[46] Plutarch says that Pericles sensed the popular mood and made the motion to keep the people happy. The conjecture is probable enough, but it should also be pointed out that Cimon's loss of a hundred loyal friends could have been a very severe setback to his political position—perhaps as severe a weakening of his power as a ten-year period of ostracism. Cimon would have to construct new alliances if he were to continue a political career. Thus he might now prove useful to Pericles.

whereby Cimon would be commissioned to command two hundred ships on a naval expedition against the territory of the Persian king while Pericles would exercise power in the city."[47] One of the provisions of this arrangement may have been that Cimon, in a fashion long familiar to Athenian families contracting political alliances, marry Isodice, a relative of Pericles.[48]

There is perhaps a further indication of cooperation between Pericles and the family of Cimon. The Metiochus who, according to Plutarch, was general and superintendent of roads and bakeries, was a *hetairos* of Pericles.[49] The name is unusual enough to suggest that he was the half-brother of Cimon, or at least a member of the same family.[50] The following genealogical chart sets forth the probable relationships among those involved in this alliance:

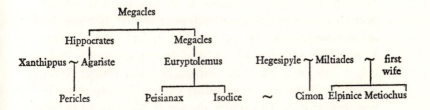

---

[47] Plutarch, *Pericles* 10. Cf. *Moralia* 812f. The context of this passage and its treatment of Elpinice seem again to suggest Stesimbrotus as the ultimate source. This would give the story a fifth century ancestry but would not guarantee it against the infection of malicious gossip.

[48] See *TAPA* 98 (1967) 67-76. A side effect would be that the wealthy son of Callias, a member of the *genos* of the *Kerykes* and husband of Elpinice, would now be tied to Pericles. If this is correct, and if a formal peace between Athens and Persia were negotiated in the late 450's or early 440's, it would be easy to see why Callias would be a logical choice as head of the negotiating mission.

[49] Plutarch, *Moralia* 811f.; See above Anecdotes Concerning Political Friendship.

[50] Herodotus 6.41 tells an exciting adventure story about Cimon's half-brother Metiochus.

What we have here, then, are the indications of a rapprochement between two important and formerly hostile Athenian families. We can conjecture the advantages to each party, the attraction of other politicians and relatives into the circle, and the wedding of Cimon and Isodice to seal the compact. The alliance represented birth, wealth, military and political prestige, and for a time it harmonized and reconciled the desires of its participants. Its value to Athens, as well as to the two families, lay in freeing the energies of capable men to deal with the crises which beset their city, in years of renewed difficulties with Persia and her subsidiaries and with other Greeks.

Yet the alliance should not be mistaken for a monopoly of political power. Cimon and Pericles were not the only leaders of Athens at this time. Their competitors are only shadowy names to us—Myronides, Tolmides, Leocrates—but Plutarch thinks it no small tribute to Pericles to point out his primacy among so many and such great rivals.[51] Nor was the alliance unshakable—by the mid-440's it had broken down. First Isodice and then Cimon died, both prematurely. Probably a little later, before the Areopagus court, Pericles prosecuted one Pyrilampes on a murder charge. The opposite side was supported by Thucydides, the son of Melesias, an in-law of Cimon.[52] The next few years saw the rapid rise of this Thucydides to the leadership of a faction in the assembly.[53] Renewed strife, followed, political bitterness and a deep divi-

---

[51] Plutarch, *Pericles* 16.

[52] See the anonymous life of Thucydides the historian, sec. 6. The passage confuses the historian with the politician, but I see no reason to doubt the story that Pericles prosecuted Pyrilampes. To be sure, Plutarch, *Pericles* 13, says he was a *hetairos* of Pericles, but considering the shifting political loyalties of the mid-fifth century such an assertion does not argue against a period of hostility. Alliances among politicians during this period are likely to have changed rapidly, as the Cimon-Pericles case indicates. Cf. A.H.M. Jones, *Athenian Democracy* 131; contrast R. Sealey, *Essays in Greek Politics* (New York 1967) 191 and n. 44.

[53] Plutarch, *Pericles* 11, anonymous life of Thucydides sec. 6, *AthPol* 28.2.

sion of the state, portending developments of the 420's and later.[54]

The Periclean building program came to be the center of a sharp controversy, with Thucydides as its most outspoken critic. The wrangling might have continued far longer if ostracism had not provided a decisive resolution. In 444/3 Thucydides was ostracized and left Athens for ten years. Plutarch says that Pericles finally "entered the ring against Thucydides, despised the risks of ostracism, threw him out, and undid the *hetaireia* that had been ranged against him."[55]

Thus the alliance between the circles of Cimon and Pericles came to an end.[56] It had lasted at most a little more than a

[54] Plutarch, *Pericles* 11, says that it was at this time that the long-standing tension in the state between citizens of popular and those of more aristocratic persuasion began to take the form of a deep division, and that the use of *demos* and *oligoi* as contrasting terms for the two groups dates from this period. This is an interesting assertion and I believe it is approximately correct. Earlier in the century one refers to both the *demos* and *oligoi*, but not, to my knowledge, as contrasting terms in political discourse. Likewise, the word *demokratia* exists before the 440's, but only later does it occur in clear and sharp contrast to *oligarchia*. That contrast is implicit in Herodotus 3.80-83 and 6.43.3, clear in pseudo-Xenophon's *Constitution of Athens* 2.17 and 2.20, and on Critias' tomb as described by the scholiast on Aeschines 1.39 (*VS* 88 A 13). See also Thucydides 3.62.3 and the papyrus of the speech of Antiphon the orator in his own defense, conveniently available in the Loeb *Minor Attic Orators* (ed. K. Maidment) I 294. It is true that none of these documents are dated to the 440's, but the significant fact is that this mode of speech, so common in the fourth century, seems not to have been adopted *before* the 440's. Plutarch's statement has often been understood as a reference to the emergence of two political parties, "Demos" and "Oligoi." But the intention of the passage seems to be to describe a division between classes and broad attitudes in Athens, rather than the constitution of new political organizations. Cf. above, Chapter 1, n. 36.

[55] Plutarch, *Pericles* 14 *ad fin.* The earlier part of the sentence used wrestling metaphors, appropriate to the son of a famous wrestling master. Cf. Wade-Gery, *Essays in Greek History* (Blackwell, Oxford 1958) 245. The implication of the latter part of the sentence is, I think, that the ties that held the *hetaireia* together were primarily personal ones, and that it was therefore not easy for a new man to take over the leadership of the group once Thucydides was removed.

[56] It is likely, however, that Pericles had some say in the appointment of Cimon's son Lacedaemonius to one of the commanding positions of the expedition to Corcyra in 433/2; Thucydides 1.45.2; *IG* i² 295 (*SEG* x 222). On Pericles' motives see Plutarch, *Pericles* 29.

decade and involved many of the characteristic political devices of the day: marriage alliances, political trials, *hetaireiai,* debates in the assembly, ostracism. Class interests, national policy, questions of right and of morality were involved, of course, but the basic pattern seems still to be one of personal ties and loyalties.[57] Success in politics comes to that man who most assiduously cultivates connections through family and friendship, who makes the strongest alliances, who most skillfully manipulates ostracisms and political trials, and the other customary weaponry of Athenian politics; in short, success belongs to the master of political friendship.

The Political Function of Friendship

ὄργανα γὰρ οἱ φίλοι ζῶντα καὶ φρονοῦντα τῶν πολιτικῶν ἀνδρῶν εἰσι. . . .

. . . for friends are the living and sentient instruments of politicians....

Plutarch, *Moralia* 807 d

So far this chapter bears out the truth of Plutarch's observation. Much of what has been said could be generalized to apply, with slight modifications, to other societies, for friendship is a universal phenomenon. But *philia* is a distinctly Greek form.[58]

In Athens during the fifth century friendship became especially important because it fulfilled a role which in other societies is often handled by other institutions. In a city without political parties, without much of the formal organizational apparatus which in modern times is so regularly associated with the word "politics," friendship became a principal

---

[57] Cf. the comments of R. Sealey in *Hermes* 84 (1956) 234-247.

[58] Republican Rome with its emphasis on *amicitia* suggests many interesting analogies. See Lily Ross Taylor's *Party Politics in the Age of Caesar* (Sather Lectures, vol. 22, Berkeley 1949) 7ff., and more recently Mother Adele Fisk, *TAPA* 96 (1965) 119-138, and J. Hellegouarc'h, *Le vocabulaire latin des relations et des partis politiques sous la republique* (Paris 1963, Publications/ Lille XI) esp. 42-56 and 63-90. Note also C. Meier, *Res Publica Amissa* 182-190.

means of getting the business of the city attended to.[59] *Philia* created political groups and held them together, just as it could bind several groups together to act for their mutual good. Through such ties the apolitical man might find a way to make his voice heard in the councils of the city or a politician might find the support and the confidence which he needed to operate effectively.

Having the right friend in the *boulē* or as a speaker before the assembly might assure an interest group of being successfully represented or a minority of being fairly heard. When Xenophon advises the clever cavalry commander to see to it that there are well-disposed politicians (*rhetoras epitedeous*) in the *boulē* to look after the interests of the cavalry (Xenophon, *Hipparchicos* 1.8), he recognizes the importance of the well-placed friend. Similarly, Socrates advised Crito to provide himself with a friendly politician who would protect him from harassment. (Xenophon, *Memorabilia* 2.10. 4-8). It was probably in this way that the *hetaireiai* took on political significance.[60] In another society they might have been and might have remained innocuous drinking clubs; but under the peculiar circumstances of Greek life they came inevitably to affect politics.

In a city the size of Athens such reliance on *philia* ties was not totally pernicious. To be sure it may have encouraged favoritism, put an undue emphasis on the congeniality and other purely personal qualities of the leader, but it had some compensatory advantages. For example, the less politically-minded citizens were provided with a source of advice and

---

[59] Cf. L. R. Taylor, *Party Politics in the Age of Caesar* 7: "The old Roman substitute for party is *amicitia*, friendship."

[60] It is not entirely clear what the *AthPol* 20.1 means when it says "when Cleisthenes was defeated in the political clubs, he won the support of the common people by promising to give the state into their hands" (trans. K. von Fritz and E. Kapp). Nor is it certain that the interpretation is free from anachronism. But for what it is worth, the implication is that Cleisthenes and Isagoras battled first in the political clubs, and that Cleisthenes turned to the common people when he found the tide running against him.

knowledge that could assist them with their problems. Through friendship the man who did not pursue an active political career might yet have some say in the decisions of his city. The state itself could also benefit. Friendship ties could provide it with some of the stability and continuity that might otherwise be lacking when the *boulē* went out of office at the end of the year and a totally new one, chosen by lot, came into power. The policies espoused in the previous year might be carried on by men who were friends of the original formulators, and thus knew intimately the background of the proposals. Most important, perhaps, conversations among friends could prove the best way of publicizing problems that the city faced, and of winning a consensus about the best course to follow. Finally, through personal ties with the city's leaders, the citizen might find himself better informed and more closely bound to the city herself.

Toward a New Model

There were no proper party organizations about 1760, though party names and cant were current; the names and the cant have since supplied the materials for an imaginary superstructure. A system of non-Euclidean geometry can be built up by taking a curve for a basis instead of the straight line, but it is not easy for us to think consistently in unwonted terms; parliamentary politics not based on parties are to us a non-Euclidean system, and similarly require a fundamental readjustment of ideas and, what is more, of mental habits.

Sir Lewis Namier, *The Structure of Politics,* Preface x-xi

The readjustment of ideas of which Namier speaks is even more essential, and even more difficult, for the understanding of the fifth century B.C. than it is for the reign of George III. We have already seen the difficulties created by the improper use of words such as "political party"; to impose upon this

66

period the axioms of parliamentary regimes can lead only to further confusion and misapprehension. What is needed is a new kind of political geometry, a construct that may seem surprising to eyes long familiar with other patterns, but one that can more readily accommodate the data preserved for us. If our minds work largely by analogy, and if our approach to truth is made through the slow, sometimes infinitesimal, progress of successive approximations, we may perhaps be justified in adopting the terminology of other specialists, and speak of constructing a new "model" for the politics of the period. This word implies no arrogant rejection of the understanding that has been won, often at great price, in the past. Rather it is an admission of our need for some schema that will enable us to put the accumulated data in some intelligible order. And it emphasizes that any such schema is only approximate and, hence, must be subject to change, as problems in its operation are discovered or as new information emerges. But some features of this new model can now be made out; we can begin to describe it more explicitly, to test it, to modify and refine it until it seems satisfactory. Four main characteristics can readily be listed.

Many Small Groups

First, the model must allow for many relatively small groups to be in operation at any given time. As was noted in Chapter 1, The Political Club, it is impossible to determine the number of *hetaireiai* that existed in ancient Athens; *a fortiori* it is not feasible to attempt to estimate the number and varieties of the less formal ties which might bind a citizen and a politician together. But though precision is not attainable, some answers at least can be excluded. It seems improbable, for example, that there were regularly only two or three groups in operation. Even if we bracket together all the *hetaireiai* and individuals who were supporting each politician, we must still allow, I believe, for many such conglomerates. There were many politicians in Athens and only the most prominent are well known to us, but all of them are likely to have been the nucleus of some group of friends and allies.[61]

Greek terminology is well suited to this state of affairs. The commonest Greek phrase for a political group is *hoi peri* or *hoi amphi*, followed by the name of a politician—literally, "the ones around so-and-so."[62] The idiom, as so often in Greek, is revealing. Its metaphor suggests that the political group is a circle around a prominent man, and although it does not intimate how large or how numerous these circles were, it makes it easy to envision a quite literally *polycentric* system, with many politicians each the center of a group of *philoi.*

This does not mean, of course, that all political groups were of equal size and significance. Some leaders must have much wider and stronger followings than others. Some may even have won a temporary hegemony where they enjoyed concentrated and undisputed power. But we must, I think, be careful not to be taken in by reports of long and unchal-

[61] On pp. 124-127 of *Theopompus* I attempted to show that our literary tradition about the domestic history of Athens has become distorted, and has focused unduly on the most prominent figures to the exclusion of others less well known, but also important. Figures of the first rank tend to expand in prominence, while those of the second and third magnitude tend to disappear. The full seriousness of this distortion is hard to assess, but one effect is obvious. It tempts the modern student of ancient Athens to underestimate both the diversity of her political life and the number of groups in operation.

The criticisms of the literary tradition advanced in *Theopompus* were partly based upon distribution figures for the more than 1500 ostraca which were published in 1966. Since then German excavators in the Cerameicus have turned up another large group, which should allow my generalizations to be tested. If the argument in *Theopompus* is correct, the new finds should include some significant groups of ostraca for men not prominently attested in the literary traditions. One hopes for a rapid publication of this important find.

[62] A good group of examples is collected in Calhoun's *Athenian Clubs*, 7 esp. n. 3. Calhoun assumes that *hetairoi* should be understood in the phrase, but he concedes that the phrase can also be used of "close political followings which, while they may or may not have been regularly organized hetairies, pursued the same objects and accomplished similar results."

lenged rule. The classic case is that of Pericles, who for fifteen years allegedly held "single and continuous rule and sway in the annual generalships" (Plutarch, *Pericles* 16). We need not doubt that Pericles was the most important politician in Athens from the expulsion of Thucydides son of Melesias to his own death. But that he was the only important politician or that his decisions were unchallenged is neither what Plutarch meant nor historically correct. Plutarch quotes the comic poet Hermippus (fr. 46) to show that well before his death Cleon was causing him trouble (Plutarch, *Pericles* 33) and that he was frequently under attack. A law case against his friend, the sculptor Pheidias, was clearly directed against his own power in the state, and there may also have been trials of his associates Damon, Anaxagoras, and Aspasia during this period. But most telling is the indisputable fact reported by Thucydides that Pericles was fined just two and a half years before his death.[63] Neither Pericles nor any other politician in ancient Athens could be sure of a lasting and unshaken rule. If one man managed to hold power for a long time, it was because of his ability, his skill, his agility in maneuvering, not because he was unchallenged. The inadequate surviving accounts of so many political figures, our ignorance of many men of the second rank, the inevitable tendency for the unsuccessful rival to disappear from the pages of history tempt and deceive us. There were no long periods of tranquil dominance in fifth century Athens; politics was regularly and vigorously polycentric.

[63] Thucydides 2.65.3. Thucydides' comment later in the same chapter, that in Pericles' time there was a nominal democracy but in fact the first man ruled, has often been taken out of context and misunderstood. It is not an indication that there was no opposition to Pericles but a tribute to his ability to control the often unruly *demos*. Compare the the speech ascribed to him in Thucydides 1.140-144. These do not seem to me the words of a man whose will was supreme and undisputed.

I have little confidence in Ephorus' account of the start of the Peloponnesian war (*FGrH* 70 F 196), and hence do not wish to adduce it in support of my view.

Coalitions

Since, as we have seen, many political groups were in existence at any given time in Athens, and since none of them could regularly be sure of winning a majority over all the others, the process of politics through much of the century would have consisted largely of efforts by individual groups to increase their followings, and efforts to combine in order to secure their objectives. The desired result could be achieved in several ways, most notably by suasion in the assembly and by the construction of coalitions. The first of these techniques is more commonly discussed and more thoroughly understood; the second, however, is also important. Several groups could be brought together to cooperate on specific issues, and to form either a majority or at least a sufficient base of support on which a majority could be assembled through oratorical and other appeals. We are not normally in a position to discuss the formation of coalitions in any detail, but once again Greek terminology is suggestive. Plutarch, *Nicias* 11, for example, speaks of οἱ περὶ τὸν Νικίαν καὶ τὸν Ἀλκιβιάδην, "the ones around Nicias and Alcibiades," and the *Oxyrhynchus Hellenica* (6.2 ed. Bartoletti) refers to οἵ τε περὶ Θρασύβουλον καὶ Αἴσιμον καὶ Ἄνυτον, "the ones around Thrasyboulos and Aisimus and Anytus." The implication, I believe, is not that there was some permanent group with two or three leaders, but rather that several leaders decided to cooperate on an issue or group of issues, and brought their separate groups into a coalition.

Something similar may lie behind another idiom, found in passages such as the following: "When the *rhetores* around Thucydides [Melesias' son] kept denouncing Pericles on the grounds that he was squandering the public funds and wasting the revenues . . ." (Plutarch, *Pericles* 14); ". . . that ill fated love of Sicily . . . which the *rhetores* around Alcibiades later fanned into flame . . ." (Plutarch, *Pericles* 20). The language here suggests that several *rhetores* might gather around a prominent leader. We cannot be sure who these speakers were or how strongly or permanently they were tied to the leader.[64]

Coalitions only rarely grow into more enduring alliances; their nature is to endure only for a short while. But on specific issues they can prove very effective. Thucydides, in one of those rare moments in which he speaks in any detail about the domestic politics of Athens, describes what seems to be a coalition which operated against Alcibiades in the fatal year of the Athenian expedition to Sicily (Thucydides 6.28-29). Alcibiades, who had been named one of the commanders of this expedition, had enemies who were anxious to remove him from command and get rid of him, since, says Thucydides, they recognized that he stood in the way of their advancement to the leadership of the *demos*. They were thus happy to take advantage of the suspicion raised by two sacrilegious affairs that had recently been reported—the mutilation of the sacred Herms and a parody of the holy mysteries. Alcibiades' enemies saw that this suspicion might be directed against him, and that he might thereby be removed from his command and perhaps condemned. When he outmaneuvered them in their first attacks, they turned to a new strategy. They sent other *rhetores* into the assembly to make another pro-

[64] C. N. Jackson, "The Decree-Seller in the *Birds* and the Professional Politicians at Athens," *HSCP* 30 (1919) 95. The phrase *hoi peri* need not, as Calhoun 7 n. 3 thought, always refer to the *hetairoi* of a politician but may refer to the leaders of other groups that came into coalition with a more prominent politician, such as Thucydides or Alcibiades. Sometimes it may be better to understand *rhetores* rather than *hetairoi* with the phrase *hoi peri*. Coalitions involving several prominent men are rather better known from the mid-fourth century than from the fifth. See for example Aeschines 1.34, 2.74, and 3.7. But these later groupings are perhaps not of exactly the same type, for they often brought together one or more generals with a *rhetor* or several *rhetores* (cf. Demosthenes, *Olynthiac* 2.20, Plutarch, *Moralia* 486 d) and were thus a sort of symbiosis between two rather specialized forms of political life. There is a movement toward such specialization in the late fifth century, but there are not many signs that the symbiosis had yet fully developed.

posal: that Alcibiades be allowed to sail with the expedition, but that he be obliged to return on a stated day and face the charges against him. This was not all that they had initially hoped for, but they consoled themselves in the thought that with Alcibiades out of the city the campaign against him could more readily run its slanderous course. We are not given the names of these politicians nor any description of their following. But it very much appears that they constituted a coalition. They had a common cause, the removal of Alcibiades, on which they could temporarily cooperate. But ultimately their goals were irreconcilable, for each wanted leadership of the *demos* for himself. Once Alcibiades was out of the way, they would turn to competition among themselves for primacy. The old coalition would dissolve and, perhaps, new ones would form.

Politics of the sort we have been describing is polycentric and kaleidoscopic—new combinations constantly emerging as new interests and new personalities join together, cooperate on one issue, then part and later find themselves on opposite sides of a new issue. To the historian attempting to describe and clarify the politics of such a period the diversity, especially combined with peculiar and spasmodic documentation, can be a source of frustration and a constant temptation to oversimplify by talking of "the right" and "the left," "the conservatives" and "the radicals," "democrats" and "oligarchs."[65] But in spite of our annoyance at this fluctuating,

[65] It is only rarely that we can detect the operation of these coalitions and the evidence for them is often very peculiar. For example, Plutarch, *Solon* 15, mentions a group of friends of Solon to whom he is alleged to have given advance information on his plans to cancel debts (*sic*) and who betrayed his confidence and profited unjustly from this advance word. They were "the ones around Conon and Cleinias and Hipponicus." It has long been recognized that the story betrays an origin in the tendentious factional literature of the late fifth century, cf. Wilamowitz, *Aristoteles und Athen* i (Berlin 1893) 62-63. All three men mentioned were ancestors of politicians active in the final decade of the war. The grouping of the three together in the story suggests a common animosity against them: possibly at some point their descendents formed a coalition or were the common enemies of the originator of this story.

almost chaotic pattern, it must be conceded that a system of this sort could serve as a means for expressing and accommodating the divergent interests and demands of various segments of Athenian society. Politics when viewed in this way, even if non-Euclidean, is still the classic pattern of accommodation of interests and preferences, and the traditional process of forming alliances and coalitions to attain common goals.

Personal Ties

It may seem gratuitous to mention once again that the "groups" to which we so frequently refer were held together primarily by personal ties. But the point is important, for on this premise, perhaps only on this premise, can some distinctively Athenian features of politics be understood. Consider, for example, the strange institution of ostracism. The Athenians annually decided whether or not to hold an ostracism. If the decision was affirmative, and if a minimum of 6000 voters cast ballots, the man named by the largest number of citizens, even if not by a majority, would be compelled to leave Athens for ten years. To a modern observer the institution is a curious one, not simply because of the strange image it conjures up of semiliterate Athenians scratching names on potsherds—or asking the obliging Aristides to write his own name on a sherd—and then filing through narrow gates to cast their ballots in an inverted popularity contest. All this is curious, but to a serious student it is less puzzling than the institution's peculiar concentration on the leader rather than on the group which supports him. Modern nations have had some experience in the suppression of political groups whose influence is regarded as pernicious. The method of harassment, however, usually differs in one important respect from the Athenian technique: it is not normally directed against a single leader but at the whole organization, and sometimes against the rank and file membership as well. The leader may, of course, be imprisoned or punished in some other way. But in modern times the action normally does not stop there, for a very good reason. If the head of such a group is arrested, another will be chosen to take his place. The mere removal of the leader accomplishes little; the second and third levels of leadership must be attacked as well, until no capable successors can be found. Or it may prove simpler to direct a broad attack against the whole membership. In any case the contrast to Athenian procedure is striking.

In Athens a follower of Cimon, the day after his old leader and friend had been ostracized, was free to meet with associates and other members of the group, free to select a new leader, free to advocate measures which Cimon had supported, free to vote as he chose and act as he chose. Since another ostracism could not be held before a year was up, the group which had supported Cimon had time to reorganize itself before the next serious challenge was directed against it. We do not hear of harassment directed against the supporters of ostracized politicians. Ostracism operated exclusively against a single leader, not his subalterns or followers.

The framers of ostracism were neither fools nor incompetents. They devised an instrument that endured, was imitated and admired, and one nicely adapted to the political conditions of democratic Greek *poleis*. Behind it was a recognition that what was most to be feared was not ideas or policies but men. The institution worked well because it was adapted to a system of politics in which political ties were in the first instance personal ties. As long as this was the case the removal of the leader would dissolve or at least temporarily incapacitate the group. Ostracism would tend, as Plutarch once phrased it, to "undo the *hetaireia*" by dissolving the ties which held it together.[66] But if political groups come to be based primarily on interest or ideology, then ostracism will

---

[66] κατέλυσε δὲ τὴν ἀντιτεταγμένην ἑταιρείαν (Plutarch, *Pericles* 14), compare above, The Alliance of Pericles and Cimon.

no longer prove effective. New leaders are likely to arise quickly, when old ones are removed, and ostracism will become an exercise of factional vindictiveness.[67] This is the reason, I believe, that ostracism came into being and flourished in a society where *philia* ties were extremely important.[68] It may also give some clue to the disappearance of the custom in the late fifth century. And finally it is also worth noting that the way in which ostracism operated is quite consistent with our other observations about Athenian politics. Clearly it could function effectively only when there were several political groups active at any given time. Its effects in a society where there were only two or three groups in existence would probably be a disastrous concentration of power: the expulsion of the leader of one group would increase the power of the surviving ones. After a few ostracisms the probable result would be a monopoly of power in the hands of one faction, or perhaps a bitter struggle between two or three units, each faced with the prospect of imminent extinction. Only in a society with many political groups could ostracism be used without pernicious results.

Were the Poor Included?

There remains a final and perplexing problem. We have been describing a model of politics that emphasizes personal

[67] The personal basis of ostracism is also suggested by the comments occasionally scribbled on the ostraca, e.g. *moichos* (adulterer) in one case. Cf. [Andocides] 4.33 on the ostracism of Cimon: "Remember our ancestors—how good and sensible they were; they ostracized Cimon because of his immorality (*paranomia*) since he cohabited with his own sister Elpinice."

[68] I do not wish to enter into the vexed questions of when and for what reasons ostracism was first introduced. My point is simply that it will work effectively only when personal ties serve in the first instance to bring people together into politically significant groups. Naturally leaders can, and often did, embody different policies, or represent conflicting interests. Hence ostracism could sometimes serve to give "Athenians a chance to decide on a major issue of policy with absolute finality where indecision might be dangerous or where feelings ran so high that civil strife might result" (W. G. Forrest, *The Emergence of Greek Democracy* [London 1966] 201-202; see also D. Kagan, *Hesperia* 30 [1961] 393-401). But this can only have been the case when the

ties and loyalties and the groups that arose from them. The roles of the *hetaireiai,* of family ties, and of marriage connections among prominent families have been stressed. What has not as yet been considered is the comprehensiveness of this model. Does it include all Athenian citizens, some of them, or only a relatively small segment of the wealthiest and most nobly born?

It would not be difficult to show that most Athenian politicians, at least during the middle decades of the century, were relatively well-to-do. The demands on their time were normally sufficient to exclude most poor farmers, day laborers, or artisans of only moderate means from any extensive political career.[69] Pericles and Cimon had extensive estates; Thucydides' mother was probably a Thracian princess; the families of Cleinias and Callias were notorious for their wealth. Even the allegedly poor politicians, Ephialtes and Aristides, were probably poor only by comparison to the often extraordinary wealth of their competitors. Themistocles entered politics with holdings of around three talents—far less than the 80 or 100 talents confiscated by the city, according to legend, when he fled to Asia—nonetheless three talents was no contemptible fortune.[70]

Given the necessity of some wealth, and the further presumption (cf. Chapter 1, The Political Club) that the *hetai-*

---

ostracized leader had come to be identified with a policy. The ostracism of Thucydides son of Melesias may be a good example, but it would be dangerous to assume that this was a thoroughly typical case.

[69] During the middle decades of the century most of the prominent politicians would seem to have been generals. This was a time-consuming and exacting job, not suited for a man without independent means. All that we know of the generals of this period confirms what Eupolis said:

> We old 'uns didn't act like this; the men we chose
> for leading
> Were scions of the noblest houses, first in wealth
> and breeding.

(Eupolis fr. 103, trans. Edmonds, cf. fr. 205.) There is a rumor that a minimum financial qualification was set for the generalship: see C. Hignett, *History of the Athenian Constitution,* 191ff.

[70] Plutarch, *Themistocles* 25, Critias, *VS* 88 B 45; see also *Theopompus* 21.

reiai did not normally include the lower segments of the Athenian citizen population, it is not likely that most poor people were fully included in the system of friendship ties which we have suggested constituted the basic pattern of Athenian politics. What was true in the fourth century, that "according to established opinion politicians ought to be economically independent," was probably also true in the fifth century.[71] Since politicians would naturally tend to marry, to join *hetaireiai*, to form friendships among their own social and economic peers, the poorer citizens would not be as well represented as the rich in the political groups which have been described. The Greeks knew the truth of the saying: "Poor friends are an acquisition that nobody wants" (Euripides, *Electra* 1131), and of Jason's self-damning self-justification: "Everyone gets out of the way of a poor friend."[72]

A high-minded Greek might deplore the cynicism of these sentiments and might discount the idea expressed in one of Sophocles' plays: "Money brings a man friends, and then honors, and finally a position nearest the thrones of loftiest tyranny."[73] He might prefer to agree with Heracles in Euripides' drama:

> The man who prefers to win wealth or strength
> rather than good friends should think again.
> Euripides, *Heracles Driven Mad* 1425-1426

But when he rose from his seat in the theater he would return to his familiar haunts, dine with his usual *hetaireia*, discuss the play and the affairs of the city with his old friends, and resume the reassuring confinement of his ways. He would probably be quite surprised if one asked him if he had many *thetes*, peasants, day laborers, or oarsmen in the fleet as

---

[71] S. Perlman, *Athenaeum* 14 (1963) 335.

[72] Euripides, *Medea* 561, cf. Euripides fr. 152 (Austin).

[73] The lines are from the *Aleadae* of Sophocles, fr. 85 (*TGF*). In the last line, τυραννίδος θακοῦσιν ἀγχίστην ἕδραν, there is a textual problem. The manuscripts read either τ' ἄγουσιν (A) or ἄκουσιν (SM). Nauck's text, which I have translated, adopts Salmasius' conjecture θακοῦσιν.

friends; just as he might be annoyed if it were suggested that these poorer citizens deserved a voice equal to his own in the running of the city. If we continued to press him on the point, he might argue that the poorer citizens were not really interested in politics and did not aspire to an equal share of power. The conversation might even resemble an exchange between the young Socrates and the stranger with whom he converses in Plato's *Politicus*:

> STRANGER: Well then. What about those free citizens who willingly enter into service occupations for the other sectors of society just enumerated, those who interchange the products of agriculture and the other crafts and keep trade in balance, some within the local market, some in transactions between cities whether by sea or land, both those who buy and sell, and those who barter? I mean the ones we call moneychangers, and merchants, and ship owners and traders. Will they claim some expertise in political science?
> SOCRATES: They might claim some expertise in merchandising science.
> STRANGER: But surely those whom we see working as hired laborers and *thetes*, servants to all and happy about it, we won't find them making pretensions to the royal science, will we?
> SOCRATES: How could that be possible?[74]

The poor, despite their obvious economic interest, would seem often in antiquity to have been less strongly motivated to take part fully in the affairs of the city than many of their better-off fellow citizens. We may concede this point to our imaginary interlocutor. But this does not mean they were incapable of being organized and of becoming a powerful force in politics. In war or in hard times, when their livelihood and even their lives were in danger their complacency could not be relied upon, and the way was open for a clever man to de-

[74] Plato, *Politicus* 289 e-290 a.

velop a new pattern of politics in which the poor and less well-connected citizenry played a much more significant role.

A Test Case: The Ostracism of Hyperbolus

The model developed in the last sections can now be given an initial test, to see what results emerge when it is applied to a specific case. The problem chosen comes from rather late in the century, and should test both the adequacy of the model and the extent to which it can be applied to the last few years of the period under investigation.

The ostracism of Hyperbolus is known in part from Thucydides (8.73.3), also from Theopompus (*FGrH* 115 F 96), and Plutarch (*Nicias* 11 and *Alcibiades* 13). A speech preserved among the works of Andocides purports to have been delivered just before the voting, and may give us some idea of the later tradition about the ostracism, if not an actual contemporary view.[75] These and other scattered allusions provide enough information for a fairly full account of the ostracism. At first it might seem that Plutarch's account in the *Nicias* is both full and accurate:

> At the risk of oversimplification, it was a struggle between the young who wanted war and the old who wanted peace. The first were against Nicias, the second against Alcibiades. . . . The split created an opportunity for the most reckless and unscrupulous leaders, among them Hyperbolus of the deme Perithoidae. He was a man whose arrogance was not based on power, but who had acquired power through arrogance. He was the embodiment of the disrepute of his city and for that he won his reputation in the city. He thought that he was safely out of the range of ostracism at that time, since he was indeed a more likely candidate for the whipping post. He hoped that when one of the other

[75] The authenticity of the speech and the date of ostracism are both disputed. The most recent discussion is C. Fuqua, *TAPA* 96 (1965) 165-179, from which most of the relevant bibliography can be gathered.

two was driven out, he would be a match for the remaining one. He was obviously pleased at the dispute and egged the people on against both of them. Those in Nicias' circle and in Alcibiades', recognizing his worthlessness, met secretly, discussed the matter, combined forces and arranged it that neither of them was ostracized, but Hyperbolus instead.

Plutarch, Nicias 11.3-5

But there are difficulties in this account. We become suspicious, for example, as we read on and find that Plutarch concludes his remarks with the confidence-shaking comment, "I am not unaware that Theophrastus says that Hyperbolus was ostracized when Phaeax, not Nicias, was contending with Alcibiades. But most authorities are agreed on the version presented here" (Plutarch, *Nicias* 11 *ad fin.*). Theophrastus is no light authority, and it is disquieting to find that the alleged agreement of the anonymous sources had less influence on Plutarch when he came to write the *Alcibiades*.[76] In this life he is willing to give a much more prominent role to Phaeax, who was so curtly dismissed in the *Nicias*. Now (*Alcibiades* 13) he admits that Alcibiades "had brought down all the other demagogues but was still in contest with Phaeax, the son of Erasistratus, and Nicias, the son of Niceratus." Surely this is more satisfactory; Phaeax must not be left out of the account of the ostracism. He is securely attested as an important personage of the time by Thucydides, the comic poets, and, significantly, by several ostraca.[77] If Plutarch deemphasized his role in the *Nicias* it was perhaps because he

[76] The *Alcibiades* would seem to be the later work, since chapter 13 of this life refers to chapter 11 of the *Nicias*. But note C. Stolz, *Zur relativen Chronologie der Parallelbiographen Plutarchs* (Lund 1929: Lunds Universitets Årsskrift N.F. Aud. 1 Bd. 25, Nr. 3) 132, who shows that the works are close to contemporary and that arguments about priority must not be pressed.

[77] The literary testimony is conveniently gathered in *PA* 13921. The ostraca were published by W. Peek in *Kerameikos* III 78-80 (no. 149), and by H. A. Thompson in *Hesperia* 17 (1948) 194. Note also Diogenes Laertius 2.63 who implies Phaeax was a general.

was reluctant to admit that other politicians shared the stage with the character whose prominence he wished to stress.

The same motive, compounded with Plutarch's regular dislike of "demagogues," may account for the deemphasis of the political significance of Hyperbolus which is apparent in these accounts. The implication that Hyperbolus was a man of little standing or importance at the ostracism, but notorious enough to be the victim of the collaboration of Alcibiades and others is not warranted. It is true that Thucydides abandoned his customary restraint, and sneeringly branded Hyperbolus "a rascal, ostracized not from fear of his power and prestige but from his depravity and the disgrace he brought to the city," but the words must not be misconstrued.[78] Hyperbolus, whatever his faults, was surely a man of some considerable importance in Athens. We are not well enough informed about him to construct a continuous account of his life, but the following tabulation should dispel the notion that he had an insignificant or only very brief role in the affairs of his city:

Probable Date	Event	Evidence
before 426	First mentioned in Comedy	Cratinus, *Horai* fr. 262
424	mentioned in Aristophanes, *Knights*	lines 1303f.
? 424/3	Hieromnemone (sacred delegate to Delphic Amphictyony)	Aristophanes, *Clouds* 623-625, but cf. scholia *ad loc.* and Camon, *GIF* 16 (1963) 49ff.
ca. 422	mentioned in Eupolis, *Poleis*	fr. 238
before 421?	trierarch	Aristophanes, *Thesmophoriazusae* 837; cf. Eupolis fr. 195
421	member of the *boulē*?	*IG* i² 84
421?	attacked in Eupolis, *Maricas*	frs. 193 and 194
421?	mentioned in Leucon, *Phrateres*	fr. 1

[78] Thucydides 8.73.3. Note the exact wording: Thucydides does not deny that Hyperbolus had power and influence in the city.

Probable Date	Event	Evidence
ca. 420	attacked by Hermippus in *Artopolides*	Aristophanes, *Clouds* 551-552, and scholia *ad loc.*
ca. 420	attacked by Plato Comicus in *Hyperbolus*	frs. 166-172
Uncertain date, but before ostracism	elected general?	scholia on Aristophanes, *Acharnians* 346, and *Peace* 1319; see Camon, *GIF* 16 (1963) 46ff.
	attacked Nicias?	Himerius, *Or.* 36.63
	mentioned by Polyzelus	fr. 5
417	proposed amendment to	IG i² 95 (*SEG* xii 32)
416 or 415	ostracized	see below
Uncertain date, after ostracism	probable allusion in Plato Comicus	fr. 153
411	murdered on Samos	Thucydides 8.73.3[79]

Nor does this tabulation exhaust the evidence. Theopompus attests his political prominence; the fury of these remarks by Andocides indicates an importance which the speaker might try to deny which was too great for mere contempt: "I am ashamed to speak of Hyperbolus, whose father is a branded slave laboring in the public mint, and who is, himself, a foreigner, a barbarian, a lampmaker."[80]

If it was a surprise that Hyperbolus was ostracized, as Plutarch asserts, the reason was not that he had never been a significant politician. It would be more reasonable to argue that he seemed too powerful and too secure for Athenians to imagine that he could be so swiftly defeated. If those who have written about the period have deemphasized his importance, they may have been misled by the notion so common in late antiquity and in modern times that Athens was a city

[79] Most of the information in this table has been gathered from *PA* 13910. Subsequent studies of Hyperbolus will benefit, as has this table, from the useful articles by F. Camon in the *Giornale Italiano di filologia*, vols. 15 and 16 (1962 and 1963).

[80] The fragment of Andocides is quoted in the scholia to Aristophanes, *Wasps* 1007, and is conveniently available in the first volume of the Loeb *Minor Attic Orators*.

where only two or three leaders were active at any one time.[81] As long as one thinks of politics in these terms, it is tempting to reject any suggestion that Phaeax had a significant role in these events, and to place no stress on Hyperbolus' standing, while hinting luridly at the revulsion which his unnamed depravities provoked. But our new model of politics makes it possible to understand this ostracism far more easily and with far less violence to the facts. The reasonable inference—that at least four politicians were involved—can be readily admitted. Phaeax, Nicias, Alcibiades, and Hyperbolus can each be given a significant part.[82] Theophrastus' authority need not be impugned, nor Hyperbolus' political importance denied. Granted that Plutarch's accounts must be viewed more critically and in some measure amended, much of what he says will not seem implausible. For example, he is probably correct in asserting that since it was clear that the citizens would turn the ostracism against one of the three (sc. Phaeax, Alcibiades, or Nicias), Alcibiades brought the fac-

---

[81] Modern scholarship tends either to deny Phaeax any importance, to insist that he was merely a figure of the second rank, or to insist that he was a subordinate of some more famous politician. See the summary in F. Camon, *Giornale Italiano di filologia* 16 (1963) 145. Most of these treatments seem to me Procrustean and have little to commend them. J. Carcopino, however, has constructed a more sophisticated argument in *L'ostracisme Athenien* (Paris 1935) 228-229. He believes that Phaeax was an ally of Nicias, and supports his view by pointing out that both men are associated with Dionysius Chalcous. But the associations are very tenuous: the reference to Phaeax in fr. 4 of Dionysius Chalcous is questionable (see Gulick's index to the Loeb Athenaeus s.v. "Phaeacian"). Nicias' association with Dionysius is even more problematic. Plutarch, *Nicias* 5, says he adopted a boy who pretended to be Dionysius' son. This surely does not suggest that the politician and the poet were especially close friends. But granting Carcopino's point for a moment, what shall we say of the logic of the argument? Would the fact that both Phaeax and Nicias were associated with Dionysius prove, or even suggest, that they were in alliance with each other?

[82] Indeed since the ostraca against Cleophon are from the late fifth century, perhaps from this ostracism, he too may have played a part in this affair. For the ostraca see E. Vanderpool, "Cleophon," *Hesperia* 21 (1952) 114-115; *Hesperia* 37 (1968) 120. F. Camon, in *Giornale Italiano di filologia* 16 (1963) 147-151, suggests that Cleophon and Hyperbolus may have been in coalition, but for this there is no evidence.

tions (*staseis*) together and, conversing with Nicias, turned the ostracism against Hyperbolus (*Alcibiades* 13). It is perfectly reasonable that a coalition was formed and that Hyperbolus was its victim.[83]

The case of the ostracism of Hyperbolus works well in the model we have constituted—with one anomaly, Hyperbolus himself. The sources suggest there was some sort of difference between him and the other politicians, though they are vague about its exact nature. Comedy seems to share the widespread dislike of this man, and makes it clear that he lacked the acceptability of the wealthy and well-born politicians of earlier years, or even of his opponents in this ostracism. Nor do we hear of a *hetaireia* or *stasis* supporting Hyperbolus. His base of support is not clearly defined. Thus the ostracism, but not the man himself, is easily accounted for in the scheme of Athenian politics developed so far. To understand Hyperbolus a rather different approach is needed.

[83] Since in an ostracism only a plurality was required, it does not follow that the identifiable groups opposed to Hyperbolus were very large. By discreet campaigning, by having ostraca prepared in advance to hand out on the day of the voting, and perhaps by other less commendable methods, even relatively small groups could accumulate enough votes to ostracize a man.

3. The New Democracy

Introductory

Cleon's Repudiation of His Friends
Cleon's Style in Thucydides—Cleon's Style in Comedy

The New Vocabulary of Politics
Philodemos and *Misodemos*—*Philopolis* and *Misopolis*—Parallel Developments—Effects and Implications

New Terms for the Leader
Demagogos—*Prostates tou demou*—*Rhetor*—Effects and Implications

Pericles and Cleon
Pericles: Traditionalist and Innovator—The Indispensable Expert—Pericles' Resemblance to Cleon—Cleon and His Friends—Cleon's Style

Two Models of Politics

3. The New Democracy

Introductory

THE system which we have described in the last chapter is a strange one to modern eyes, far different from anything with which we are familiar. Yet for a small and relatively tranquil city it could prove workable, and perhaps highly advantageous. As we have already seen, such a system had its virtues: it could provide means to represent the interests of many citizens and to reconcile and adjudicate their demands; built into it were ways of testing the competence of leaders before they rose to great prominence; it could bind at least some citizens closely to their city. As long as the safeguards that had been developed within this system—for example, ostracism—were functioning properly, excessive concentration of power in any one group could be avoided and civic strife mitigated. In a larger city or in one where public business was more complex, where fewer citizens knew each other, where tensions between classes were strong, the system might prove far less satisfactory. Only a few men would possess the expertise needed to formulate and implement intelligent policies; many politicians would prove inept and hopelessly amateur. Suspicion, distrust, and the proliferation of political groups would retard the formation of coalitions and make it more difficult to obtain an effective governing majority.

As the century went on, Athens faced many of the problems to which we have just alluded. She grew greatly in size, and the complexity of her affairs increased immeasurably as she changed from an archaic town to the imperial ruler of half the Greek world. Her power, moreover, came increasingly to depend upon her fleet, and that fleet in turn depended on the Athenian lower classes to provide the bulk of the oarsmen and sailors. The situation that resulted was anomalous and potentially dangerous: the city was relying on precisely those

87

citizens who had the least political influence. Since many of them were members of the thetic class, the lowest of the four property assessment groups, they were theoretically excluded from certain offices.[1] But far more important was the exclusion of these citizens from the system of *philia* ties, the importance of which we have already seen. Not all of them could have belonged to *genē*; very few of them are likely to have been included in the symposia and *hetaireiai* of the powerful. Thus they constituted a group outside the centers of real power in their society, one likely to suspect that the government which was called a "democracy" did not always live up to its professions, and one which might look upon existing friendship groups with some suspicion. They would not be likely to overlook or to excuse the ethical problems in political friendship.

For the life of the city this situation had serious implications. The possibility of tension was present—tension between the more or less wealthy, usually well-born and socially prestigious citizens, the *chrestoi*, and some of the poorer, less distinguished Athenians.[2] The *chrestoi* were the "useful ones," the men who expected to lead. The poorer citizens, though numerous and potentially powerful, not only lacked the wealth and background for a political career but were without close personal connections with those who exercised pow-

---

[1] *AthPol* 7.3, cf. B-S 899 n. 2.

[2] In the fifth century the wealthier and more prestigious citizens would call themselves *kaloi kagathoi* (gentlemen) or *agathoi* (good people) or *beltistoi* (the best people) or perhaps simply *andres* (real men). *Chrestoi* could be substituted for any of these words in most contexts, but it emphasizes the value and reliability of these men and their implicit claim to leadership. The word is cognate with the verb *chraomai*, meaning, *inter alia*, "use." Its range extends from "useful" to "good" or "desirable." *Chrestos* seems not to have been in common use before the fifth century, but then becomes a widely used term, e.g. Ion of Chios *FGrH* 392 F 6 (*ad fin*), Aristophanes, *Frogs* 735, Euripides, *Heracles Driven Mad* 670 etc. From time to time, especially in Euripides, it is used as a purely moral term—"virtuous." But frequently it has class connotations and suggests good genealogy and some wealth. Note, for example, its use in Pseudo-Xenophon, *Constitution of Athens* 1.2 and 4, and Thucydides 6.53.2. Its common antonyms are *phaulos, poneros,* and *achreios,* later *archrestos.*

er. These poorer citizens suffered only rare formal disabilities; by Greek standards they had extraordinary rights and privileges. In theory at least the affairs of the city were in their hands in a way quite unparalleled in most modern governments. But in practical terms the influence of these *phauloi* or *poneroi* was disproportionately small.[3] For, despite their numbers, they lacked the one essential element for political power, organization. Without it they might witness, discuss, approve the decisions which were made, but still not exercise their full force in the affairs of their city.[4]

[3] The etymology of *poneros* is "full of *ponos*" (toil). Hence it comes to mean "working class," "unpleasant," and ultimately "bad." O. Reverdin, *Museum Helveticum* 2 (1945) 210 notes the parallel to the French *vilain*. See also the useful comments of L. Whibley, *Political Parties in Athens* . . . (Cambridge 1889) 48 n. 2. The word comes to be used as an antonym of *chrestos*, in its moral sense (hence "evil"), in its social sense (hence "low class," "poor or ill-born"), and in its civic usage ("unable to perform civic functions," cf. Adkins, *Merit and Responsibility*, 214). Note the contrast with *chrestos* in pseudo-Xenophon's *Constitution of Athens* 1.1 *et alibi*, and Thucydides 6.53.2. *Mochtheros* is a similar, though less frequently used, word.

Although *poneros* was in common use in the fifth century, it is not a word a man would chose to apply to himself. Its unfavorable connotations could be avoided by selecting *phaulos* instead. This word, too, contrasts with *chrestos*, e.g. Xenophon, *Memorabilia* 2.3.17, but it is usually not deprecatory. As E. R. Dodds points out in his note on Euripides, *Bacchae* 430-433, "The φαῦλοι are the 'simple' people both in the social and in the intellectual sense: Eur. frequently contrasts them with the σοφοί . . . and not always to their disadvantage. . . ." It is perhaps the best term to describe those without politically influential friends, cf. Plato, *Meno* 94 d.

[4] In my view the developments toward democracy (and toward tighter control over the allies) which took place before the 440's or even the 430's were not primarily due to agitation by the *thetes*, "the naval mob," "the proletariat," or whatever term one chooses for the poorer citizenry. Most of the changes in those years could command a consensus and would have been acceptable to a broad segment of Athenian citizenry, many rich citizens and many of hoplite status, for their effect was largely to strengthen, stabilize, and embellish the city, and to so order its domestic affairs that power was not readily monopolized by a few families or cliques.

The fallacy in attributing these developments to the activity of the *phauloi* is the assumption that only some citizens benefited from them; further, that all segments of the citizenry were politically conscious to the same degree and equally active in politics. There is some reason to believe that then, as so often now, the poorer citizens were less active than those of moderate or considerable means. The poor might be stirred to action by some great issue or passionate cause, but the problems of organization were great, and they

Under such circumstances growing tensions and animosities between citizen classes were possible, even likely. But there is a further possibility in this situation that is obvious to us and was not neglected in antiquity. The reward would be great if means could be found to activate and organize the *phauloi,* the "unpretentious" citizenry. Herein is the origin of a new kind of democracy, a new pattern of politics that was to become increasingly conspicuous as the century went on. If we are to understand the origin and appeal of leaders such as Hyperbolus, then it is to the attitudes and disaffection of these citizens that we must turn. Admittedly, we should not imagine that in the late fifth century Hyperbolus and others confronted a totally new situation that no Greek had ever faced before. On the contrary, even when the city was far smaller and ideas of equality far less developed, similar circumstances and politicians to exploit them could sometimes be found. For example, Herodotus gives this account of an episode in the rise of Cleisthenes to power, late in the sixth century: "In Athens two men were powerful, Cleisthenes, a man of the Alcmaeonids . . . and Isagoras, son of Teisander, who was of a prominent house though its early origin is not known to me. (His kin sacrifice to Carian Zeus.) These men formed factions (*estasiasan*) to win power, and when Cleisthenes was getting the worst of it, he made the *demos* his *hetairos.*"[5]

---

seem often not to have sought positions of political leadership for themselves. Note especially Aristophanes, *Knights* 178-189 and Plato, *Politicus* 289e-290a.

[5] Herodotus 5.66: ἐν δὲ αὐτῆσι δύο ἄνδρες ἐδυνάστευον, Κλεισθένης τε ἀνὴρ Ἀλκμεωνίδης, . . . καὶ Ἰσαγόρης Τεισάνδρου οἰκίης μὲν ἐὼν δοκίμου, ἀτὰρ τὰ ἀνέκαθεν οὐκ ἔχω φράσαι· θύουσι δὲ οἱ συγγενέες αὐτοῦ Διὶ Καρίῳ. οὗτοι οἱ ἄνδρες ἐστασίασαν περὶ δυνάμιος, ἑσσούμενος δὲ ὁ Κλεισθένης τὸν δῆμον προσεταιρίζεται. The final word, *prosetairizetai*, is cognate with the word for associate, clubman, *hetairos*. The verb is rare in Greek; the only other occurrences in Herodotus describe the formation of Otanes' conspiracy against Smerdis (3.70.2 and 3). Its common sense is to bring someone into the *hetairos* relationship, compare Plutarch, *Cato Minor* 4, and the cognate in Thucydides 8.100.3. See also M. Ostwald *Nomos and the Beginnings of Athenian Democracy* (Oxford 1969) 142-143.

The way in which Cleisthenes went about making the *demos* his *hetairos*

Cleisthenes' technique proved successful and was imitated. Throughout the fifth century politicians such as Cimon were assiduous in winning the good will of the common run of citizens by timely acts of generosity and by a sustained affability of manner. This was the politics of largess, the effectiveness of which we have already noted. The good will of citizens who were not tied to any politician by close *philia* bonds could prove decisive in a vote of the assembly or of a jury. But the full realization of the power to be gained from a systematic cultivation of the *demos* and the full development of the steps that led to that support came only in the last third of the century, by a process which is the theme of this chapter and through a much reviled man whom we must now strive to understand.[6]

Cleon's Repudiation of His Friends

". . . Cleon, when he first decided to take up political life, brought his friends together and renounced his friendship with them as something which often weakens and perverts the right and just choice of policy in political life."[7]

is not clear. The sequence of argument in chapter 66 might lead one to conclude that it was his tribal reforms that brought this about, but 5.69.2 indicates that the reform was the result rather than the cause of his good standing with the demos. The version of the affair in *AthPol* 20.1 reads ἡττώμενος δὲ ταῖς ἑταιρείαις ὁ Κλεισθένης προσηγάγετο τὸν δῆμον, ἀποδιδοὺς τῷ πλήθει τὴν πολιτείαν . . . , and the beginning of chapter 21 of the treatise suggests that the record of hostility between the Alcmaeonidae and the Peisistratids helped him win the confidence of the *demos*. The meaning and relationship of the passages in Herodotus and in the *AthPol* are still obscure; see most recently R. Seager, *AJP* 84 (1963) 287-289. My suspicion is that Cleisthenes brought the *demos* over to his side by quite informal means, by promising to treat them as his *hetairoi*, to look after their interests, to give them a say in political decisions.

[6] I propose to approach Hyperbolus by first studying Cleon. I do not wish to equate the two men, nor to regard Hyperbolus simply as a caricature of Cleon (cf. F. Camon, *Rivista di studi classici* 9 [1961] 196-197). But if it is correct to regard Cleon as an innovator in the art of politics, then it is likely that Hyperbolus, a man of similar class and background and confronted with similar problems in his political career, would learn from him and adopt some of his techniques.

[7] Plutarch, *Moralia* 806 F, trans. H. N. Fowler in the Loeb Classical Li-

The anecdote is again from Plutarch, and belongs to that same group of stories about friendship and its political implications which was investigated in chapter 2. It is a surprising passage, not only for the slight and quickly passing hint of a favorable assessment of Cleon, but also for its suggestion that an Athenian politician of this period might deliberately throw away the support of a group of friends. From what has been said in the last chapter, this would seem an irrational and foolish action. Friends were the basis of a political career in fifth century Athens, and as we read on in the passage it becomes clear that the friends Cleon turned away were substantial and important.[8] How could anyone, least of all a clever politician, deny himself the advantages such friends could supply? Was Cleon mad?[9] Is the story to be rejected?

Before dismissing it as an unbelievable ascription of unparalleled altruism to an unprincipled politician, it will be wise to consider the whole story carefully. Plutarch's comments are revealing. The hint of approval passes quickly; he deplores Cleon's action, but not as political folly:

---

brary. Plutarch contrasts the story with Themistocles' comment, that he would not want to sit on the archon's throne if he couldn't see to it that his friends received better treatment than his enemies. It is likely that these stories have a common origin—I suspect Theophrastus. See above, Chapter 2, n. 33.

[8] It may still be objected by some that Cleon was too impoverished to have such important associates. But this has long been shown to be incorrect; see Chapter 4 below, Cleon's Wealth.

[9] *Mania* was, of course, precisely the charge brought against Cleon and other politicians by some contemporaries, e.g. Cratinus, fr. 217 b (and note Thucydides' characterization of Cleon's promise to win at Pylos in twenty days [4.39.3] as *maniodes*). Cleon is perhaps also intended in pseudo-Xenophon's attack on the Athenian leaders as *mainomenos* in 1.9 of the *Constitution of Athens*; and the first hand in the Venetus manuscript of Aristophanes seems to me to be correct in writing *mainomenos* in *Wasps* 1232; compare the scholia on line 1235. Demostratus (scholion to Aristophanes, *Lysistrata* 397) and Diopeithes (Teleicleides fr. 6) are also accused of madness, as is the whole Athenian *demos* in pseudo-Plato, *Axiochus* 368 d.

Sophrosyne is the opposite of *mania* and is sometimes used for "sensible" politics, e.g. Thucydides 3.82.8, Aristophanes, *Frogs* 727, Teleicleides fr. 41. It does not seem, however, to have been the slogan of any one group. Note Cleon's use of it in Thucydides 3.37.3. On the word see H. North, *Sophrosyne* (Ithaca 1966) esp. 77, 90, and 115 and G. Grossman, *Politische Schlagwörter* (Zürich 1950) 137-145.

But he (Cleon) would have done better if he had cast out from his soul avarice and love of strife and had cleansed himself of envy and malice; for the city needs not men who have no friends or associates (*hetairoi*), but useful (*chrestoi*) and sensible (*sophrones*) men. As it was, he drove away his friends. "But a snake-like mass of flatterers writhed" [Aristophanes, *Peace* 756] about him, as the comic poets say; and being rough and harsh to the better classes (*epieikeis*) he in turn subjected himself to the multitude in order to win its favour—"The gerontagogue, donor of reiterated wages" [Anonymous fragment of Old Comedy, 11]—making the most unpretentious (*phaulotaton*) and unsound elements his associates against the best (*aristoi*).[10]

Plutarch's criticism is not that Cleon's action was political suicide, but that he was irresponsible in turning the *phauloi* against the "best people." Far from being folly, Cleon's act, to judge from Plutarch's reaction to his sources, contributed to the extraordinary influence and power which he enjoyed in the Athenian assembly. By turning his back on a coterie of influential supporters, Cleon could more easily present himself as a man of the people and thereby forge an alliance between himself and the poorer and hitherto ill-represented sections of the populace. The ambitious, dynamic, and prosperous entrepreneur becomes the spokesman for the poor and disaffected.

In adopting these tactics Cleon would be following a course which not only had some precedent in the careers of Cleisthenes, Aristides, and Pericles, but also is familiar in modern times. The demand has sometimes been made, for

---

[10] Plutarch, *Moralia* 806 F-807 A. I have taken the translation of H. N. Fowler in the Loeb and modified it extensively to bring over more of the word play (e.g. γεροντανωγῶν in Fr. Com. Adesp. 11, a parody of Sophocles fr. 447 *TGF* and a pun on δημαγωγῶν), and to keep closer to the tone of the Greek. For "make his associates" at the end of the passage Plutarch uses the verb *prosetairizomai*, the same verb Herodotus used in the passage quoted in the introduction to this chapter (5.66).

example, "in certain working-class sections of the French and German Socialist parties that the leaders should break off all social relationships with the bourgeois world . . . and should have no other companions than 'regularly inscribed members.'"[11]

If Plutarch were to prove correct in stating that Cleon once renounced his friendship with this group of men, he may have provided us with a very important clue about a significant development in Athenian politics, one that carried the examples set by some politicians earlier in the century to their logical conclusion, that at the same time marked a departure from the familiar pattern of organization by *philia* ties, and that might substantially change the distribution of political power within the society. The great question, then, is whether Plutarch's account can be believed. Is it a scrap of dubious reliability, or is it perhaps the exact piece which will enable us to solve a perplexing puzzle?

The answers to these questions are fortunately relatively easy to determine. The story can be tested, for if what Plutarch reports is correct, there should be other signs of the change in politics brought about by Cleon. Plutarch's story may be the most explicit indication of Cleon's approach, but it should not be the only one. Even though the documentation of Cleon's life and career is less adequate than might be hoped, we can still expect to find, in our primary sources for the period, notably in Thucydides and in Aristophanes, some reverberations of this change.

Cleon's Style in Thucydides

One indication is to be found in a speech by Cleon which Thucydides reports. To be sure, Thucydides does not pretend that the speeches in his history are an exact rendering of the words used by the politicians and orators on the occasions he

[11] R. Michels, *Political Parties*, trans. E. and C. Paul (Glencoe, Illinois 1958) 343. The entire chapter, "The Postulate of Renunciation," is apposite to our investigation.

records. Modern scholars have sometimes contended that the speeches are practically free compositions by Thucydides himself, with no basis in historical fact. Yet many of the speeches are carefully drawn and even individualized—suggesting that Thucydides not only mastered the situation sufficiently to know what arguments would be necessary, but also knew his characters well enough to determine the style and approach they would use.[12] Thus the words Thucydides assigns to Cleon in his speech on the Mytilene question may well suggest the tone of his argument, even though they cannot be a verbatim transcript of the speech: "For the most part the less pretentious people—in comparison with the more knowledgeable—administer cities better. The latter want to be thought wiser than the laws . . . while those who are less confident in their own knowledge are content to be less learned than the laws" (Thucydides 3.37.3-4).

The wording is interesting; οἵ τε φαυλότεροι τῶν ἀνθρώπων πρὸς τοὺς ξυνετωτέρους ὡς ἐπὶ τὸ πλέον ἄμεινον οἰκοῦσι τὰς πόλεις: Thucydides represents Cleon as the spokesman for those Athenians without intellectual or other pretensions, for the *phauloi*. The verbal coincidence with Plutarch's anecdote is striking. But far more significant is the whole tone of the passage. Cleon appears as the anti-intellectual, the opponent of the pretentiousness and snobbishness of some segments of

---

[12] The contrast between the speech by Archidamus (1.80-85) and that by Sthenelaidas (1.86) seems to me instructive. Thucydides knows he does not have the exact words and that to render the speeches in Doric would be fraudulent. But he draws a sharp contrast between the two speakers and writes for each a brilliant and highly individual speech. Similarly, Cleon's words in the history are distinctive and individualized. It does not follow that Thucydides has all details of Cleon's style right. Yet surely enough of Thucydides' audience knew the oratory of Cleon first-hand to be severe judges of "free compositions." My disposition is to admit that Thucydides normally kept as close as he could to the general line of approach of a speaker, even though he had to guess about the exact wording. I am also impressed by the arguments of J. Finley, *Thucydides* (paperback reprint, Ann Arbor 1963) 94-104 and in chapter VIII of that valuable work. For a different view of Thucydides' speeches in general, and especially of this speech of Cleon, see A. Andrewes, *Phoenix* 16 (1962) 64-85.

Athenian society, a true man of the people.[13] If we can indulge in anachronistic categories for a moment, this is Athenian Populism—with its characteristic confidence in the ability of the voter to reach expeditious decisions without the guidance of any elite. In this sense the passage helps confirm what Plutarch tells us of Cleon—his repudiation of "the best people" and his ostensible devotion to the *phauloi*.

Cleon's Style in Comedy.

Nor is Thucydides our only confirmation of Plutarch's anecdote about Cleon's political style. Comic poetry, for all the ambiguity and difficulties of interpretation which it presents, has the same effect. The comments of Aristophanes, Eupolis, and other comic writers were intended to raise laughs— never to be read with the sober faces worn by historians when they cull historical facts from comic poetry. Old Comedy has a large element of caricature; it distorts, exaggerates and parodies in order to entertain. Thus Paphlagon, the ranting, fraudulent, bombastic servant of old man Demos in the *Knights*, the character who both in antiquity and in modern times has been recognized as a caricature of Cleon, is no more an exact portrait of the politician than the comic mask which the actor wore was a photographic likeness. But since the technique *is* caricature, some features of the real man must have been recognizable—to the Athenians if not always to us. Consider one small example.

There is a recurring phrase in the play which has often been suspected of echoing the actual words of Cleon, taken out of context and made ludicrous in a new setting. Paph-

---

[13] If we could accept Sotion's story *apud* Diogenes Laertius 2.12—that Cleon indicted Anaxagoras on a charge of impiety—we would have a further example of the anti-intellectual nature of Cleon's policies. But the story inspires little confidence: Satyrus, quoted in the same passage of Diogenes, says it was Thucydides (i.e. the son of Melesias) who indicted Anaxagoras. The attempt to reconcile these authorities by D. Kienast, *Gymnasium* 60 (1953) 210-229, seems less probable to me than the assumption that both authors are rather freely embroidering the only sure fact: that the Athenians did at some point take legal action against Anaxagoras.

lagon continually professes his loyalty and devotion to Demos, the personification of the Athenian people, and uses the most flamboyant language for his protestations: "I love you, Demos, and I'm your *erastes*" (*Knights* 732). Paphlagon claims to be a suitor in a love affair, and the object of his attention is not some fair maid or pretty Athenian youth, but silly old Demos. The situation is ludicrous and Paphlagon's language is absurd. It might be dismissed as pure comic fantasy if a later passage in the play did not provide a strong argument for thinking that the words are not Aristophanes' own free invention, but "flowers culled from the oratory of Cleon."[14]

The reader can judge for himself; the passage is *Knights* 1340-1344. The Sausage-seller, Paphlagon's rival, admonishes Demos to be less gullible and criticizes him for being taken in by speakers in the assembly. The discourse moves, almost imperceptibly, from comic fantasy to political reality: "First off, whenever someone said in the assembly, 'Oh Demos, I'm your suitor (*erastes*) and I love you and care for you, and I'm the only one who looks after your interests'—whenever someone used these preambles, you crowed like a rooster and proudly shook your head." The lines allude back to Paphlagon's outlandish phrase in line 732, but the emphasis has

[14] B. B. Rogers in his commentary on *Knights* 1341 (London 1910). Cf. A. Burckhardt, *Spuren der athenischen Volksrede in der alten Komödie* (diss. Basel 1924) 40. The obvious objection to this view, namely that the language is too shocking and exotic to have come from political discourse, will not bear examination. According to Thucydides, Pericles just a few years before the performance of the *Knights* had used the same metaphor in a context that was only slightly different. In the Thucydidean version of the funeral oration he is made to say, "What I prefer is that you should fix your eyes every day on the greatness of Athens as she really is, and should fall in love with her" (Thucydides 2.43.1, trans. Rex Warner), ἀλλὰ μᾶλλον τὴν τῆς πόλεως δύναμιν καθ᾽ ἡμέραν ἔργῳ θεωμένους καὶ ἐραστὰς γιγνομένους αὐτῆς. . . . Gomme's commentary on the passage is very useful on the origin and development of the conceit. The extravagance of the language is fully appropriate to Pericles' love of the vivid phrase and to Cleon's florid oratory. (On Cleon's style of speech see *AthPol* 28.3 and Theopompus, *FGrH* 115 F 92, a commonplace repeated frequently in antiquity, e.g. Plutarch, *Nicias* 8, *Tiberius Gracchus* 2, Cicero, *Brutus* 28). Similar phraseology may be found in Herodotus 3.53.4 and Aristophanes, *Acharnians* 143.

shifted to its use *in the assembly* and to the *demos'* foolish reaction. Thus the arrow which hits Paphlagon nicks Cleon as
well, and it would appear that we have in the *Knights* an echo
of Cleon's oratory.

Discount this example of comic caricature as seems proper.
Deny, if it seems best, that Cleon actually used such flamboyant language, and that Aristophanes was parodying it in
the *Knights*. Yet the direction of Aristophanes' attack may yet
be significant. He presents Paphlagon, a readily detectable
comic Cleon, as a man who speaks in extravagant terms of his
devotion to the Athenian citizen body and who claims to have
the interest of those citizens at heart. This devotion is expressed through the language of personal relationships, transferred to political affairs. Paphlagon takes the language of the
most intense *philia* and translates it to a new sphere.[15] The
demos becomes his *philos*. Whatever we think of this passage
it must be admitted that this manner of speech is fully consistent with that of a man who turned his back on a group of
influential *philoi* and built his power on mass support.[16]

[15] Some irony may be intended, especially if certain upper-class politicians
were thought to have had love affairs with handsome youths, and if Cleon, as
Knights 875-878 may hint, attacked them for it. Aristophanes would not have
missed the perfect opportunity for comedy if Cleon, having attacked some
opponents on this charge, proceeded to express his love for the *demos*.

[16] There is an interesting parallel to what we have observed about Cleon
in a passage in Euripides' *Hecuba*, probably produced in the 420's (see A.
Lesky, *Tragische Dichtung der Hellenen* [Göttingen 1956] 170 esp. n. 2).
Hecuba attacks Odysseus for betraying her:

> ἀχάριστον ὑμῶν σπέρμ', ὅσοι δημηγόρους
> ζηλοῦτε τιμάς· μηδὲ γιγνώσκοισθέ μοι
> οἳ τοὺς φίλους βλάπτοντες οὐ φροντίζετε,
> ἢν τοῖσι πολλοῖς πρὸς χάριν λέγητέ τι.

> Yours is an ungracious tribe, all you
> who are after the honors of a public
> speaker. Don't expect any recognition
> from me, you who don't care if you hurt
> your friends, as long as you say some-
> thing pleasing to the masses.

Euripides, Hecuba 254-257

Thus, in effect, Hecuba likens Odysseus to an orator in the assembly who
abandons his *philia* ties to ingratiate himself with a wider following. The

The New Vocabulary of Politics

We have spoken so far of likelihoods. It is likely that Plutarch's story of Cleon's repudiation of his friends is correct; it is likely that Thucydides and Aristophanes corroborate it. But we are still far from certainty. Yet more evidence can be found that will allow us perhaps to be more precise and more confident. By the time with which we are concerned our knowledge of the development of the Greek language begins to improve. There are still great gaps in our documentation and more material would be welcome, but the record is far more complete for the 430's and 420's than for any preceding decades. And Attica is the best documented region within Greece. Thus it becomes possible at roughly this time to learn how Athenians were speaking about politics. And since the way people speak often contains important clues to the way they act, the study of political vocabulary may prove a valuable instrument for understanding Athenian history. Sir Lewis Namier has noted what seems to be an encouraging example in the history of eighteenth century Britain, when changes in terminology give a clue to historical developments. "In 1706 it was 'faithful service to your country'; in 1760 'service of one's friends.' The community had become atomized and individualized, and when another half-century had passed and the idea was proclaimed that the greatest common good is to be reached by everyman pursuing his own individual advantage, this was not so much a eulogy of egotism as an apologia for an existing practice."[17]

There is one development, or rather one group of developments, in Athenian political vocabulary which may allow us better to understand the events of the time and further to test

audience at the first performance of this play might for a second be reminded of a politician of recent memory against whom the same charge had been made. Cf. L. Pearson, *Popular Ethics in Ancient Greece* (Stanford 1962) 145.

[17] Sir Lewis Namier, *The Structure of Politics at the Accession of George III* (second ed., London 1963) 18.

the validity of Plutarch's anecdote about Cleon. The generalizations which we draw for this period may in some respects
be the opposite of those Namier derived for the eighteenth
century, but the approach is very much the same. Once again
friendship enters directly into politics, but now in a different
way: during the last third of the century the terminology of
friendship is applied to the city and especially to the *demos*.
The individual's relation to his *polis* comes to be spoken of in
ways that had formerly been reserved almost exclusively for
his relations to persons.[18] And this change betokens changes
in thought and ultimately in conduct. For the first time in
Greece people begin regularly to profess that they will show
the city the kind of loyalty which was formerly promised to
friends. We begin to hear men called "*demos*-lovers" or
"*demos*-haters," apparently without ironic intent. The city begins to share the language of devotion and fidelity that was
appropriate to *philoi*. Although this development bears an
obvious resemblance to the manner of speaking which Aris-

---

[18] It seems odd to us that it is first in the fifth century that one begins
commonly to hear the injunction to love one's country. There were of course
strong precedents earlier: Odysseus went back *philen es patrida gaian*, "to
his own fatherland," and earlier Greeks surely felt strong emotion for their
cities, perhaps even for Hellas. But it is only relatively late that the feeling
finds clear expression as a moral duty. The idea is implicit in Sophocles'
Antigone 182-183, usually dated 441 B.C., but the earliest explicit statements
come from the 420's: "Wise men ought to love their children, their parents,
their country—and this they should build up and never tear down" (Euripides,
Suppliants 506-508). (On the date of the Suppliants see A. Lesky, *Tragische
Dichtung*, 176.) In the *Erechtheus*, perhaps produced the same year as the
Suppliants (see Lesky, *Tragische Dichtung*, 177-178), Praxithea, who has
decided to sacrifice her child for the city, expresses the wish, "Oh fatherland,
if only everyone who lives in you loved you as I do" (*Erechtheus* fr. 360
TGF [fr. 50 Austin], lines 53 and 54, cf. fr. 360 A in Snell's supplement
to *TGF*). A passage in the *Phoenissae* is similar,

> —Fatherland, it seems, is the dearest thing to mortals.
> —It's impossible to express how dear it is.

> Euripides, *Phoenissae* 406-407

See also Adespota fragment 411 and Euripides fr. 729, *Medea* 328-329,
642-651, and Aristophanes fr. 898A. Note the implications of what Pericles
is reported to have said in 2.60.2-4 (430 B.C.), the necessity for self-sacrifice
for common good.

tophanes uses in his caricature of Cleon, we cannot positively assert that Cleon introduced some or all of the new usages which appear in his day. But the fact that they are a part of a movement toward a new arrangement of politics from which he cannot be disassociated increases rather than decreases their significance. The new terminology of politics provides the background for Cleon's political operations, and increases the plausibility of the story of his abrupt break with the old pattern of political friendship.

Philodemos and Misodemos

The word *philodemos*, "friendly to the *demos*," first appears in extant Greek literature in 424 B.C. in Aristophanes' *Knights*.[19] Demos has been impressed by the services of Paphlagon's rival, an ingratiating if ill-bred and loud-mouthed sausage-seller from the agora. Finally, in lines 786 and 787 Demos asks him: "Who are you, man? You're not some descendant of Harmodius [the tyrannicide], are you? That surely was an act of yours that was noble and *philodemos*." A year later we find the word applied to a human being for the first time: "Old Solon was *philodemos* in his nature" (Aristophanes, *Clouds* 1187).[20]

Thus we find the first signs of this interesting compound in the 420's; its antonym, *misodemos*, appears at almost exactly

[19] The word *demos* is ambiguous in Greek; it can refer either to the people as a whole (*populus*) or to the lower segments of it (*plebs*). Since the ambiguity is vital in political sloganeering and argument, I have transliterated the word rather than translated it.

Compounds with *philo-* are treated in a useful monograph by M. Landfester, *Das griechische Nomen "philos" und seine Ableitungen* (Hildesheim 1966) (*Spudasmata* xi); pp. 160-174 are especially relevant to our discussion.

[20] The idea of loving the *demos*, as has been pointed out above, is present in lines 732-734 of Aristophanes' *Knights*. Note also the expression [κ]αὶ φιλέσο τὸ[ν δῆμον τὸν Ἀθεναίον . . .] in line 47 of the Athenian treaty with Colophon, usually dated 447/6 B.C. (For the text see D 15 in vol. II of B. D. Meritt, H. T. Wade-Gery and M. McGregor, *The Athenian Tribute Lists* [*SEG* x 17]). *Philodemos* occurs as a proper name in the first half of the century (*PA* 14481), but it is not clear whether the sense of the name is "friendly to the *demos*" or "befriended by the *demos*."

101

the same time, in Aristophanes' *Wasps* 474 (422 B.C.). The speaker is the chorus, a group of old men, ardent admirers of Cleon who fear that Bdelycleon will destroy the jury system from which they benefit. The chorus rings the changes on the charge of subversion and calls Bdelycleon a *demos*-hater and monarchy-lover (ὦ μισόδημε καὶ μοναρχίας ἐραστά).[21] *Misodemos*, unlike its antonym, becomes a popular word of political parlance; it is Theramenes' charge against Critias (Xenophon, *Hellenica* 2.3.47) and reportedly the attack made against Andocides (Plutarch, *Alcibiades* 21) and against the speaker in the fourth oration ascribed to Andocides (pseudo-Andocides 4.8, cf. 16). Clearly in appealing to the *demos* it could be a very powerful word.

Philopolis and Misopolis

Philopolis and *Misopolis* show a development similar to, but not identical with, that of the pair discussed in the preceding section. *Philopolis* (or *philoptolis*), "friendly to the city," would seem to be an old word that acquires new vitality in the late part of the fifth century. The earliest attested use is Pindar, *Olympian* 4.16 (452 B.C. or earlier), where *Hesychia,* tranquility, is called "friendly to the city." In the Euripidean *Rhesus* 158 it is applied to a character in the play, Dolon. According to Thucydides 2.60.5 Pericles boasted that he was one who loved his city and was unbribable, φιλόπολίς τε καὶ χρημάτων κρείσσων. This is the first instance of the application of the word to a political figure, a usage which becomes common in subsequent years. In the late fifth century the word is frequently used, and often in very interesting contexts. Alcibiades uses the expression *to philopoli* in his ruminations about patriotism in the sixth book of Thucydides.[22] The band of lady conspirators in Aristophanes' *Lysis-*

---

[21] The word also appears in fr. 108 of Aristophanes (*The Farmers*) and refers to the Spartan fig. The date is probably around 424 B.C. (see Edmonds I 599ff.). Cleon seems to have been mentioned in the play (see fr. 101). Did he make one of his charges of treason or conspiracy against the fig?

[22] Thucydides 6.92.3-4. On the passage see N. M. Pusey, *HSCP* 51 (1940) 215-231.

trata claim that they possess a whole thesaurus of virtues—
physis, charis, sophon, and *philopolis aretē phronimos,* "a native suitability, grace, wisdom, and a discreet civic-minded
competence" (lines 545-548). The sycophant's claim in *Plutus*
900 is not far different. Even Meletus, who indicted Socrates
on the vague charges that eventually caused his death,
claimed to be *philopolis* in his speech for the prosecution
(Plato, *Apology* 24 b).

Misopolis, though a rarer word, also begins to be heard
during the late part of the century. In one case the context is
especially interesting. The source is once again one of Aristophanes' "anti-Cleon" plays, the *Wasps,* and the speaker is
again the chorus of old admirers of Cleon, who are upset at
Bdelycleon: "Run and shout and tell Cleon this, and demand
that he come to grips with this damned city-hater . . ." (Aristophanes, *Wasps* 410-413). This appeal, if any, seems likely
to work with Cleon, perhaps, we might suspect, because the
chorus is speaking Cleon's own language.

Parallel Developments

At roughly the same time several other related words and
expressions come into use. It seems, for example, to be in the
420's that the expression *eunous toi demoi,* "well disposed to
the *demos,*" begins to have currency.[23] The first example is
again from Aristophanes, and again calls Cleon to mind. His
comic *alter ego,* Paphlagon, asks old man Demos to convene
an assembly and put him and the Sausage-seller to the test to
see which is better disposed to him.[24] At almost the same time
as the production of the *Knights* (424 B.C.), the so-called Old

---

[23] *Eunous tei polei,* "well disposed to the city," is slightly older; first example: Sophocles, *Antigone* 209. Note also Adkins' discussion of a similar
phrase used by Lysias, *Merit and Responsibility,* 210. For *dysmeneis tei polei*
see Sophocles, *Antigone* 187, and note Darius' claim that the *mounarchos*
is the man best suited to protect the citizenry from those hostile to it, the
dysmeneis, Herodotus 3.82.1; cf. Appendix I. The contrary sentiment is expressed in Euripides, *Suppliants* 429. *Dysnous tei polei* is an expression ascribed to Pericles in Thucydides 2.60.6.

[24] Aristophanes, *Knights* 748; for Demos' decision: *Knights* 873-874.

Oligarch was implying that *eunoia* was one of the qualities commonly attributed to the *poneros* when he rose to advise the assembly (pseudo-Xenophon, *Constitution of Athens* 1.7).[25] The *chrestos* on the other hand is suspected of *kakonoia*. The author of the pamphlet does not deny the suspicion; indeed, by the end of his essay he fully accepts it: "In no city is the better segment well disposed to the *demos*, rather the worst in each city is well disposed to the *demos*" (3.10). We should not naïvely accept what this polemicist says as an accurate description of Greece in his day, but it would be equally wrong to fail to recognize the value of this pamphlet as a clue to the way some Athenians thought and spoke about politics. The pamphleteer may be copying the language of public orators and politicians. In any event it is clear that by his day *kakonoia* and *eunoia* were terms of political discourse.

Now at last we approach the point where the significance of the data we have been observing becomes apparent. In the last third of the century we find numerous signs that words like *philodemos* and *misodemos, eunous toi demoi* and *philopolis*, were being applied to political figures. In some cases the terms were in use earlier, or have earlier precedents; in others, they seem first to come into use in the late 430's or in the 420's. They are all in frequent use, however, within a few years of the curious erotic imagery in Aristophanes' *Knights,* and at the approximate time when Cleon would have repudiated his friends.[26] The convergence of these events is, I believe, extremely important for the under-

---

[25] On the date of the pamphlet see Appendix II.

[26] The date of Cleon's entry into politics cannot be precisely fixed, but it must come before Pericles' death in 429 B.C., as Hermippus fr. 46 shows. There may also be some basis for Idomeneus' story that he was one of the accusers of Pericles in 430 B.C.; see Plutarch, *Pericles* 35; but this may simply be false inference from the comic poets. Cf. Jacoby in the commentary to *FGrH* 338 F 9. For Theopompus' account of Cleon's entry into politics see *Theopompus* 50-58.

standing of Greek politics. In isolation any of these data might be dismissed as insignificant, the result of accident, poor documentation or unreliable speculation. But when considered together a pattern emerges too clearly, I think, to be denied. What is common to all these developments is an ostensible transfer of primary loyalties from individuals, relatives, or friends, to the city or its citizenry. Cleon turns away from his friends; the language of politics turns words and images which formerly or properly applied to relationships between individuals to a new kind of civic discourse.

Effects and Implications

The Greeks loved their native land and said so, even in the earliest recorded times. They had for long spoken of their homeland as their "fatherland," and one need only open the *Odyssey* to detect the yearning that the Greek away from home felt as he tried to return *philen es patrida gaian*. They had also, perhaps from the first days of planned emigration, spoken of the colonizing city as the "mother" of the colonies and had expected that new foundations would fulfill specified obligations to their *Metropolis*. All these are personal terms transferred to civic uses, and contain the seeds of later developments. But however much emotion and latent patriotism was present in early Greece, there is still a significant change in the fifth century. Now, in the Athens of Cleon's lifetime, affection for the city takes a new form. Its new expressions convey far more than the venerable feelings of homesickness or pious devotion to a founding and protecting city. The new terminology goes further, affirms loyalty to the city, and even implies that that loyalty is a requirement for political advancement. Thus it marks a new stage in the enunciation of Greek values. For before this time the Greeks had not often or clearly expressed, let alone resolved, the conflict between devotion to the city and devotion to a friend. The new vocabulary did not bring with it an automatic resolution to a persistent and difficult problem, but it did permit a new clarity of discussion and it did imply a new series of priorities. The politician who presented himself as *philopolis, eunous toi demoi, philodemos,* or the like, implied that he was willing to accord the city the place which friends had so often enjoyed in earlier periods of Greek history, and that he was willing to transfer his "primary loyalties" from the *philia* group to the wider circle of the *polis* or the *demos.*[27]

We should like, of course, to know who was responsible for the development of this new kind of political discourse. Some signs point to Pericles, some to Cleon; much may have been due to more obscure politicians.[28] We cannot speak with finality. Nor can we say whether the politicians who used this terminology were sincere, or to what extent they lived up to the principles which it implied. But these are not the most important questions. It is far more vital to recognize the full significance of the change we have detected. These developments of language mark the emergence of a new hierarchy of values in the Greek city, one that emphasizes civic virtues and devotion to the well-being of the whole city. They form both the natural culmination of a progression toward popular rule, and the essential preconditions for a successfully functioning democratic system. Their importance for political life, political theory, for the course of subsequent history could be explained at great length. But it is also important to note the ambiguity of the new developments, for possibilities of civic improvement rarely are free from the threat of new and sometimes more insidious dangers. The logical sequence to the line, "Oh Demos, I'm your suitor and I love you and I care

[27] Cf. Adkins, *Merit and Responsibility,* 230-231.

[28] One would like in particular to know more about Eucrates (*PA* 5759) and Lysicles (*PA* 9417) and a Callias all mentioned in the scholia on Aristophanes, *Knights* 129 and 132, in a context that suggests that they enjoyed political prominence shortly before Cleon. They seem to be of the same social class as Cleon and perhaps anticipated or shared some of his traits.

for you," is exactly that which follows in Aristophanes, "and I'm the only one who looks after your interests."[29] The new vocabulary is more than a new way of ordering the priorities of loyalty; it is also a new technology of political power. It is, or can be used as, a device for suggesting that its user is the *only* truly dedicated servant of the whole city, and that his rivals are suspect, perhaps even traitors. It has potential for slander and invective as well as for a loftier definition of the politician's calling.

The fact that the words which we have studied often occur in pairs, *philopolis* and *misopolis*; *philodemos* and *misodemos* indicates the double-edged power which they accorded to their skillful manipulator. The politician could build himself up as *philopolis* or *philodemos* and at the same time he could tear down his opponent as the enemy of the citizenry. Language is power and its development, like any new technology, is morally ambiguous. If the new vocabulary of politics could lead to a greater degree of devotion to the common weal, it might also supply the means to attack the innocent and encourage fear and suspicion. Aristophanes, fairly or unfairly, accuses Cleon of precisely this abuse, and implies that Cleon was constantly breathing the fire of conspiracies and subversion, tyrannies and treason, the whole drearily paranoid rhetoric so familiar from modern times.[30] Cleon may have

[29] *Knights* 1341-1342. The final words are probably also an echo of political oratory, presumably Cleon's. Compare A. Burckhardt, *Spuren der athenischen Volksrede in der alten Komödie*, 41.

[30] Note especially Aristophanes, *Wasps* 488ff. The essay of M. I. Finley in *Past and Present* 21 (1962) 12 suggests that the instability and insecurity of the leader's position in a direct democracy may have had important psychological effects on Athenian politicians. Perhaps one might go a step further and speculate whether the "paranoid style" (the phrase, I believe, is Richard Hofstadter's) adopted by so many politicians, ancient and modern, is not the result of a transference of the leader's feelings of insecurity from his own personal world to the affairs of the city. The politician whose own standing is threatened sees subversion and treachery everywhere and imagines the city beset by similar dangers. If he is skillful enough and times are troubled enough he may find a way to make his anxiety and that of his fellow citizens the basis of a successful political appeal.

been rather different from what Aristophanes makes of him—
we must never forget the distortions of Socrates in the *Clouds*
when we read of Cleon in the *Wasps* or the *Knights*—but
Aristophanes has succeeded in pointing out some of the dangers implicit in these otherwise apparently hopeful developments. And this is perhaps a greater accomplishment than
achieving exactitude in the presentation of any individual.[31]

New Terms for the Leader

We have set for ourselves a difficult task: persuading
changes in language to teach us about changes in politics.
Since words are often reluctant or recalcitrant witnesses, we
cannot expect easy progress. Yet sometimes their testimony
surprises us by its clarity and by the insight it affords into developments that might otherwise escape notice. C. S. Lewis'
comments on a more recent change in political terminology
remind us how revealing words can sometimes be. He noted
that "ruler" has given way to "leader" in common parlance:
" 'Leaders' is the modern word. . . . This is a deeply significant
change of vocabulary. Our demand upon them has changed
no less than theirs on us. For of a ruler one asks justice, incorruption, diligence, perhaps clemency; of a leader, dash, initiative and (I suppose) what people call 'magnetism' or
'personality.' "[32]

The philologist thus can sometimes help the historian or
political scientist to see a little more clearly the phenomena
with which they are concerned. Athens in the last third of the
fifth century provides a further example, for there too the

[31] Yet, once again Thucydides and Aristophanes, for all their differences,
agree not only in general but also in detail about Cleon. One may dismiss
their agreement as the result of accident or shared bias, but it should be noted
that Thucydides' version of Cleon's speech on the Mytilene problem contains
the insinuation that his opponents neglect the interest of the city for personal
gain. Thucydides 3.38.3.

[32] The passage is to be found in Lewis' Cambridge inaugural lecture "de
descriptione temporum," reprinted in *They Asked for a Paper* (London 1962)
18.

terminology for the political leader was changing in significant ways. Older terms, to be sure, persist in use, *hegemon*
(leader), for example, a word built up on the root meaning
"to track out." *Archon* (used for any magistrate) and
strategos (general) and other traditional titles continue as
well, but other terms begin now to appear. Some of these, for
example *demagogos*, have cognates familiar to us from modern languages; others, such as *prostates tou demou* (protector
of the *demos*) will sound strange to our ears. But if we are
patient and exact in our study of these expressions, they may
reward us with an increased understanding of Athenian politics. The words bear the mark of a new era and may help
convey to us a clearer impression of the city in which they became the common coin of political commerce.

Demagogos

The most famous of these words, *demagogos*, was brought
over into English during the controversies of the mid-seven-
teenth century and has now become a part of our standard
political vocabulary. But what Milton called the "Affrighten-
ment of this Goblin word" seems not originally to have been
present in Greek.[33] Although the word eventually acquired
unfavorable connotations, neither its etymology nor the early
instances of its use give reason to believe that it was originally
a derogatory term. It is a combination of *demos* and the root
"to lead." In origin, then, there is no pejorative force to the
word.[34] The earliest preserved uses are often sharply critical

[33] J. Milton, *Eikonoklastes* sec. iv (1649) found on p. 392f. of Vol. III of
the Yale edition of Milton's works (New Haven, Connecticut 1962). The
New English Dictionary indicates that the word first occurs in its pejorative
sense in a pamphlet called *Eikon Basilike* (London 1648) p. 19, the authorship of which Milton imputed to Charles I. After calling it a "Goblin word,"
Milton goes on to remark that "the King by his leave cannot coine English
as he could money"—thereby confirming the editors' view that the usage was
new in Milton's day.

[34] *Demos*, as has been pointed out above, is ambiguous. It can be the equivalent of either *populus* or *plebs*. In the mouth of a *chrestos*, then, the word
could be used in an adverse sense, "the leader of the *plebs*," but the reaction

of contemporary politicians, but it is the context, not the word itself, which conveys that criticism. For example, consider the earliest known use of the word, these lines spoken to the Sausage-seller in Aristophanes' *Knights*: "The *demagogia* is no longer for a cultured man, nor for someone *chrestos* in his manners, but for the ignorant, and the obnoxious" (Aristophanes, *Knights* 191-193).[35]

Even in the fourth century one can speak of "good demagogues" without seeming excessively oxymoronic.[36] The reasonable assumption then seems to be that when the word first came into use it was not pejorative, unless it was spoken among a group that was agreed and united in its hatred of the *demos*. In ordinary discourse it would be neutral, perhaps even complimentary.

Prostates tou demou

As Moses Finley has pointed out, the word *demagogos* is surprisingly rare in fifth century Greek.[37] Far commoner

---

provoked by the word would depend on already existing attitudes toward the *demos*. Thus the ambiguity of the component *demo-* makes it difficult to use the word as a "smear word," except among those who were already ill-disposed to the *demos*. As the century goes on and *demos* comes more and more frequently to be used in the narrower sense, it becomes easier to represent the *demagogos* as a factional leader. (On the development of the word *demos* note the comparative rarity of the sense "plebs" in literature before the late fifth century, and the change that can be detected in Herodotus 1.196.5 and pseudo-Xenophon, *Constitution of Athens* 1.2 et alibi. By the late fifth or early fourth century the word is quite frequently used for the poorer citizenry, e.g. Xenophon's report of Socrates' conversation with Euthydemus in *Memorabilia* 4.2.37, or Thucydides 2.65.2.)

It is Xenophon, *Anabasis* 7.6.4 which seems to me the first locus where a word related to *demagogos* is itself clearly deprecatory. Thucydides 8.65.2, however, indicates that in 411 *demagogia* in oligarchic circles was a very serious charge. The latter passage underlines my main point: the connotation of the word in the first years of its use depended upon the circle within which it was used. Among oligarchs it was an insult; among democrats it could be neutral or complimentary.

[35] In this passage the related word *demagogia* is used. Another example of an early use of this group of words is restored in line 4 of fragment a of P. Heidelberg 182. On this papyrus see the important article by M. Gigante in *Maia* 9 (1957) 68-74.

[36] Lysias 27.10, cf. Isocrates 15.234.

[37] M. I. Finley, *Past and Present* 21 (1962) 4.

through the last third of the century is the phrase *prostates tou demou*. *Prostates*, "one who stands before," hence, a protector, occurs in Aeschylus and Herodotus, and thus seems an older word than *demagogos*.[38] But it is only in the 420's that the word comes to be securely attested in the sense of a leader of the citizen body of contemporary Athens.[39] The earliest secure instance is Aristophanes' *Knights* (424 B.C.), an important passage to which we must later return. For the moment let us simply note that the lines foretell the replacement of Paphlagon by his rival the Sausage-seller, and also seem to express Aristophanes' wish that the current real-life *prostates* of Athens, Cleon, would also be replaced.[40] Euripides uses the word in his tragedies to describe characters, some of whom resemble contemporary politicians.[41] But the most interesting use of the word is Thucydides'. He never adopts it in his sketch of the fifty years from the end of the Persian war to the beginning of the Peloponnesian, nor does he ever apply it, or its cognates, to any politician of the early part of

[38] Aeschylus, *Seven Against Thebes* 408, 798, 1026, *Suppliants* 963. Of these only *Suppliants* 963 has the political sense which is of concern to us, and there is good reason to suspect that this portion of the play is not by Aeschylus; see A. Lesky, *Geschichte der griechischen Litteratur* (second ed., Bern and Munich 1963) 278. In Herodotus the word occurs in 1.127.1; 2.178.3; 5.23.2 and compare 1.59.3 and 3.82 (discussed below). The word is also found on an early Locrian inscription, *apud* R. Meiggs and D. Lewis *A Selection of Greek Historical Inscriptions to the End of the Fifth Century* B.C. (Oxford 1969) no. 20, line 34 (p. 36).

[39] In Herodotus we hear of *prostatai* of barbarian states or of other Greek cities (e.g. 9.41.3) and of factions within Athens (1.59.3) but not of the whole citizenry of Athens. 3.82.4, as we shall see may, however, have been written with Athens in mind.

[40] Aristophanes, *Knights* 1128. Compare *Frogs* 569; in *Peace* 684 the word is applied to Hyperbolus, and in *Ecclesiazousae* 176 to the politicians as a group. Note also *Ploutos* 920 and *Wasps* 419. O. Reverdin, *Museum Helveticum* 2 (1945) 204, lists eight fifth century politicians to whom the title *prostates tou demou* was applied by contemporary writers: Cleon, Hyperbolus, Androcles, Cleophon, Archedemus, Thrasybulus, Archinus, and Agyrrius. To this list Pericles should probably be appended, as will shortly appear. Many of these eight politicians were also called *demagogos*, and the two words are treated as synonymous in the scholia to Aristophanes, *Knights* 1128.

[41] *Orestes* 911, and compare line 772 of that play with his *Suppliants* 243. In each case Euripides' attitude seems to be hostile to the person called *prostates*.

111

the century.[42] But in his account of the years of the war the word *prostates* is frequently used, for the leaders of Corcyra (3.75.2), of Megara (4.66.3), of Syracuse (6.35.2), and in 3.82.1 in a generalization about many Greek cities that were afflicted with revolution during the war. In 8.89.4 he applies it to politicians in Athens and in 2.65 cognates of the word are used in such a way as to make it clear that Thucydides regarded Pericles as a *prostates*, at least during the last years of his life.[43]

Does Thucydides mean to suggest by this that the word only came into use during Pericles' lifetime? Perhaps not, for even Thucydides' famed exactitude cannot be expected to extend to the finest points of terminology. Nonetheless it does appear that Thucydides, perhaps quite accidentally, has paralleled the chronological development of this term in the fifth century. Originally a way of referring to any protector, divine or human, some time in the second half of the century it adds a more technical sense—it comes, as we have seen, to be applied to political leaders in the city.[44] We cannot date the beginning of the new use of the word with precision, but it is clear that the development must have taken place before the production of the *Knights* in 424. Since in that play the word does not seem to be strange or new, we might suspect that it had already been in use for some years, perhaps while Pericles was still alive. The evidence that it was current before his prominence in the city is slim and unsatisfactory.[45] It is most

---

[42] Thucydides seems concerned to emphasize the importance of collegiality in the early part of the century. Cf. K. J. Dover, *JHS* 80 (1960) 61-77. Note, however, that in 6.89.4 Alcibiades applies the term *prostasia tou plethous* back to the period of the Peisistratid tyranny.

[43] Cf. Xenophon, *Memorabilia* 1.2.40.

[44] Divine protectors: Sophocles, *Trachiniae* 209; cf. line 9 of the Themistocles decree. The word is also the standard term for the patron of a resident alien (metic) at Athens; see e.g. Lysias 31.9 and note the metaphorical usage in Aristophanes, *Peace* 684.

[45] Although fourth century works (especially the Aristotelian *AthPol* e.g. 2.2 and 28) apply the term back to earlier politicians, even to those of the sixth century, arguments that the word was used in a political sense before

likely, I believe, that the term came into use when politicians began to represent themselves as the protectors of the whole city or of the *demos*. It should be noted that although we often speak of *the prostates*, and sometimes hear of neat successions of such leaders, contemporary writers sometimes use the plural of the word and imply that there might be several *prostatai* at any one time. Hence we should not assume that the *prostates* enjoyed a monopoly of power, or that there was a diadochy of single leaders of the city.[46]

Pericles' time must ultimately depend on Aeschylus, *Suppliants* 963 (now dated 466-459 B.C., see A. Lesky, *Tragische Dichtung der Hellenen*, 59-60), but, as has been pointed out in n. 38 above, this line is from a portion of the play widely rejected as a later addition. Without some contemporary evidence, I am reluctant to conclude that the word was in use in the early fifth or sixth century. The evidence of fourth century authors cannot be pressed, for their terminology is frequently that of their own day.

V. Ehrenberg, *Polis und Imperium* (Zürich 1965) 278 n. 1, and H. Schaefer, *RE* s.v. *prostates* Suppl. 9 (1962) 1293-1296, argue for an earlier beginning of this use of the word. Other useful discussions can be found in B-S I 414ff., V. Ehrenberg, *People of Aristophanes* (Oxford 1951) 353ff., and O. Reverdin, *Museum Helveticum* 2 (1945) 203f.

[46] On the concentration of power in a single leader, see Aristophanes, *Knights* 1121-1130, *Peace* 680-681. And note also Thucydides 6.35.2 (concerning Syracuse) and Aristotle, *Politics* 1279 a 8ff. To judge from Euripides, *Phaethon* fr. 776 (*TGF*), the tendency to rely on a single leader was a matter of concern during the last ten years of Euripides' life.

Important as this evidence is, it must not be stretched too far. In particular it must not be assumed that it applies with equal force to earlier parts of the century. Then, as I have argued, collegiate sharing of power was generally operative. Nor should it be assumed that a *prostates*, even in the late part of the century, enjoyed any formal position or even temporarily unchallenged power. The use of plural forms of the word is one indication that several such leaders often existed at any one time and that the concentration of power had not reached the extreme state joked about in Aristophanes' *Knights*. Note the plurals in Thucydides 4.46.4 (Corcyra), 4.66 (Megara), and 3.75.2 (Corcyra). In 8.89.4 Thucydides refers to the competition among various Athenian politicians to become "first" *prostates tou demou*. Since the adjective clearly indicates preeminence, not chronological priority, the passage shows that in Thucydides' day it was at least conceivable that there might simultaneously be more than one *prostates tou demou*.

Fourth century authors sometimes constructed neat successions of leaders of the *demos*, see e.g. *AthPol* 28, Theopompus, *Philippica* X (cf. *Theopompus* 73 and 165 n. 69). In these schematizations one *prostates* succeeds another, and political rivalries tend to appear as struggles for succession, without much room for the operation of factors other than the participants' desires for aggrandizement. These schematizations contributed to the tendency noted earlier

There remains one passage which may shed some light on the origin and development of this term. It is found in the midst of the debate between Darius and others, reported in the third book of Herodotus' history. We have already studied part of this passage and seen that it has relevance not only to Persia but also to fifth century Athens. It is now time to look at it more carefully.[47]

Darius speaks to advocate monarchy over oligarchy or democracy. He believes it is the best form of government for Persia to adopt, far superior to either of the alternatives. It is better than oligarchy, he contends, because in an oligarchy the individual leaders use public affairs to fight out their private animosities and

> this is the engendering of *staseis*, and *staseis* give birth to assassination and from assassination monarchy is the result. And in this it reveals by how much this [sc. monarchy] is the superior system. Now when the *demos* rules there is no escape from trouble, and when this trouble comes, it takes the form not of animosities among the troublesome but of strong friendships. For the troublemakers put their heads together and arrange public business in a cabal. This sort of thing continues until someone protecting the *demos* puts down such men. Afterwards the man is admired by the *demos*, and since admired, turns out to be a monarch. And in this situation even this man bears testimony to the fact that monarchy is the most superior system.
>
> Herodotus 3.82.3-4

in this study to simplify the pattern of Attic history, and have made it easy for modern writers on the subject to impose the terminology of present-day political parties upon the history of ancient Athens. They may also have contributed to confusions such as the one detectable in the scholion on Aristophanes, *Clouds* 624, which implies that Hyperbolus' career began only after Cleon's death. This is surely wrong, as the allusion to Hyperbolus in the *Horai* of Cratinus (fr. 262) shows, but it may have been the natural inference to draw from some diadochy of political leaders of Athens.

[47] See also Appendix I.

The sentences on democracy in this speech outline a process remarkably similar to that which emerges from our study of Athenian politics. Darius feels there is an inevitable progression in democracy, from strong friendships to governments by a narrow clique, to a reaction in which a single leader emerges. Our study has led to the recognition of the extraordinary importance of *philia* in Athenian politics, and the possibility that a relatively small segment of the population might dominate public affairs. In Cleon's repudiation of his old friends we may have the act of an astute politician who wished to appeal to those citizens who felt excluded from the older pattern of democratic politics. As we have seen, the new political vocabulary of Cleon's day emphasized devotion to the city rather than narrow loyalty to one's friends. *Prostates tou demou* is a title well suited to convey the impression that a politician has the best interest of the citizenry at heart. Thus it is striking that Herodotus has Darius use that expression for the leader who suppresses the strong friendships that had hitherto dominated the state. The phrase, if our examination of the evidence is correct, was one of recent coinage when Herodotus wrote, and might well serve to remind his audience that the debate in Persia was not an antiquarian digression into history, but a discussion of contemporary and wide concern.[48] It is true, to be sure, that no *prostates tou demou* in fifth century Athens ever became a true *monarchos*, but the fear was present even if the reality was not. A desire for single rule was often imputed to Pericles, and Cleon and Hyperbolus seem both to have enjoyed an extraordinary concentration of power.[49]

---

[48] From what has been said it follows that both the debate in Herodotus 3 and the allusion back to it in 6.43.3 are most likely to have been composed after the introduction of such terminology and after the successful exploitation of the fear that public affairs might come to be dominated by groups of *philoi*. This implies a relatively late date for the passages, late 430's or 420's. See also Appendix I.

[49] Note the attacks made against Pericles in Old Comedy, e.g. the anonymous fragment (Edmonds 60) *apud* Plutarch, *Pericles* 16, and Thucydides'

Rhetor

Another new term for politician which became popular in the last third of the century was *rhetor*, "one who speaks." Since the word is an easy development out of the cognate verb *ereo*, used often in Homeric assembly scenes, it seems plausible that it was in use well before its first attested occurrence, an Athenian inscription of around 445 B.C.[50] By the 420's it seems to have become a popular word for politicians.[51] Dicaeopolis in Aristophanes' *Acharnians* uses it for the politicians he plans to heckle in the assembly; later Eupolis applies it to Pericles and his rivals and successors.[52] The term is expressive and exact. The politicians of this period were naturally thought of as *rhetores*, for they led by their eloquence. They were not primarily backroom manipulators, cloakroom advisors, or quiet professional administrators. Being a politician meant being a speaker. "It was . . . perfectly

laudatory comments in 2.65.9. On the power of Cleon and Hyperbolus note Aristophanes, *Knights* 1121-1130, *Peace* 680-681. Single rule, *monarchia,* is closely identified with tyranny in Euripides, *Suppliants* 404ff., Aristophanes, *Wasps* 464-470. The fear that a *prostates tou demou* might become a tyrant may have influenced the fourth century treatment of tyranny, e.g. Aristotle's anachronistic view (*AthPol* 28.2) that Peisistratus was a *prostates tou demou.*

[50] Note Homer, *Iliad* 1.76 *et alibi.* The regulations for a colony at Brea *IG* i² 45 (*SEG* x 34) contain the word, partially restored, in line 21. Sophocles fr. 1090 also uses it, but in the sense "judge." Fourth century authors, as often, apply the term back to earlier periods, e.g. Isocrates 15.231-236, a succession of famous politicians beginning with Solon.

[51] There are useful discussions of the word in C. N. Jackson, *HSCP* 30 (1919) 89-102, F. Camon, *Giornale Italiano di filologia* 15 (1962) 364 n. 1, and in W. Pilz's dissertation, *Der Rhetor im attischen Staat* (Weida i. Thür. 1934). Pilz argues that the word was restricted in application to the helpers of the major politicians and that in classical times the leading statesmen, e.g. Cimon, Pericles, Nicias, were never called *rhetores* (p. 13). Although it is true that the word is sometimes better translated "spokesman" than "speaker," and although it is a perfectly appropriate term for an "untergeordneter Helfer," Pilz does not adequately explain the reference to Pericles as a *rhetor* in Eupolis fr. 98, nor does he seem to recognize the force of passages such as Aeschines 1.25 and Demosthenes 18.25 in his discussion of them. From this insufficiency follows another: "Das Wort *rhetor* ist zum Begriff für eine bestimmte Kaste geworden" (p. 24), thence eventually to the ill-supported notion that Sophistic education normally played a large part in the training of the *rhetores* of the late fifth century.

[52] Aristophanes, *Acharnians* 38, cf. 680 and *Knights* 60. Eupolis frs. 98 and 99. Note also Euripides fr. 597 (*TGF*).

precise language to call political leaders 'orators,' as a synonym and not merely, as we might do, as a mark of the particular skill of a particular political figure. Under Athenian conditions . . . much more is implied. . . . Everyone, speakers and audience alike, knew that before night fell the issue must be decided, that each man present would vote 'freely' (without fear of whips or other party controls) and purposefully, and therefore that every speech, every argument must seek to persuade the audience on the spot, that it was all a serious performance, as a whole and in each of its parts."[53] Oratory was power, and a very independent kind of power: ". . . the man who ventures to use force needs no small number of allies, but the man who can persuade needs no one" (Xenophon, *Memorabilia* 1.2.11).

Xenophon's comment has the trial of Socrates in mind, but the principle can be generalized. The skillful speaker in Athens had a source of power that freed him from many of the encumbrances of the old style of politics. He could be more independent, he could neglect, even offend, influential groups, he might even dare to bypass the old process of building up alliances through the often aggravatingly slow sequence of discussion, concession, compromise, and coordination. Through his eloquence a politician could swiftly attain a lofty position in the city—but a perilous one. What rhetoric gave, rhetoric could take away. If that technique could elevate him to the pinnacles of power, it could also abandon him to sudden gusts of popular fancy and plunge him quickly to the depths of obscurity, or to the chastisements of the assembly or the law courts.[54]

Effects and Implications

The terminological developments discussed in the last three sections may be clues to an *imperii arcanum* which was divulged in the late fifth century: it was possible to acquire

[53] M. I. Finley, *Past and Present* 21 (1962) 12-13.
[54] Cf. P. A. Brunt, *CR* New Series 11 (1961) 143-144.

political power by direct appeal to the citizenry without the tedious apprenticeship imposed by the system of political friendship, without the slow aggregation of alliances and coalitions. A man could win prominence by offering to protect the interests of the *demos*, by presenting himself as a *prostates tou demou,* and through his success as a *rhetor* become the leader of the people, the *demagogos.*

The new terminology brought with it a new style and a new technique. It made possible, as we have seen, a rapid rise to power based on the power of hitherto ill-organized segments of the citizenry. A new pattern of politics came into being, in which the allegiance of large numbers of citizens came to be as important, even more important, than alliances with narrow circles of influential men. The new politician worked by "shaping mass alliances rather than by negotiating with different power groups to obtain a balance."[55]

New techniques bring with them new practitioners. The older, more familiar forms of politics do not disappear. Their practitioners remain, survive, sometimes even succeed, but new faces and new techniques become conspicuous. Cleon is one example. It is not precisely clear what role he played in the development of this new technique of politics, but his importance cannot be overlooked. If he was not the chief developer, he was one of the chief beneficiaries. In his hands the new style of politics was perfected. It was he, I believe, who found political wisdom where others could see only madness.

[55] The phrase is a quotation from an article by F. M. Hechinger on the Columbia University riots in the spring of 1968 (*New York Times,* May 2 1968, p. 43). The author notes that the administration at Columbia used a classic American political science approach to settle the problem, and proceeded by "negotiating with different power groups to obtain a balance." But, the article suggests, the problems were not amenable to such tactics; the real question was one of shaping mass alliances and it was precisely in the personal contact and persuasion essential to these alliances that the administration was deficient. The Columbia situation thus is not only an example of the intense emotions which can be released when old political techniques suddenly are found to be obsolete and new styles of politics appear, it also provides a partial parallel to the kind of techniques which were competing in fifth century Athenian politics.

He turned his back on influential friends, and won by this apparent folly even greater power. He did not originate all the terms prominent in the 420's, but so many of those words occur in contexts where he is being discussed, attacked, or parodied, that the inference that he exploited the new political vocabulary seems secure.[56]

Thus whatever one thinks of the morality or wisdom of Cleon, his place in the development of politics is indisputable. He was the master of a new technology of political power, an innovator and a perfector. His accomplishments, like any great technological change, are a break with past traditions and ways, and a source of imitation and emulation in the future. But they are also a culmination of earlier developments. It will not detract from Cleon's accomplishment to observe the extent to which his actions had already been anticipated by Pericles.

Pericles and Cleon

Pericles: Traditionalist and Innovator

For all his wealth and lineage, for all his friends and his expertise in the traditional techniques of politics, Pericles is nonetheless an ambiguous figure in the development of Athenian politics. Modern scholars have not reached a consensus about his policies or his personality; ancient writers were equally divided. To some he was the austere aristocratic leader, unswayed by the passions and the vulgarity of the mob; to others he was a demagogue in both the ancient and the modern sense. Sometimes these two viewpoints coexist in the

---

[56] Cf. above sections on *Philodemos* and *Misodemos*, *Philopolis* and *Misopolis*, Parallel Developments, *Demagogos*, and *Prostates tou demou*. If I am correct in suspecting that it was a habit of Cleon to make great use of words such as *philodemos*, *philopolis* and their antonyms, then the opening of Aristophanes' *Wasps* takes on an added humor. Note the great series of *philo*-compounds in the servants' speeches, lines 74-90, culminating in the diagnosis that the master is *phileliastes*, a law-court-lover. Then in 133 it emerges that his name is Philocleon—the perfect nomenclature for a follower of the great user of *philo*- words.

same author, harmoniously or in ill-concealed conflict.[57] Pericles remains enigmatic; the reason for this, I believe, is that although a master of time-honored political techniques, he originated some of the innovations which Cleon was later to perfect. Aristocratic in birth and upbringing, Pericles was far-sighted enough to see the possibility of quite a new arrangement of politics. For this reason too, Cleon sometimes appears as a distorted Pericles, mouthing his words and exaggerating his policies.[58] And thus too, later writers, depending on their political bias and outlook, have chosen to emphasize one or the other of Pericles' two sides, or, like Plutarch, have attempted to integrate them by positing an abrupt change in character.

Pericles the traditionalist, the master of political friendship, remains the better known, but traces of his more innovating *alter ego* can be detected in policies which he shared with his more radical successors: belief in the necessity of the empire, reluctance to yield to Spartan demands, professions of concern for the *demos*, the use of pay for public services. He was, moreover, long the standard for oratorical excellence, the *rhetor par excellence*.[59] Thucydides, to whom so much of the impression that he was an aristocratic leader is due, provides nonetheless the basis for showing that he could also be regarded as a *prostates tou demou*.[60] Isocrates calls him a

---

[57] Thucydides is one of the principal sources for the view that Pericles was a politician of aristocratic style. But as early as the fourth century some writers criticized him as an undesirable *demagogos*; see *Theopompus* 43-46, and note Plato, *Gorgias* 515 d ff. B. Perrin's article, "The Austere Consistency of Pericles," *Transactions of the Connecticut Academy of Arts and Sciences* 15 (1909) 219-224, argues that Plutarch attempted, not always successfully, to reconcile these two views of Pericles.

[58] Note the parallels collected by J. de Romilly, *Thucydides and Athenian Imperialism*, trans. P. Thody (Oxford 1963) 163-166, and cf. A. G. Woodhead, *Mnemosyne* Ser. IV, 13 (1960) 289-317; A. Andrewes, *Phoenix* 16 (1962) 75.

[59] Note Eupolis fr. 98. The anecdote in Plutarch, *Demosthenes* 6, wherein Eunomus the Thriasian praises Demosthenes' style of speaking as the closest to Pericles, indicates the high esteem in which Pericles' oratory was held.

[60] Compare above, *Prostates tou demou*.

120

demagogos.[61] *Demagogos, prostates tou demou, rhetor*: the attributes of the new-style politician are already found in Pericles. His too is at least some of the new vocabulary of politics: "What I would prefer is that you should fix your eyes every day on the greatness of Athens as she really is, and should fall in love with her."[62]

There is one other story about Pericles which deserves careful consideration as a possible precedent for Cleon's withdrawal from his friends. Plutarch in his biography gives a short sketch of Pericles' conduct during one portion of his career: "It was noted that he travelled only on one street in the city, the one that led up the *agora* and the council chamber. He turned down invitations to dinner and all similar forms of sociability and familiarity. In fact during all his long political prominence, he never dined with any of his *philoi*, except when Euryptolemus his cousin got married, he stayed until the libations and then immediately withdrew" (Plutarch, *Pericles* 7.5).

Plutarch treats this story as an illustration of Pericles' desire to maintain his reserve and dignity, and goes on to point out that he avoided that "satiety which springs from continual intercourse."[63] But he also makes it clear that this was a means of winning the support of the *demos* of the city. There are perhaps two ways in which such restraint contributed to obtaining that support. The first is by presenting Peri-

---

[61] Isocrates 8.126; 15.234. The latter passage makes Isocrates' admiration for Pericles quite clear.

[62] Thucydides 2.43.1, trans. Rex Warner, cf. above, Cleon's Style in Comedy. Pericles, like Paphlagon in the *Knights*, transfers the word *erastes* to political vocabulary.

[63] The sequence of thought in Plutarch, *Pericles* 7, is difficult to follow. The story quoted in the text follows on the statement that Pericles began to court the favor of the multitude rather than of the *kaloi kagathoi*. We expect an example of Pericles' demagogy or popularity-seeking to follow. Instead Plutarch describes his austere way of life. To judge from *Nicias* 11, Pericles' actions cannot have been considered demotic. Thus the story seems awkward in this chapter; it fits far better into context in *Moralia* 800 c, as a hortatory tale enjoining circumspection on the man who enters public life.

cles as the indispensable expert in the complexity of public business; the second is by presenting him as an impartial public servant, without dangerous obligations to *philoi*.

The Indispensable Expert

Of these two ways the first is perhaps the more important. For the growth of Athens from small town to imperial city imposed new demands upon her politicians—as the city grew the function of the politician changed. In the old quiescent town there were, to be sure, moments of intense and complex difficulties: wars with other states, financial problems, factional strife among the citizens. But these, as best we can tell, were not frequent and could be handled by a kind of crisis politics—short periods of intense effort by leaders who were still essentially amateurs. A campaign season or two, perhaps only a few days of concerted effort, could restore tranquil normality.

But as the new century progressed new problems became more common. In its opening years two great invasions from Persia posed difficulties of a hitherto unexperienced dimension. And even if they could still be handled by a new version of the old crisis politics, they indicated the need for more consistent and long-range planning. The aftermath of the wars taught the same lesson. Athens soon took on the leadership of the confederacy against Persia, the Delian League, and thereby assumed the military and, what was more important, the administrative burden of coordinating defensive and offensive operations in the Aegean. As time went on the treasury of the league was moved to Athens (454 B.C.) and efficiency seemed to demand that Athens exercise more and more direct control over what was rapidly becoming an empire rather than a league. The survival of extensive fragments from the inscriptions recording the annual quotas and divine offerings of this confederacy gives us a good indication of the attention to detail necessary for its proper operation.

122

But this is only a small part of the story. Treaty negotiations, supervision of religious sites and festivals, and eventually an ambitious building program increased the burden of public administration. And at the same time the growth in the population of Attica created new problems. Yet, although Athens had come to be the ruler of a great empire, the master of a fleet that dominated the whole eastern Mediterranean, the bulwark of Greek defense against Persia, and increasingly the protagonist in a conflict with Sparta, Corinth, and their allies, the formal political structure under which the city operated was still basically that of the small town that a few generations earlier had cast off tyrannic government and designed a new pattern of civic life. Constitutional changes had been rather common in the early decades of the century, but after 462/1 few important modifications of this sort were made. Athens seems to have reached a consensus on constitutional matters that lasted until the attrition of war and the strains of defeat began to take their toll. Yet the more we consider the situation of Athens, the more perplexing this agreement appears. The city was confronted with ever-increasing responsibilities and dangers, which imposed upon her inherited political forms stresses which Cleisthenes and his contemporaries at the end of the sixth century could only dimly have foreseen. The use of lot to fill important state offices, the emphasis on the principle of collegiality, the strictly limited terms of many major officials, might have been effective ways to prevent a recurrence of tyranny or of *stasis*, but they were less likely to meet the needs of a major imperial power. While Athens needed continuity and expertise of leadership, her constitutional procedures provided instead limited tenure of office, collegiality, and frequent changes of personnel.

Yet Athens constantly surpasses our expectations. To be sure, after twenty-seven years of war she lost her empire, her freedom, and her democratic constitution—temporarily. But it is not her eventual defeat which causes wonder. Rather it

123

is the fact that a city with a political organization such as Athens' should have survived so long against such opposition which demands explanation. The causes which we might adduce are varied: the even more archaic constitution of Sparta, the advantage which sea power accords, the endurance and adaptability of the Athenian citizenry. But part of the reason was also, I believe, the skill and competence of her leaders. The growth of the city created a new situation and demanded a new kind of political leadership. The city could not hope to be successful with the old crisis politics. Instead it needed, and found, a new breed of specialized semi-professional politicians who could master and explain the complex details of their city's business.

Pericles is the great and least controversial example. He served repeatedly as general, spoke on major matters in the assembly with care, precision, and rhetorical virtuosity. He supervised the vast building program which transformed the appearance of Athens and which appropriately bears his name. To attain the leisure he needed, he entrusted the management of his farm to an overseer, Evangelus, who ran it with an exactitude that provoked admiration and amazement (Plutarch, *Pericles* 16). His own concentration on duty, reflected in Plutarch's story of his avoidance of all social activity save the marriage feast of Euryptolemus, is probably part of the same pattern of attentiveness to detail and a self-sacrificing determination to master the complicated business of the city.

Pericles' devotion to the city has won recognition both in antiquity and in modern times: it was largely responsible for the ability of Athens' political institutions to survive in an increasingly complex world. But if Pericles is to be praised, so must other less widely admired politicians of the late fifth century. As has recently been pointed out, "Kleon and his like were not simply the people's leaders on the comparatively

124

narrow political front which Thucydides examines: a large part of the point is their mastery of finance and administration. The bulk of business is an important factor. It needed more than a few clear headed experts."[64] The first book of Aristotle's *Rhetoric* outlines the principal topics with which a public speaker must be prepared to deal and the types of problems he is likely to be confronted with (Aristotle, *Rhetoric* 1.4.1359 a 30ff.). It is an impressive, even frightening, array and the burdens of public life are not likely to have been less in the fifth century than they were in the fourth. Politics, in short, had by the period with which we are concerned become a full-time career that demanded from its practitioners "a comprehensive grasp of the resources and interests of their own and other cities," and "a constant readiness to advise on all manner of questions."[65] It created what Professor Andrewes has called "the indispensable expert."[66]

[64] A. Andrewes, *Phoenix* 16 (1962) 83.

[65] P. A. Brunt, *CR* New Series 11 (1961) 144.

[66] The need for such experts could not have been clearly been anticipated by Cleisthenes, whose experience had been of a city suffering under an excessive concentration of leadership. He naturally devised a structure which would divide and limit power. What was perhaps needed was a throughgoing constitutional revision sometime in the 440's or 430's to bring the formal structure of power more closely into line with the needs of the city. But without this revision, some informal changes were necessary. Hence the growth of the new style of politics. The appearance of "indispensable experts" naturally imposed a further strain on the old constitutional forms. Since these men often held no official position, they were not necessarily subject to the scrutiny which elected magistrates had to undergo both before and after their terms of office. (Hence it was easy to make charges of foreign birth and malfeasance against them.) Their power was great and quite outside the existing system of constitutional control.

This seems to me the situation which would give rise to the *graphē paranomon*, the regulation which allowed an orator to be prosecuted for bringing a motion that was contrary to existing law. Although the introduction of the *graphē paranomon* is commonly dated in the late 460's (cf. C. Hignett, *History of the Athenian Constitution* 210ff.; B-S 896 n. 1), a later date seems to me more probable. It is noteworthy that the earliest datable example of its use is 415 B.C. (Andocides 1.17) and the other early examples cannot be far from this date (Antiphon frs. B 2 and 5 [Loeb]). It seems likely to me that these law cases arose relatively soon after the law was in-

Pericles' claim to the title is indisputable. But if we turn from what the ancient authorities *felt* about Cleon and Hyperbolus to the facts that they report about these men, it can be seen that these "demagogues" deserve it as well. We have, for example, two decrees of Hyperbolus, one which he moved, one that he amended.[67] When we study them, the impression that emerges is not that of a flamboyant orator, but of a competent legislator who knows his legal procedure and who has mastered the details of the subject before him. This is not to say that men like Cleon and Hyperbolus were really dull and uncontroversial technicians, but it should remind us that they, like Pericles, devoted themselves to the minutiae of politics as well as to the great issues and the occasions for spectacular oratory. And it may lead us to suspect as well that their mastery of public affairs was part of their appeal to a citizenry that recognized its inability to keep fully informed on matters that were often as difficult to understand as they were vital to the city's welfare. Athens needed her experts and found them not so much among her officials as among the *rhetores* who led the *demos*.[68]

---

stituted and that the absence of earlier indications is not just an accident of preservation. Otherwise one is compelled to posit a 45-year gap between the establishment of the *graphē paranomon* and its first recorded use.

The strongest objection to dating the *graphē paranomon* as late as I have suggested is based on the notion that it fulfilled the same function of preserving the constitution as the Areopagus *boulē* had before Ephialtes' reforms. Hence it seems logical that the *graphē* should have come in very shortly after 462/1. But there are difficulties in this argument, not least that a crucial passage, *AthPol* 25.2, does not readily support such a view.

[67] *IG* i[2] 84 (*SEG* x 93); *IG* i[2] 95 (*SEG* xxii 11).

[68] The growing need for specialization, I believe, provided the politicians with a new way of appealing for support. They could represent themselves as the masters of the complexities of public affairs. That Cleon did this is perhaps suggested by Aristophanes, *Knights* 75, and Eupolis frs. 290-292, which perhaps echo Cleon's oratory (cf. A. Burckhardt, *Spuren der athenischen Volksrede in der alten Komödie* 40ff.). Note also the use of the same verb, *ephorao*, in Herodotus 3.53.1.

That Cleon originated this appeal is unlikely. The expression "turn the city (or her affairs) over to someone" seems to have come into use rather earlier. Note Herodotus 1.64.2 and especially Thucydides 2.65.4 (the Athenians turn affairs over to Pericles). See also Thucydides 6.15.4 and Plato,

Thus part of the significance of Plutarch's story about Pericles' single-minded devotion to business is that it reflects imperial Athens' need for "indispensable experts." Pericles, like Cleon and perhaps many politicians of the last decades of the century, recognized this need and was prepared to fill it.

Pericles' Resemblance to Cleon

Plutarch's story about Pericles' austere and reserved way of life (above, Pericles: Tradionalist and Innovator) emphasizes not only his devotion to the details of public business but also an almost fanatical zeal in avoiding his own *philoi*. He turned down invitations to dinner and all similar forms of sociability and familiarity . . . he never dined with any of his *philoi*. . . . The extravagance of Pericles' actions impresses us, as it did Plutarch. And even if we allow that Plutarch and his sources may have exaggerated the facts, it still appears likely that Pericles himself intended his actions to impress. We suspect here a kind of political posturing and gesturing, a kind of dramatic extravagance not uncharacteristic of Pericles. For example, when the Periclean building program was criticized as excessively expensive, Pericles is said to have replied in the assembly, "All right, put it on my bill, not on yours, but I'll put up the inscriptions of dedication with *my* name on them."[69] Or again, when gossipers predicted that Archidamus of Sparta would see to it that Pericles' farm was

---

Lysis 209 d, Xenophon, *Hellenica* 2.4.23 for similar uses of the verb *epitrepo*.

The verb *epitropeuo* ("be guardian of") suggests the same way of looking at the politician. Note its use in *Knights* 212 and 426 and *Peace* 686; also Thrasymachus, *VS* 85 в 1 (p. 322 line 6) Herodotus 3.82.2. On Cleon as the *epitropos* of slaves see Aristotle, *Rhetoric* 3.8.1408 b 25.

Other expressions which indicate the use of this appeal are *hikanos prattein* (Xenophon, *Memorabilia* 2.9.4) and *epimeles* (Xenophon, *Memorabilia* 2.8.4).

[69] Plutarch, *Pericles* 14. H. Mattingly, *Historia* 10 (1961) 164-165, suggests that the story refers not to a dispute about the whole building program, but to a disagreement about a relatively small building. This is attractive, but the inscription which Mattingly adduces to support his argument (*IG* i² 54; *SEG* x 47) implies the Athenians accepted the offer. The whole point of Plutarch's story is that they refused.

spared by the invading Peloponnesian army, Pericles said he would give his farm to the city if it were spared.[70] He was indeed as much the master of the flamboyant action as of the telling oratorical phrase.

Thus the extravagance of his actions in avoiding his friends is consistent with other features of his political style. It is a gesture and an impressive one, designed, like so many gestures, to have multiple significance. It points, as we have seen, to his devotion to business. It reminds the observer of his devotion to the common good and emphasizes that Pericles is a public man, more concerned with the city than with his own pleasures, willing to subordinate his personal fancies and friendships to the needs of the city. Though it is not a repudiation of the traditional politics of friendships, though Pericles continues to use friends, discreetly, for his political goals, it does affirm his willingness to follow wider interests than those of his own *philoi*. Thus it anticipates developments which in a few years' time were to give a dramatically different tone to the politics of Athens. It has in it something of Cleon's extravagance and foreshadows his more notorious repudiation of his friends.

Cleon and His Friends

Cleon's withdrawal from his friends was thus not entirely without precedent, nor did it amount to a total and perpetual renunciation of the aids which *philia* might bring a politician. He turned his back on one group of influential supporters, but, as Plutarch points out, he soon found himself surrounded by other, and to Plutarch's way of thinking far less desirable, associates.[71] The gesture of renouncing one set of friends made the point: Cleon was not going to be the representative of one faction but rather the devoted friend of all citizens.

[70] Thucydides 2.13.1 and Plutarch, *Pericles* 33. See also Chapter 2 above, Friends and the City.
[71] Plutarch, *Moralia* 807 a, cf. above, Cleon's Repudiation of his Friends.

This gesture did not preclude the future accumulation of new allies and assistants.

But, of course, when these associates appeared, opponents of Cleon would attempt to call attention to them, and especially to their undesirable qualities. Aristophanes alludes to the "hundred heads of flatterers" that serpentlike surrounded Cleon.[72] The Sausage-seller's description of Paphlagon and his followers in the *Knights* was probably also intended as an attack on Cleon: "Don't you see the battalion of young leather-sellers that accompany him? Around them live the honey-sellers and the cheese-sellers, This crew has put their heads together so that if you fume and decide to play potsherds [i.e. try an ostracism] they'll seize their arms at night and run down to seize the grain importeries."[73]

The Sausage-seller is playing Cleon's game—discovering treason and conspiracy in every dinner-party and chance meeting.[74] We should not assume that his is a fully accurate picture of Cleon and his supporters. But in the *Wasps* Aristophanes is more specific, as he parodies a symposium of

[72] Aristophanes, *Peace* 756, quoted by Plutarch in *Moralia* 807 a. "The picture here recalled is that of the hundred-headed hydra slain by Heracles, but the details of it are derived from Hesiod's description of . . . Typhoeus in *Theogn.* 824 sqq. . . . As are snakes the 'hair' of Typhoeus, so were flatterers the 'hair' of Cleon" (M. Platnauer, *Aristophanes' Peace* [Oxford 1964] 133).

[73] Aristophanes, *Knights* 852-857. The passage is an important one, first for its hint that an ostracism might be tried (we know of no ostracisms between the death of Pericles and the Hyperbolus affair). Further, although the allusions to the granaries cannot fully be made out, the allusions to grain supply recur in this play. Note especially line 1100 in which Paphlagon promises to supply Demos with grain, and cf. 1166-1167. The prominence of this theme in the play suggests that the Athenians were much concerned with keeping their food-supply lines clear and safe at this time. This is attested independently (e.g. Thuc. 2.94.4, cf. 8.90.5 and *CP* 58 [1963] 116-118). But the *Knights* gives basis to the conjecture that Cleon responded to this anxiety and exploited it.

[74] Note the extraordinary tie between this passage and the debate on the best form of constitution in Herodotus' third book. *Knights* 854 and Herodotus 3.82.4 both refer to groups who put their heads together against the interests of the state. Both use the word *synkypto*. For a fuller discussion of the passage in Herodotus see Appendix I.

129

Cleon and his allies. He mentions Theorus, Aeschines, Phanus, and a foreigner named Acestor.[75] From other comedies we can glean some information about these men, or at least gain some idea of the attitude of the comic poets toward them. Theorus, for example, is the butt of many jokes in the *Wasps* and is elsewhere called a perjurer and an adulterer.[76] Some of the allusions to him in the *Wasps* suggest that he may have looked after Cleon's interests in the law courts.[77]

Comedy also found cause for merriment in the character of Aeschines, who boasted about great wealth which he did not in fact possess. His pretensions to culture were regarded as equally ludicrous and were mocked with casual sarcasm in *Wasps* 1244.[78] Phanos is an unusual enough name to justify identifying this man with Cleon's signer of accusations, mentioned in *Knights* 1256. Acestor, the most obscure of the group, is frequently trounced for his allegedly foreign origin; his name, however, is a perfectly acceptable, if rare, Athenian one. He is said to have been more skillful at conning himself a dinner than at his profession of tragic poetry.[79] Although comedy has no sympathy with any of the four, Cleon seems to have found them useful, perhaps congenial.[80]

---

[75] Aristophanes, *Wasps* 1220-1221.

[76] *Wasps* 42ff. and 599ff., *Clouds* 399ff., and note the scholion on *Wasps* 42. A Theorus is mentioned in *Acharnians* 134-174, an ambassador who came back from Thrace with a long expense account, but short on results. He may be the same as this Theorus, or the name may be a comic personification of *theorus*, "envoy."

A Theorus is listed as a commander of the fleet on a casualty inscription of approximately 409 B.C. published by D. W. Bradeen in *Hesperia* 33 (1964) esp. 48-49. He is quite possibly the same Theorus denounced in Comedy.

[77] Note *Wasps* 418 and 599.

[78] The evidence concerning this Aeschines is gathered in *PA* 337. As Kirchner there points out, "Sellus" seems not to be a proper patronymic, but the name for any fraudulent claimant to wealth. Cf. *PA* 737.

[79] *PA* 474 to which add Eupolis fr. 159. Note the name Acestor among the descendants of Philaios in the Marcellinus *Life of Thucydides*, 3. It also occurs on a red figure vase mentioned in *PA* 472.

[80] It might be argued that the four were not in fact associates of Cleon. Perhaps Aristophanes was simply grouping together various obnoxious characters without regard to their actual political affiliation. Yet, the allusions to

To these associates of Cleon one or two more can be added. Theophanes, mentioned in *Knights* 1103, is said in the ancient notes on that passage to have been an undersecretary of some board or project, also a cheat and a flatterer of Cleon.[81] Thoudippus, the man who proposed the increase of tribute in 425/4, named his son Cleon and has sometimes been presumed to be a son-in-law of the famous politician. In any event the choice of Cleon's name for a son points to some close connection.[82]

The evidence about these men is fragmentary and in many ways unsatisfactory. We can say little about their standing in society, their wealth, their family background, their exact roles in politics. Even the one clearest fact, that the comic poets felt no admiration for them, could be predicted from the poets' attitude toward Cleon himself. Yet their very existence is a matter of some significance. It indicates that Cleon, like Pericles and many of his predecessors, had his allies and associates, some of whom at least played a role in politics. Cleon was not some lonely eminence in civic affairs. Like any Athenian politician he needed and used others in his career. What distinguishes Cleon is his style, for it is that which sets him apart from so many of his predecessors.

Phanos in *Knights* 1256 and to Theorus in *Wasps* 418 and 599 imply that these two at least had some close association with Cleon.

[81] Theophanes is, I believe, the first Athenian whom we hear called a *hypogrammateus*, an undersecretary for some board or project. The office presumably developed with the growing complexity of public business in the fifth century. It is first mentioned on inscriptions in *IG* i² 374 lines 110 and 258, accounts for the building expenses of the Erechtheum, 408/7 B.C. On the office see B-S II 1058 and 1042. Another associate of Cleon, Phanos, is called in *Knights* 1256 *hypographeus dikon*, an obscure title which caused the scholiast on the passage some difficulty and which LSJ interprets, "signer of accusations *on behalf of another.*"

[82] *PA* 7251 and 7252. The decree is *IG* i² 63-65 *SEG* x 75. On the relation of Thoudippos to Cleon see H. T. Wade-Gery and B. D. Meritt, *AJP* 67 (1936) 392 n. 36.

Theogenes the Acharnian (*PA* 6703) may be an associate of Cleon, but the evidence is not decisive. See A. Andrewes and D. M. Lewis, *JHS* 87 (1957) 180, and Thucydides 4.27.3.

Cleon's Style

It was, moreover, Cleon's style which later antiquity remembered best. In recent times historians have suspected that Cleon was involved in, perhaps chiefly responsible for, the revision of the tribute assessments in 425/4, the exile of the historian Thucydides, the fining of Pericles, indeed many of the most important events of the 420's. And yet the ancient writers provide little information that would either confirm or refute these suspicions. When they talk of Cleon, they tell not what he did but how he did it. There was, for example, the story that he strode into the assembly and dismissed it with the comment, "I have some foreign guests to entertain" —a brash and seemingly offensive action, but one which amused rather than annoyed the Athenians. Plutarch and the others who mention this episode say nothing about the circumstances, who these "foreign guests" were, and why the Athenians found the comment so entertaining. We can conjecture, with distinguished scholarly support, that the "guests" were Spartans captured at Pylos and that the assembly was postponed in celebration of the great victory which Cleon and Demosthenes had won there. But our conjecture, though plausible, will lack the definitive seal of ancient testimony.[83]

What the ancient sources chose to record in this and in other instances was Cleon's style rather than his accomplishments. Even Thucydides, most restrained and impersonal of historians, stresses Cleon's style rather than his actions. He introduces him as "most violent . . . and most persuasive," not "most radical and severest in his policies toward the empire" (Thucydides 3.36.6). There follows a speech which is perhaps more revealing about the character and techniques of

---

[83] The story of Cleon's dismissal of the assembly is first found in Theopompus, *FGrH* 115 F 92, compare Plutarch, *Moralia* 799 d and *Nicias* 7. On the setting of the story see Wade-Gery, *Essays in Greek History* (Blackwell, Oxford 1958) 233-235.

Cleon than informative about the motivations and policies of the Athenian assembly.[84]

From fourth century writers we learn a good deal about the manner of Cleon's speaking but little about the content: "He was the first who shouted on the public platform, who used abusive language and who spoke with his cloak girt up about him, while all the others used to speak in proper dress and manner."[85] The contrast with the past was a sharp one. Before Cleon's time, we are told, all speakers kept their hands tucked in their cloaks and made no use of gestures.[86] Cleon broke with tradition and introduced the gesture into demagoric oratory.

Later this innovation, like so many of his changes, was universally and complacently accepted by the bourgeois republic of the fourth century. But when it was introduced it must have seemed shocking and vulgar to many Athenians—and not least to Aristophanes, who mocked Cleon's oratory in the *Knights*.[87] And if the mere raising of a hand could cause a stir, it is easy to imagine the reaction to some of Cleon's more radical departures from tradition. His repudiation of political friendship could account for a great deal of the emotion which the mere mention of his name could provoke.

[84] The speech is a brilliant piece of oratory. Cleon begins by lashing out at the Athenians, "I've often thought that a democracy was incapable of ruling others; now your change of heart about the Mytileneans proves it." He then proceeds to develop the emotion of anger provoked by such a statement and skillfully to turn it against the advocates of a more humane policy. They are made to appear suspect and then—the greatest triumph of art is to conceal art—Cleon denounces the Athenians' excessive love of oratory! We may dismiss the speech as a fabrication of Thucydides, but, if we do so, we must hypothesize other equally brilliant speeches for Cleon in order to explain how his oratory held such sway over a public accustomed to the rhetorical finesse of Pericles.

[85] *AthPol* 28.3, trans. K. von Fritz and E. Kapp. The description is common in antiquity; cf. Theopompus *FGrH* 115 F 92 apud scholia to Lucian, *Timon* 30 (Rabe 115, 13); Plutarch, *Nicias* 8; *Tiberius Gracchus* 2; Cicero, *Brutus* 28.

[86] Aeschines, *Against Timarchus* 25.

[87] Note especially *Knights* 136-137.

It would be natural, then, for the writers of antiquity to stress Cleon's changes in the style of politics, while neglecting his policies. For what Cleon proposed seems not to have been so drastically different from what Pericles had recommended—a strong hand on the empire, no concessions to the Peloponnesians, popular democracy at home. The difference between the two men was one of degree, of temperament, of approach, and of expression—in short, of style. Perhaps the ancient writers stressed what was truly most distinctive in the man.

Two Models of Politics

The style which Cleon developed poses an especially difficult problem for the student of Athenian politics. As we have seen, he utilized friends and drew upon many of the techniques of Pericles and other earlier politicians, but he created a new mode of political action which may properly be distinguished from all its predecessors. That he succeeded depended on the existence of narrow and often powerful groups of *philoi* and on feelings of animosity against them. But although an understanding of these friendship groups is important for an understanding of Cleon, the model which explains them cannot also readily account for Cleon himself.

Thus our inquiry has taken a strange turn. What began as a search for a more adequate model of Athenian politics has detected not one pattern, but two. One, the older and more traditional, has as its constituent groups relatively small bands of *philoi*; these groups form coalitions that can produce a majority in the assembly or the *boulē*, or influence policy in other ways. In this model there is little room for those citizens outside the friendship groups, for the poor and the "unpretentious." They might, to be sure, be useful at a crucial vote in the assembly or by showing their enthusiasm and support for one politician over another. Indeed, on an issue that provoked great attention and emotion, or when their interests were palpably threatened, they might take matters in hand and follow a quite unexpected course. Such were their prerogatives. But in the daily sequence of business, when emotions were not stirred and tedium cloaked the operation of economic interest, it was the *philia* groups that had the organization, the leisure, the concern, the power to control decisions.

The second pattern is quite different. It deemphasizes the power of the friendship groups and stresses the mass allegiance which skillful and eloquent leaders can win. It focuses on precisely those segments of the citizenry which had least influence in the first pattern.

These two patterns are, of course, schematizations for our convenience. Both are oversimplifications of a complex and changing reality, but they are useful because they can help us analyze Athenian politics more clearly. We should not mistake the models for reality. Yet, in a sense, the models represent systems of politics that actually existed and competed over a long period of time. Some elements of the first system are still detectable in the fourth century; parts of the second system can be traced back to the sixth. Yet, from what has been said above, it appears that the second pattern emerged in its fully developed form only after Pericles had come to prominence. Thus it can be expected that the model based on this system would work most effectively for Cleon and his successors.

Late in the century it is apparent that the new pattern has still not fully displaced the old. Indeed the complexity of events in the last two decades of the century can sometimes best be understood by the use of both models. In the ostracism which resulted in the expulsion of Hyperbolus, for example, Nicias, Alcibiades, Phaeax, and their coalition can best be accounted for under the first model: they each have a *stasis*, or closely-bound body of supporters. They unite, in time-honored fashion, against another politician, Hyperbolus.

135

But our sources suggest that Hyperbolus was a politician of a rather different sort. He seems to have lacked an organized *stasis* and to have been without the connections of his rivals. His importance is more easily accounted for in the second model: a leader with broad but loosely organized support, one who relied on his oratory and his skill at representing himself as the friend of all Athenians.

In the struggle that culminated in his ostracism we can see the old style of politics and the new in sharp conflict. The traditional devices, alliances and coalitions, are used against the practitioner of new techniques. The old order, as the outcome of this ostracism reminds us, does not lightly give way to the new. But the ostracism of Hyperbolus was a battle, not the whole war, and it was fought on grounds peculiarly unfavorable to the new style of politics. Ostracism was itself an old-fashioned device by this time. It had not been successfully used for years; it would never be used again. Since it provided little opportunity for eloquence, a man of Hyperbolus' type was at a considerable disadvantage.[88] A great premium, moreover, was placed on well-disciplined followers in an ostracism, for the widely scattered vote meant that a relatively small body of united citizens could often produce the plurality needed to drive a man out of the city.

Thus when Hyperbolus was defeated, the new style of politics was not discredited. It endured and contributed in varied and often quite surprising ways to the distinctive form of Athenian political life in the late fifth century.

[88] R. Jebb, *Attic Orators* I (London 1893) 132-135, emphasized that ostracism provided no good occasion for oratory. The point is perhaps overworked by Jebb, who was eager to press his case against the authenticity of the fourth speech of Andocides (purportedly given at this ostracism), but there is force to his observation.

4. Toward Revolution

The New Style of Politics

Two New Developments
The Decline of the Generalship—Youth in Command—Cause and Effect

The Social Standing of Cleon and His Successors
Cleon's Wealth—The Wealth of Other Politicians—Family Background

Culture and Education

Old Comedy and the New Politicians
Foreign Birth—Class Prejudice—Cleon's Offense

Withdrawal from Politics
Comedy—Tragedy—Aristophanes' Way Out—Otanes' Withdrawal

Toward Revolution

4. Toward Revolution

The New Style of Politics

CLEON was not the only flamboyant politician of the late fifth century. His contemporaries and those who survived him were a colorful lot with styles that often resembled his. Syracosius, for example, followed Cleon in abandoning the old restrained manner of public address and was described by one comic poet as "running about the *bema* yelping like a hound dog."[1] Cleophon, like Cleon, made a dramatic entrance into the assembly with a speech ready against peace negotiations and his breastplate girded on.[2] The nicknames of the politicians of the period further indicate how colorful they were: "Bleary Eyes," "Smoky," "Hempy," "Quail."[3] The flair of some of these men was remembered long after their policies, their offices, their family connections, and almost all else about them were forgotten. Their names became proverbial, and a thousand years after their deaths collectors of proverbs knew phrases such as "beyond Hyperbolus," denoting the extremely litigious, or "more cowardly than Peisander" for the exceedingly timorous.[4] Even the courtroom—Paches falling

---

[1] Eupolis fr. 207. The testimony on Syracosius is gathered in *PA* 13041. He is best remembered for his law restraining comedy, mentioned in a scholion on Aristophanes, *Birds* 1297, cf. Phrynichus fr. 26.

[2] *AthPol* 34.1, scholion on Aristophanes, *Frogs* 1532.

[3] "Bleary Eyes": Archedemus, Lysias 14.25, cf. Aristophanes, *Frogs* 588 and Eupolis fr. 9; "Smoky": Theogenes, Eupolis fr. 94; cf. scholion on Aristophanes, *Birds* 822; "Hempy": Eucrates, Scholion to Aristophanes, *Knights* 129 and see the entry in *PA* 5759. (He was also called "The Boar of Melite" and "The Bear.") "Quail": Meidias; Aristophanes, *Birds* 1297-1298 and scholia *ad loc.*

[4] Hyperbolus: Apostolius, *Centuria* 17.68 (in E. Leutsch and F. G. Schneidewin, *Corpus Paroemiographorum Graecorum* II [Göttingen 1851]; Peisander: Apostolius 14.14; compare "more ambitious than Cleophon" in the scholia to Aristophanes, *Frogs* 1532; "more cowardly than Epeius" in Apostolius 7.69, Zenobius 3.81; "more crooked than Simon" in Suidas s.v. *Simon* (Adler, Sigma 447). Most of these expressions seem to have originated in Old Comedy, e.g. Cleophon: Aristophanes, *Frogs* 679; Epeius: Adespota fr. 31. For the most part they refer to men active in the period 420-400.

139

on his sword while being tried on the conduct of his general-ship—provides evidence of a vehemence and impetuosity never wholly lacking in Greek politics, but rarely so clearly represented as in the teens and the twenties of the fifth century.[5]

Cleon is not of course responsible for all that was done in this period, but traces of his style turn up in unexpected places. We cannot be sure that they indicate his influence, but they warn us not to underestimate his importance. Plutarch's recognition that there was more than a little of the *dema-gogos* in Nicias may perhaps be discounted. Cimon, not Cleon, may have shown him the way.[6] But Alcibiades mas-tered the new politics, as Plutarch again noted: "Although his genealogy, his wealth and his military distinction opened wide doors to him for a political career, and though he had many *philoi* and close supporters (*oikeioi*), he preferred to base his power with the populace on the favor his speech won rather than on anything else" (Plutarch, *Alcibiades* 10.3).

And in his case there is more reason to suspect Cleon's in-fluence. At least in one instance Alcibiades' technique seems remarkably similar to Cleon's. Consider the following two passages, both attacks on Nicias. The first describes Al-cibiades: "He raised a clamor against Nicias and slandered him with plausible sounding accusations, for example that when he was general he had not wanted to capture the enemy

---

[5] On Paches' death see Plutarch, *Nicias* 6, *Aristides* 26. Cf. the poem in the *Greek Anthology* VII 614 (Stadtmüller).

[6] Plutarch's life of Nicias in chapters three and four refers to his use of wealth to acquire the *demagogia* and detects something *agoraion* in his extrav-agance. Compare A. B. West, *CP* 19 (1924) 136-137. And note the similarity to Cimon in chapter 10 of Plutarch's *Cimon* and *FGrH* 115 F 89 (cf. *Theo-pompus* 33-35). Both men built up a following in the *demos* by judicious use of their wealth.

The conventional two- or three-party schematizations of Athenian politics are particularly inadequate in dealing with men like Nicias and Cimon. Since they seem less "radical" than Pericles or Cleon, they are labeled "aristocrats," though Nicias has no genealogical claim to this title, or grouped with various reactionaries, sometimes even with oligarchs, quite without justification.

troops blockaded on Sphacteria and that when others had seized them he let them go and gave them back as a favor to the Spartans" (Plutarch, *Alcibiades* 14.4).

The second describes Cleon: "And pointing at Nicias the son of Niceratus, who was general, he spoke, revealing his enmity, and he attacked him saying it was no great task—if our generals are real men—to sail and capture those on the island [Sphacteria]. That's what he'd do, if he were in command" (Thucydides 4.27.5).

Similarities of this sort inevitably raise the question: how many other politicians followed Cleon's example? Were his developments in the technique and style of politics enduring ones, or were they simply idiosyncrasies which disappeared at his death? It is true that no other politician of the late fifth century is known to have repudiated his friends, nor did any of them, as best we can tell, acknowledge a debt to Cleon. And yet, as we have seen, the terminological innovations which were made in Cleon's day persisted in Greek speech and many politicians clearly continued to emphasize that they were the friends and protectors of the whole *demos*. The probable inference is that others followed the way which Cleon had pointed out; men ilke Hyperbolus and Cleophon, who were *demagogoi* and *prostatai tou demou* are likely to have exploited his techniques.

This is probably the best explanation of the dividing line in Athenian history, drawn by several ancient sources immediately after Pericles' death. They recognize that Athenian politics were never quite the same after Cleon became prominent, even though their explanations of *why* the change came about are less than satisfactory: "As long as Pericles was the leader of the people, the state was still in a fairly good condition, but after his death everything became much worse. For then the people first chose a leader who was not in good repute with the better people (*epieikeis*), while, in the earlier period, the political leadership had always been in the hands of the latter. . . .[7] In an attack on sycophancy, Isocrates makes a similar division:[8]

> Now Pericles, who was established as *demagogos* before men of this sort came along, took over the city when it was not to be sure as reasonable as it had been before it acquired the empire, but while it was still tolerably well governed, and did not strive for his own profit. . . . But these men have shown themselves so different from him, that they dare to say that their concern for public affairs prevents them from tending to their own business; but it appears that their "neglected" affairs have made greater gains than they would have ever thought to pray for. But our citizenry, for whom they profess to care, is in such a bad way that no one can relax or enjoy life. The whole city is filled with grief.[9]

[7] *AthPol* 28.1, trans. K. von Fritz and E. Kapp. Compare the scholion on Aristophanes, *Peace* 681, discussed in *Theopompus* 62 and 161 n. 40.

[8] "Sycophancy" is used in the Greek sense: any citizen could indict another for the violation of the laws. The practice was not in itself pernicious, indeed it was an essential substitute for some formal public prosecutor. But it lent itself readily to abuses, when "sycophants" brought or threatened to bring cases against wealthy citizens without due cause. The expense and inconvenience of legal battles and the possibility of conviction could often be avoided only by bribing the sycophant.

[9] Isocrates, *On the Peace* 126 and 127. Cf. Aristotle, *Politics* 1320 a 6ff. The passage indicates that politicians of the fourth century used their devotion to public business to win gratitude and support. It also contains a faint echo of Aristophanes, or perhaps Cleon. Compare "our citizenry, for whom they profess to care" with Aristophanes, *Knights* 1341-1342: "Oh Demos, I care for you and I'm the only one who looks after you." Note also the use of the root *Ked* (care for) in Aristophanes, *Wasps* 242, 731.
The implication of the passage is that sycophancy began to be a problem shortly after Pericles; we naturally think of Cleon, but whether or not he was a sycophant is far from clear. The charge of bribery is fairly often brought against him (e.g. *Knights* 438, *Acharnians* 6 and the scholia thereon) but the charge that he was a sycophant is comparatively rare (*Peace* 653, *Knights* 260ff. applies to *euthynai* and is not apropos). It is odd that Aristophanes, who mocked the excesses of this institution (e.g. *Acharnians* 818-828), should miss any opportunity to press this charge against Cleon. Perhaps Cleon, who was himself well-to-do (see below, Cleon's Wealth), was reluctant to go to extremes in the use of this practice.

The most reasonable inference to draw from these passages is that Cleon's innovations in the style of politics were long-lasting ones and that many politicians of the next decades adopted some, if not all, of his techniques. And, as we have seen, this presumption can help us understand the careers of some of these politicians, especially Hyperbolus, Androcles, and Cleophon.[10] Furthermore, it may help to account for two other developments that can be observed during this period —the decline in the political importance of the generalship and the rapid rise of young men to positions of prominence.

Two New Developments

The Decline of the Generalship

In the fifth book of the *Politics* Aristotle contrasts the tyrannies of earlier times with those of his own day. He suggests, rather anachronistically, that in each case it was the *demagogos* who became tyrant, but notes a sharp difference in the techniques used in the two periods.[11] ". . . Then the *demagogoi* were drawn from those who held the office of general

[10] Most of Cleophon's career comes after the chronological limit of this study, but since he is best understood as a politician much influenced by the new techniques of politics, it seems appropriate to mention him. He was a much reviled and hated politician, especially for his introduction of two obol grants (Aeschines 2.76) and for his opposition to peace (Lysias 13.8, *AthPol* 34.1, Aeschines 3.150). Yet his honesty was attested by the poverty of his house at his death: Lysias 19.48. See also *PA* 8638.

[11] Aristotle is anachronistic, I think, in applying the term *demagogos* to periods earlier than the fifth century. If the argument in Chapter 3, *Demagogos*, is correct, the word came into use in the late fifth century specifically for leaders of Cleon's type. To apply it to earlier times is dangerous; this misrepresents the history of the word and also makes it easy for those less well informed than Aristotle to misunderstand Athenian political history, for the substantial differences between men like Cleon and, for example, Peisistratus are obscured. Both were eloquent men (note, *inter alia*, the apparent allusion to Peisistratus as a "Siren" in Simonides and Pindar [fr. 339 Snell], see *P. Berol.* 13875; G. Zuntz, *CR* 49 [1935] 4-7), and both held power derived in part from their good standing with the *demos*. But to suggest that they were leaders of the same type is to neglect the important developments which separate them.

(for men were not yet clever orators), but now that rhetoric has developed, the capable speakers serve as *demagogoi*, to be sure, but no longer apply themselves to military matters since they lack the experience . . ." (*Politics* 1305 a 11ff.). The passage immediately raises two questions. First, is the allegation that the generalship had declined in political power correct; second, if so, when did the decline begin?

For the Athens of his own day, at least, Aristotle seems to be quite correct. No prominent Athenian politician of the late fourth century was also a general.[12] The contrast with the period a century and a half earlier when the Persians were threatening Greece is striking; then almost every important politician was a military commander. Even in the more peaceful days after the threat of Persia had diminished, the most prominent politicians were or had at some time been generals: Themistocles, Cimon, Ephialtes, Pericles, and other lesser figures as well. The fourth century general and politician Phocion noted the sharp contrast between the divided responsibilities of his own day and the time of Solon, Aristides, and Pericles, when the same men were famous in the assembly and on the battlefield.[13]

When did the change take place? Aristotle's own reason for the change—the development of rhetoric—suggests a date after the middle of the fifth century.[14] Such a dating may be accepted, even if one wishes to demur about the cause which Aristotle proposes. As we have seen, the growth of the city and the empire were accompanied by a need for increased expertise in political affairs. Generals might find themselves away from Athens much of the year, or so busy on purely military matters that many of them could not free themselves for

[12] Cf. S. Perlman, *Athenaeum* 41 (1963) 347.

[13] Plutarch, *Phocion* 7 *ad fin.* There is a useful discussion of this passage and this phenomenon in the opening sections of G. Gilbert, *Beiträge zur innern Geschichte Athens* (Leipzig 1877).

[14] For Aristotle's date for the rise of rhetoric see Cicero, *Brutus* 12 (46). It began first in Sicily after the fall of the tyrants and only then spread to mainland Greece.

consideration of the full range of political issues. It is in such a time that one would expect the growth of specialization in political affairs and the emergence of a growing distinction between the military and political professions.

This expectation is confirmed by what scanty evidence we have. If we draw a line after Pericles' death we notice a significant change. Cleon, to be sure, was a general, as were Nicias and Alcibiades; Cleophon and Hyperbolus may have been as well.[15] But for Cleon, at least, the generalship played a part rather different from the role it had taken in the careers of many of his predecessors. Pericles, for example, had been general at least as early as the 450's and was regularly general for the fourteen years that followed the ostracism of Thucydides the son of Melesias. His proven military ability and achievements contributed to the prestige and power which he enjoyed in the city. Cleon, on the other hand, came to the generalship late and by miscalculation:

And pointing at Nicias the son of Niceratus, who was general, Cleon spoke, revealing his enmity, and he attacked him saying it was no great task—if our generals are real men—to sail and capture those on the island. That's what he'd do if he were in command. When the Athenians heckled Cleon and asked why he didn't sail right now, if it seemed no great task to him, Nicias, smarting under his attacks, told him he could take whatever force he wanted so far as the generals were concerned and try what he proposed. At first Cleon thought this mere talk and was willing enough. But when he recognized that Nicias was really yielding his command to him, he said he was not general, Nicias was. He was now quite frightened, since he had never thought that Nicias would dare to resign his command to him. But Nicias kept insisting and withdrew from the Pylos assignment and made the Athenians witness the

[15] Cleophon's generalship is mentioned in scholia to *Frogs* 679, Hyperbolus' in scholia to *Knights* 1304.

fact. They, as crowds do, egged Nicias on to withdraw and Cleon to sail, and the more he avoided the expedition and backed down on the things he had said, the more they shouted.

Thucydides 4.27.5-28.3

Cleon, in other words, became a general only after, and because, he had already become a well-known and daring politician.[16] After his success with the command he took over from Nicias, Cleon continued his military career and, indeed, died on the battlefield. But it would be hard to argue that the generalship played as important a part in his rise to power as it had in the careers of many of his predecessors. Hyperbolus' case is less clear; a late and not always reliable source says he was a general but does not mention a date.[17] But even if the generalship is historical and comes early in his career, its importance cannot have been great. Thucydides' narrative gives us a knowledge of the period detailed enough to make it clear that Hyperbolus did not command in any crucial engagement. Despite his dislike of Hyperbolus, Thucydides was probably sufficiently objective to note any military distinction which he won. His silence, thus, is a good indication that the generalship did not play an especially important part in Hyperbolus' rise, nor consume a great deal of his attention after he became prominent. The same can be said of Cleophon, whose generalship is also attested only by the scholia on Aristophanes. Again the silence of Thucydides does not disprove what the scholiast says, but it indicates the relative unimportance of the generalship in his career.[18]

---

[16] The attack on Nicias took place in 425 B.C.; Cleon was already winning some notoriety as a speaker in Pericles' lifetime, see the fragment of Hermippus (46), *apud* Plutarch, *Pericles* 33.

[17] On Hyperbolus' generalship see F. Camon, *Giornale Italiano di filologia* 16 (1963) 46-48, who dates it in 424/3.

[18] Peisander is another example. His generalship is mentioned only by Nepos, *Alcibiades* 5. Again the *argumentum e silentio* applies to the significance not to the historicity of the reported generalship.

Cleon, Hyperbolus, and Cleophon were men of great eloquence and, I believe, great masters of civic affairs. It is to this rather than their military fame that they owed their success. They would seem, then, to represent early instances of a phenomenon which was later to become common: capable speakers who rose to prominence without great and constant military achievement. They set a pattern in this, as in other respects, that later politicians would follow.[19]

Youth in Command

The second development in the years immediately after Pericles' death is one about which Eupolis complains while invoking two great men of the past: "And no longer, Lords Miltiades and Pericles, let swinging teenagers rule us, dragging the generalship around their ankles."[20]

Alcibiades was the great example of the rapid rise to power which Eupolis exaggerates and deplores. Indeed, it is likely that Eupolis had Alcibiades in mind as one of these *meirakia*, teenagers.[21] He was very young when he first began to win attention in the city, perhaps about twenty-three when the comic poets first took notice of him.[22] Later, when he was perhaps thirty, the Spartans made the mistake of snubbing him, for they thought him too young to negotiate a peace treaty for them. In another city a man of Alcibiades' age might have been kept out of political affairs, but in Athens the Spartans soon found what disastrous results came of their insult to Alcibiades' mighty ego (Thucydides 5.43.1ff.).

---

[19] Cf. B-S 1 416 n. 3.

[20] καὶ μηκέτ', ὦναξ Μιλτιάδη καὶ Περίκλεες,
ἐᾶτον ἄρχειν μειράκια κινούμενα
ἐπὶ τοῖν σφυροῖν ἕλκοντα τὴν στρατηγίαν.

Eupolis, *Demes*, fr. 118, probable around 411 B.C. For the textual problems see Edmonds' edition.

[21] It seems to have been an affectation of Alcibiades to drag his cloak behind him. Compare Archippus *apud* Plutarch, *Alcibiades* 1, *ad fin.* and note also the beginning of chapter 16 of that life.

[22] He was probably born around 450, and was alluded to in Aristophanes, *Banqueters* fr. 198 (427 B.C.).

To be sure, Alcibiades may be an exceptional case. He was, as Thucydides points out, "honored for the distinctions of his ancestors" (5.43.2), and may thus have risen rapidly to power. Nor should we conclude from the rash attempt of Glaucon, Plato's younger brother, to address the assembly before he was twenty years old that other Athenian youths shared his brashness.[23] Among the most famous men of the period, moreover, are some whose first prominence seems to have come only after they were forty. Nicias and Laches, for example, were both older than Socrates and first come to our notice in the 420's.[24] Yet Hyperbolus is known to have entered politics at what was regarded as an excessively early age.[25] And Eupolis' reiterated complaints about the youth of Athens' leaders make better sense if there was a noticeable change in this respect than if we regard them simply as the embittered grumbling of the rapidly aging.[26] He is not the only one of his contemporaries to show signs of alarm at the influence and policies of ambitious young men. Euripides' *Suppliants* displays the same concern, though of course the setting is drastically changed. The play is set in the mythic time of early Athens; Theseus is king and he attacks Adrastus for being misled by the youth of Argos: "You destroyed the city, led astray by youths who like to win honor and foment wars without any thought for justice, who destroy the citizens— one so he can become general, another to win power and do

---

[23] Glaucon's political aspirations were restrained by a sobering conversation with Socrates (Xenophon, *Memorabilia* 3.6.1ff.). Although he is not known to have had any political career, he did distinguish himself at the battle of Megara late in the Peloponnesian War. Plato, *Republic* 368 a.

[24] Cf. Plato, *Laches* 186 c. Cleon was perhaps born before 470; cf. J. Davies, *Athenian Propertied Families*, no. 8674 (Oxford, forthcoming), and is not attacked in Comedy for his youth.

[25] Eupolis fr. 238; Cratinus fr. 262.

[26] In addition to his comments in the *Demes* quoted at the head of this section and his remark about Hyperbolus noted in the last footnote, see also fr. 310 and fr. 90, where he transforms an old proverb, "Don't trust a child with a knife," to one he thinks more apposite for his day, "Don't trust a child with politics," Cf. also Aristophanes, *Acharnians* 680ff.

what he wants, another for gain, never caring if the people are harmed by his actions" (*Suppliants* 231-237).

These words of Euripides, so exaggerated in their context, remind us of the mighty oversimplification in Plutarch's account of the ostracism of Hyperbolus, "To put it simply, it was a match between the young who wanted to make war and the old men who wanted to make peace."[27] This is a vast overstatement, yet perhaps Plutarch could claim some justification for it and might even adduce more supporting evidence than is possible at this late date.[28]

Cause and Effect

For the two developments discussed in the last sections there may be a single cause. If what has been said above about the emergence of a new style of politics is correct, then both the decline in the political importance of the generalship and the lower age of many of the politicians of Athens is understandable. One of the effects of the innovations made in Cleon's time was that a politician could circumvent many of the processes that had formerly seemed essential to a political career. In the old pattern proven reliability was exceedingly important; time and military experience would test it and eventually create the backing of confidence which a politician needed. His deeds in battle or his long apprenticeship in the art of government would show that he was worthy of trust. Under the new pattern a good speaker could rout his opponents with a clever argument, emotional appeals, or addi-

---

[27] Plutarch, *Nicias* 11; cf. *Alcibiades* 17.

[28] We are rather better informed about the age of the Four Hundred, and these too seem to have included many rather young men. The following table is based on p. 307 of the useful dissertation of H. C. Avery, *Prosopographical Studies in the Oligarchy of the 400* (unpublished Ph.D. thesis, Princeton 1960):

Over 60	8
50-60	3
40-50	4
30-40	9
20-30	1

tional information. For we must not forget that if many politicians of the late fifth century spoke well, they were also well informed. If they could show themselves consistently persuasive they might become "indispensable experts" and enjoy the heights of influence and prestige.

Thus one effect of the new pattern of politics which appeared in Cleon's day was that a bright and articulate young man could rise more quickly than had formerly been possible. He might also find it desirable to concentrate his efforts at home rather than seeking election to the generalship and sailing off with his colleagues. Indeed, for many young Athenians the generalship was unattainable no matter how capable they were. It not only required leisure and its handmaiden wealth, but also an electoral miracle, for normally there were only ten generals, one elected annually from each tribe. Where our documentation is sufficient, a tendency towards iteration can be noted on the generalship lists: experienced commanders tend to be returned to office. Thus a young man was not likely to be elected if his tribe already had a famous old fighter, of less political finesse perhaps, but of unshaken military reputation. He would simply have to wait until time or an enemy arrow cleared the way for him. It might be decades before he was in command, and as long as political advancement was tied to military distinction, his role in the decisions of the city was limited.

Cleon in effect severed the connection. He showed how to separate a political career from a military one. There was no need to wait. The leadership of the city could be won before or without the generalship. This was the revelation of a momentous *imperii arcanum*. It opened, as has so often been pointed out, a rapid way to power for the inexperienced, the glib, the rhetorical charlatans; but it also meant that ability need not languish so long before winning recognition.

The new pattern of politics introduced by Cleon was both a danger and an opportunity. Sound judgment could make it work. A citizenry that could and would distinguish between a specious argument and cogent reasoning would not be threatened by it and might even benefit. Prejudice, emotionalism, and folly could destroy the pattern and the city as well.

The Social Standing of Cleon and His Successors

A study of the style of Cleon and his successors helps us in considerable measure to understand the nature of politics in his day and in the following years. Only a fuller knowledge of their position can clarify the way they operated and the reactions they provoked. And both of these must be comprehended for the proper study not only of our period of Greek history but also of the revolutionary period that follows it. Our literary sources are less abundant and more tendentious than we might hope, but the archaeologists and epigraphers will help. Let us begin with Cleon himself.

Cleon's Wealth

In Cleon's case one fact stands out. Although Comedy creates the impression that he was a malodorous, impoverished leather-peddler from some foul tannery, in truth he was nothing of the sort. His father, Cleainetus, owned a factory in which slaves worked hides into leather.[29] It was a profitable enough business.[30] Even if the inflammatory story that Cleon entered public life in debt and left an estate of fifty talents when he died is true, it speaks about his character, not his background.[31] Cleon may have been a profligate, but he was

[29] Scholion on Aristophanes, *Knights* 44, as emended. It is not entirely clear that Cleon himself followed his father's profession in his adult life. Note the scholion on Lucian, *Timon* 30 (Rabe 116), and the hint in *Knights* 248 that he may have been a tax farmer.

[30] It is now generally recognized that Cleon's father and the Cleainetus mentioned as a *choregus* in 460/59 in *IG* ii² 2318, line 34, are one and the same person. Anyone who could afford to be a *choregus* was well-to-do.

[31] Critias, *VS* 88 B 45 *apud* Aelian, *Varia Historia* 10.17. The reliability of the passage is denied by T. A. Dorey, "Aristophanes and Cleon," *Greece and Rome* N.S. 3 (1956) 132-139.

raised in a family that had enjoyed prosperity. One ancient tradition even says he was once a member of that well-to-do, long-haired group of young Athenians, the Knights,[32] but whether or not this is true, the essential fact is clear: Cleon was accustomed to wealth.

The Wealth of Other Politicians

It is more difficult to speak with confidence about the economic position of other politicians of the 420's and 410's. Some like Alcibiades and Nicias were clearly very rich, but for many our only source is Comedy or writers who depended on Comedy for their information. The case of Cleon is clear warning to beware rash inferences from such data. Indeed, when we find Hyperbolus sneeringly called a lamp-maker or a potter and notice the similarity to what is said about Cleon in the same sources, we begin to suspect that he too derived his wealth from some prosperous factory where the work was done by slaves.[33] The same skepticism makes us

[32] The scholiast on *Knights* 225 (cf. Tzetzes on *Clouds* 549 a) asserts Cleon was once a Knight, but this statement has received very little attention in modern scholarship (note however H. Diller, *Gnomon* 15 [1939] 113) although it is, I believe, quite consistent with what we know of him from Plutarch's *Moralia* 806 f-807 a. He had influential friends and then repudiated them. Were his early associates Knights? Was there thus a special animosity of the Knights against him? And were they an especially appropriate chorus for an anti-Cleon play such as Aristophanes' *Knights*?

The story that he was a Knight may also shed some light upon the difficult 94th fragment of Theopompus, given the further presumption that the Knights had, as the scholiast on *Knights* 627 (cf. Suidas s.v. *Hippeis* [Adler, Iota 537]) asserts, disciplinary powers over their members. The exercise of this authority may have forced Cleon to return a five-talent bribe mentioned in this fragment of Theopompus and in Aristophanes, *Acharnians* 6. Fragment 93 of Theopompus would then fit into place as an account of Cleon's response, "after he had been insulted and provoked by them [the Knights], he undertook a political career and . . . denounced them on a charge of refusing to fulfill their military duties." Hence also his epithet *taraxippostraton* (*Knights* 247)? On these two fragments of Theopompus see also *Theopompus* 50-59.

[33] Hyperbolus is called a lampmaker in Aristophanes, *Peace* 690, and in the scholia to Aristophanes, *Knights* 739. He is called a potter in the scholia to *Knights* 1304 and a metalworker in the scholia to *Clouds* 1064. These testimonies are not contradictory. See the discussion in F. Camon, *Rivista di studi classici* 9 (1961) 182-197. There are hints that he performed a trierarchy in Eupolis fr. 195 and Aristophanes, *Thesmophoriazusae* 836-845.

wonder whether Cleophon, the lyre-maker, was not also a wealthy manufacturer.[34] And our suspicions are increased when we learn that he may have been a general, as his father surely was.[35]

Most historians today share our suspicions about the wealth of Cleon, Hyperbolus and Cleophon, and such other politicians as Lysicles the cattle-dealer or Eucrates the flax merchant. Politics, then as now, was an easier pursuit for the wealthy than for the poor, and the increasing complexity of affairs and growing need for professionalism in the late fifth century are likely to have excluded from a serious political career anyone who did not have abundant leisure.

There was, of course, one great difference between the economic standing of many of the politicians of the late fifth century and that of Pericles and Cimon. These two and perhaps many of their rivals and allies derived their wealth from land,[36] but not many of their successors depended on agriculture. Rather they were middlemen or manufacturers,[37] men drawn from a segment that had long existed in Athens' population but which had hitherto not produced many politicians.[38] Now, in the prosperity stimulated by the Athenian

[34] Cleophon is called a lyre-maker in Andocides 1.146, Aeschines 2.76, *AthPol* 28.3, scholia to Aristophanes, *Thesmophoriazusae* 805 and to *Frogs* 681.

[35] On Cleophon's generalship see above, The Decline of the Generalship. Ostraca show that his father was Cleippides, the general of 428 (Thucydides 3.3.2). See E. Vanderpool, *Hesperia* 37 (1968) 120. Cf. below, Family Background.

[36] We learn of Pericles' estate from Plutarch, *Pericles* 16, and of Cimon's from *AthPol* 27.3 and Theopompus, *FGrH* 115 F 89.

[37] In addition to Cleon, Hyperbolus, and Cleophon note Eucrates: hemp, Aristophanes fr. 696, cf. *Knights* 129 and scholia *ad loc.* Lysicles: sheep dealer, Aristophanes, *Knights* 132. Also called a "hide-stitcher" in *Knights* 739 and scholia. Dieitrephes: wicker jars, scholion on Aristophanes, *Birds* 798 (see Suidas, s.v. Diitrephes [Adler, Delta 1054]). The evidence that Theogenes was a merchant (Eupolis fr. 110 A-B line 9) is very tenuous. Nicias' wealth was not far different from that of these men; it was based on slaves who worked in the mines, see Xenophon, *Poroi* 4.14; Lysias 19.47; Plutarch, *Nicias* 4.

[38] Callias, son of Hipponicus, nicknamed "pit-wealthy" (*lakkoploutos*), like Nicias derived his great wealth from mines and the slaves that worked them, Xenophon, *Poroi* 4.15; Nepos, *Cimon* 1.3. But his family was very old

empire, they had attained the degree of leisure, affluence, and interest required for political careers. Predictably they were turning their attention from their shops near the agora to the political assemblies on the Pnyx.

In Greek the most convenient name for most of these men was *agoraioi*, "men of the agora," a descriptive term, but also one with some emotional overtones.[39] Although this term could be applied to the poor and lowly, it was also used for the well-to-do. Socrates, for example, in one of his characteristically hyperbolic comparisons likens conversations about poetry to the symposia of these *agoraioi*. The passage makes it clear that he is thinking of relatively prosperous men, but men whom he, at least, does not admire:

> Conversation about poetry reminds me too much of the wine parties of second-rate and commonplace people (the *agoraioi*). Such men being too uneducated to entertain themselves as they drink by using their own voices and conversational resources, put up the price of female musicians, paying well for the hire of an extraneous voice—that of the pipe—and find their entertainment in its war-

---

and renowned (cf. J. Toeppfer, *Attische Genealogie*, 86ff.) and he cannot properly be grouped with men whose families, as we shall see, were far less distinguished.

[39] The word *agoraios* is first used in Greek as an epithet of gods who protect the assembly place, Aeschylus, *Agamemnon* 90, *Eumenides* 974; cf. Herodotus 5.46.2. But it very quickly takes on pejorative connotations; it is an insult in Aristophanes, *Peace* 750; cf. fr. 471 and Plutarch's comment on Nicias' dedications in *Nicias* 4. The reason for the change is probably to be found in the application of the word to "the men of the agora," those whose chief concern was to buy cheap and sell dear, as Xenophon would describe them (*Memorabilia* 3.7.6). Prejudice against these men is also clear in Aristophanes, *Frogs* 1013-1017, where they are contrasted to the tall well-born heroes of Aeschylean drama.

The range of application of this word in the fourth century is clarified by Aristotle, *Politics* 1289 b 33 and 1290 b 39-1291 a 8. The range in the fifth century is less easily determined, but Xenophon, *Poroi* 3.12 and 13, and Herodotus 2.141.4 might be taken to show that Aristotle's predecessors used the word in a narrower sense than he did and distinguished *emporoi* (merchants) and *kapeloi* (retailers) from *agoraioi*. See also M. I. Finley, *CP* 30 (1935) 320-336.

blings. But where the drinkers are men of worth and culture (*kaloi kagathoi*) you will find no girls piping or dancing or harping. They are quite capable of enjoying their own company without such frivolous nonsense, using their own voices in sober discussion and each taking his turn to speak or listen—even if the drinking is really heavy.

> Plato, *Protagoras* 347 c-d, trans.
> W. K. C. Guthrie (Penguin translation)

It is easy to see from this passage that the *agoraioi* could not claim the distinction of the old *kaloi kagathoi*. However wealthy they might be, they lacked the respectability that time, a good genealogy, and elegant manners could bring.

Our evidence points to the conclusion that many of the politicians of the last three decades of the century were *agoraioi* or *nouveaux riches*, and that they met in many quarters the prejudice so frequently accorded the newly prosperous, Cleon, Cleophon, Hyperbolus, and their like were surely not the old aristocracy of Athens. They claimed no gods or Homeric heroes in their ancestry, boasted no family distinction in the misty past. To the best of our knowledge none of these three even belonged to a *genos*. Hence some prejudice against them would be likely, for, as Aristotle pointed out: "And since that which is old seems closely to resemble that which is natural, it follows that, if two parties have the same good, men are more indignant with the one who has recently acquired it and owes his prosperity to it. . . . The same applies to offices of state. . . . The newly rich who attain to office owing to their wealth cause more annoyance than those who have long been wealthy . . ." (Aristotle, *Rhetoric* 2.1387 a, trans. J. H. Freese). Furthermore, the Greek word for *nouveau riche, neoploutos,* comes into use at just this time and is applied to men of this sort.[40]

---

[40] The first sign of the word is in the monstrous compound *neoploutoponeroi* in Cratinus fr. 208 (428 B.C.?) which implies the existence of the shorter word. The fragment refers to the politician Androcles (*PA* 870) and to someone

There is, however, one slight difficulty. What would seem from our literary sources to be one of the clearest examples of a *nouveau riche* appears from the ostraca and documentary material to be no such thing. The difficulty is instructive both about the man and about the sources with which we must work. It merits careful treatment.

The case concerns Dieitrephes, a general in 414/3 and 412/11, and a likely proposer of the decree honoring Hierocles of Sciathos in 408/7;[41] Aristophanes says he rose from being a "nothing" to military prominence, first a phylarch, then a hipparch, finally a general.[42] The scholiasts tell us that he was a manufacturer of wicker jars and that he was *neoploutos*.[43] They also report that the comic poet Plato called him "the mad man, the Cretan, the barely-Athenian" (fr. 31). So far, he appears the typical *nouveau riche*.

When we turn to the archaeological material, the problems begin. His name is a rare one and he almost surely belongs to the family of Dieitrephes I (*PA* 3753), a politician active around 460.[44] If that is correct he belongs on the Genealogical Chart on p. 157.[45]

---

whose name begins with Aischro-, possibly Aischron (*PA* 408), a *Hellenotamias* of 425/4. The last part of the fragment is corrupt. *Neoploutos* itself is first found in Aristophanes, *Wasps* 1309.

[41] The evidence is conveniently collected in *PA* 3755. Note especially Thucydides 7.29. The decree is *IG* i² 118 (*SEG* x 134). He may also be the archon of 384/3.

[42] Aristophanes, *Birds* 798-800 and note the scholia on these lines; note also *Birds* 1441 and scholia *ad loc.*

[43] Scholia on *Birds* 798.

[44] This Dieitrephes is known from ostraca, see W. B. Dinsmoor, *Hesperia* Suppl. Vol. v, 163 and E. Vanderpool, *Hesperia* 37 (1968) 117-120.

[45] The stemma follows E. Vanderpool, *Hesperia* 37 (1968) 117-120, cf. W. B. Dinsmoor, *Hesperia* Suppl. Vol. v, 143, 163-164. Dinsmoor (p. 163) is correct, I believe, in arguing that Pausanias 1.23.3-4 confused the two Dieitrephes when he implies that the subject of the statue in Athens was Dieitrephes II. This statue was actually of Dieitrephes I and was dedicated by Hermolycus II.

It is interesting to note that both Nicostratus and our Dieitrephes II commanded Thracians, Thucydides 4.129.1 and 7.29.1. The family may have had special interest or competence in this area. Cf. Asopius and his father Phormio, Thucydides 3.7.

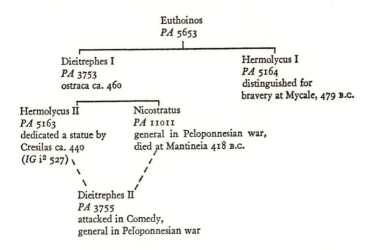

Thus Dieitrephes' father or uncle was wealthy enough to employ one of the best sculptors of the day and to dedicate what was probably a rather fine statue of a famous ancestor. Furthermore, it can be seen that Dieitrephes was not the first in his family to rise to the generalship; Nicostratus had already attained that distinction. Nor was he the first prominent politician, for his grandfather Dieitrephes I was probably well known around 460.

The disparity between our two classes of evidence, literary and epigraphical, is disquieting. Some reconciliation might be attempted: perhaps Dieitrephes' branch of the family had been only moderately wealthy and he had recently acquired a great deal of money from his manufacturing activities. Still, the difficulty remains. If good luck and the skill of the archaeologists had not combined to help us, we would be easily misled by statements that he was "*neoploutos*," "barely Athenian," "from nothing." The case of Dieitrephes does not refute the suggestion that many of his contemporaries may have been *nouveaux riches*, but it will make us hesitate before

157

drawing this conclusion in individual cases. We will want to know more about the family background and the education of these politicians before we press this generalization.

Family Background

"Though Hyperbolus and Cleophon and Demades came to the forefront of the Athenian populace, no one would find it easy to name their fathers." The sneer, representative of many comments about the background of the politicians of the fifth and fourth centuries, comes from Aelian (*Varia Historia* 12.43). And like many attacks on these politicians, it cannot be defended. Even today, after so many losses in documentation, we can produce the names of Antiphanes, Cleippides, and Demeas, nor are these fathers all hopelessly undistinguished. Cleophon's father Cleippides, from the deme Acharnia, at least, was a general in 428/7 and figured in an ostracism perhaps in 444/3.[46] As might be expected, we know less about the fathers of many other politicians of the period, and few could boast the distinguished lineage of Alcibiades, who traced his family back to Eurysaces, the son of Ajax, and thence to Zeus.[47] But gradually the progress of archaeology and epigraphy is turning up more information about these families, much of which points in an interesting direction. An inscription indicates that Cleon's father was not only an Athenian citizen but also wealthy enough to finance a chorus at a public festival. Ostraca put to rest the slander about Hyperbolus' paternity; it is now clear that his father was Antiphanes. Dieitrephes seems to emerge as a scion of an old family rather than a *nouveau riche*; Cleophon's father

---

[46] E. Vanderpool's suggestion in *Hesperia* 21 (1952) 114-115 that Cleophon was the son of Cleippides, grandson of Deinias, has been confirmed by new ostraca published in *Hesperia* 37 (1968) 120. Cleippides' generalship is mentioned in Thucydides 3.3.2, and the ostraca against him are published in *IG* i² 911, 2. Cleophon himself is said to have been a general in Aristophanes, *Frogs* 679.

[47] See (Plato) *Alcibiades* 1.121 a. For the family tree see E. Vanderpool, *Hesperia* 21 (1952) 6, cf. *Hesperia* 37 (1968) 118 n. 1.

turns out to be a general. And we have every reason to expect that further excavation and study will continue to demonstrate that the politicians of the 420's were neither barbarians nor slaves, nor the sons of non-citizens, but good Athenians, often of well-established families. It is true that, except for Alcibiades, Demostratus, and perhaps Phaeax, they apparently did not claim membership in the famous houses that traced their genealogies back to the Homeric heroes or other mythic forebears, but they were not what Comedy sometimes makes them appear to be: "I feel so strongly when I see what state our city is in I don't know what to say—though there's plenty to say. We old timers didn't used to run things like this. In the first place we had for our city generals from the greatest houses, first men by wealth and breeding (*genos*). We revered them like gods—they practically were. As a result we met no disaster. But now whatever the situation we make our expeditions with convicted scapegoats in command."[48]

If we divest ourselves of the ideas promulgated by Comedy and by writers dependent upon it for their information, we can begin to see the politicians of the period after Pericles' death more clearly. They are wealthy; they often derive their money from manufacturing or entrepreneurship rather than from agriculture.[49] Most of them benefited from the larger markets and greater security created by the Delian League and by the transformation of that league into an Athenian empire. Their families were Attic, though perhaps not of such indisputable renown as automatically to ward off slanders that they had slipped onto the citizenship rolls illegally. In a

[48] Eupolis fr. 103. Probably from the *Demes*, ca. 418-411 B.C. For an opposite view of "the good old days" see *AthPol* 26.1.

[49] I do not mean by this that these men were *emporoi*, merchants engaged in interstate trade. Nor do I think their policies were dictated by the simple desire to maintain and expand Athenian economic dominance, cf. F. M. Cornford, *Thucydides Mythistoricus*, 19ff. But they do seem to be men who benefited from the empire and who would naturally wish to maintain it. On the *emporoi* see M. I. Finley, *CP* 30 (1935) 320-336.

few cases the genealogies suggest that they were families who were marrying into older and more famous houses, and thus gradually rising in social as well as financial standing. The cases of Nicias and of Cleon are interesting and can best be studied from the genealogical charts:

Cleon, Son of Cleainetus

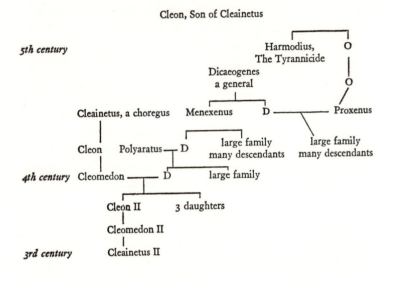

1. Nothing is known of the family before Cleon's father. J. Davies, *Athenian Propertied Families* (no. 8674) notes that Aristophanes' repeated references to Cleon as a Paphlagonian may conceal a cult, administrative, or other association somewhere in Asia Minor.

2. His son, Cleomedon, married the daughter of Polyaratus, a man apparently without noted family but of considerable wealth, pseudo-Demosthenes 40.24.

3. Polyaratus had married the daughter of a more prominent family which can be traced back to Dicaeogenes, a general who fell at a battle at Eleusis, Isaeus 5.42.

160

4. One of Dicaeogenes' many descendants, a daughter of unknown name, married Proxenus, a descendant of one of the noblest and most famous of all Athenians, Harmodius, the tyrannicide. He was of a noble family, the Gephyraioi. A great grandson of Proxenus and his anonymous wife married Eucoiline, daughter of Aristogeiton of Aphidna. It is probable that she was descended from the other tyrannicide, Aristogeiton of Aphidna.

5. Cleon's son, Cleomedon, had a large family parts of which can be traced down to the third century. For fuller discussion see J. Davies, *Athenian Propertied Familes*.

Nicias, Son of Niceratus

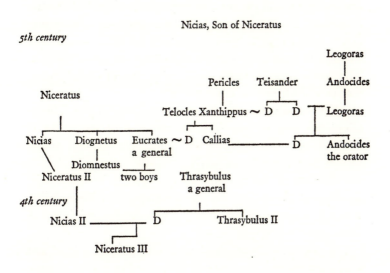

1. The family cannot be traced back beyond Niceratus I, nor can it be tied to any Athenian *genos*. Thus Nicias is not, properly speaking, one of the *aristoi*. There is, however, a tradition preserved in Diogenes Laertius 1.110 that at the beginning of the sixth century Epimenides was brought to Athens from Crete by one Nicias the son of Niceratus. On his arrival

161

Epimenides found a way of driving away a plague that had settled on Athens. This story is most probably a piece of pseudo-history promulgated by the fifth century Nicias to bolster his reputation for piety and religious devotion. Compare his comments in Thucydides 7.77.2. Such a reputation would be especially valuable in a rivalry with Alcibiades, whose orthodoxy was suspect. Cf. Wilamowitz in his edition of the *Hippolytus* (Berlin 1891) 244.

2. Nicias was one of three sons, another of whom married into the family of Telocles. This family is no better known than Nicias'; but a son of Telocles married into the extraordinarily well-attested and well-connected family of Andocides, the orator. Cf. the chart in appendix K of D. MacDowell, *Andokides On the Mysteries* (Oxford 1962) 206. This family can be traced back to the sixth century b.c. with considerable distinction. Andocides' uncle was Xanthippus, son of Pericles. The family was ultimately connected to that of Critias and to that of Callias, son of Hipponicus.

3. The family was hostile to the tyranny of the Thirty; Diognetus took no part in it (Lysias 18.9-10); Niceratus II and Eucrates were killed by the Thirty (Lysias 18.6, Suidas s.v. *apestin* [Adler, Alpha 3069]).

4. The reason for this hostility can perhaps be seen in the marriage of Nicias' grandson to the daughter of Thrasybulus, a strong opponent of the Thirty. The marriage is implied in Demosthenes 19.290.

The two genealogies show a similar pattern. Nicias and Cleon are the first members of their families known to have won any great distinction; their fathers were probably both wealthy but not especially prominent in the city. Although Cleon and Nicias rose to success, the families into which they married seem not to have been very distinguished, but in the next generation or two their descendants begin to marry into houses which, if not themselves especially famous, were at least tied to old and prestigious families. Thus Cleon's grandson could claim as remote cousins descendants of an aristocratic tyrannicide and Nicias might stop the orator Andocides, a man of extraordinary standing among the well-born families of Athens, and inquire about their mutual in-laws, the children of Telocles.

Culture and Education

If we are literal-minded enough to accept at face value what Comedy says about the wealth and the genealogy of many of the politicians of this period, we may also be misled into accepting its picture of their education and intellectual accomplishments. Comedy delights in presenting them as ignorant and uncultured; for example Eupolis' *Maricas*, a thinly (and obscenely) veiled Hyperbolus, boasts: "And of culture, I know only my ABC's."[50] A few years earlier Aristophanes had used a variant of the same joke in the *Knights*. The barb was then directed against Cleon, but in a more indirect and slightly more subtle fashion. When the Sausage-seller is informed that he is to become the greatest man in the city he replies with amazement:

> But my good man, I don't know anything about culture (*mousikē*), except the alphabet, and that just barely.

And he is then told

> That's your only drawback, that you know it, even "just barely." The *demagogia* is no longer for a cultured or well-behaved man, but for the ignorant and the obnoxious.

Aristophanes, Knights 188-192

The implication is that the current leader of the *demos*—Paphlagon in the play, Cleon in real life—excelled in ignorance and boorishness.

---

[50] Eupolis fr. 193. Compare Plato Comicus fr. 168 on Hyperbolus' pronunciation. Did he vocalize the gamma as modern Greeks do? F. Camon, in *Rivista di studi classici* 9 (1961) 186-187, compares this fragment to Aristophanes fr. 685 and suggests that Hyperbolus spoke the dialect of the city, a rather vulgar sort of Attic.

The treatment has its modern analogies, not all of them from Comedy. When, for example, John Quincy Adams refused to attend the commencement at which his *alma mater* gave an honorary degree to President Andrew Jackson, he wrote, "I *would not* be present to see my darling Harvard disgrace herself by conferring a doctor's degree upon a barbarian and a savage who can scarcely spell his own name."[51] Comedy may of course be distorting for reasons even less substantial than President Adams'. When it wants to make us laugh, it does not scruple about the means. But in some cases one suspects some of the humor is in the subject himself and that all is not comic fantasy. If a politician or his pretensions are potentially ludicrous, the comic poet may not need to distort very much to make us laugh. But let us forget Comedy a moment and turn to another source. The Socratic dialogues should provide more reliable information. Yet they agree with Comedy that some politicians, at least, were ludicrously unsuited for their careers and quite ill-educated and uncultured. One such dialogue, preserved with the works of Plato and entitled *Alcibiades* (1) presents Socrates in conversation with the young Alcibiades, who is eager to start a political career. Socrates leads him on in a passage heavy with irony:

> Turn your attention to Meidias the gambler and others like him who manage our politics; in whom, as the women would remark, you may still see the slaves' cut of hair, cropping out in their minds as well as on their pates; and they come with their barbarous lingo to flatter and not to rule us. To these I say you should look, and then you need not trouble yourself about your fitness to contend in such a noble arena: there is no reason why you should either learn what has to be learned or practice what has to be practiced.[52]

[51] Quoted in R. Hofstadter, *Anti-intellectualism in American Life* (New York 1963) 160 n. 5.
[52] *Alcibiades* 1.120 a, trans. B. Jowett, modified. Wilamowitz, in his *Platon*

164

In another Socratic dialogue, Plato's *Meno,* the Socratic irony is again turned against one of the politicians. His lack of proper education is accentuated both by the fullness of Socrates' introduction and by the irony of the final devastating phrase. The man is one who later prosecutes Socrates on those vague charges that brought about his death, a politician of some importance in democratic Athens, Anytus.[53] Socrates sees him approaching and turns to Meno and says:

> Why look here, my dear Menon, in the nick of time here is Anytos; he has taken a seat beside us. Let us ask him to share in our search [to determine whether virtue can be taught]; it would be reasonable to give him a share. For in the first place, Anytos has a wealthy father, the wise Anthemion, who became rich not by a stroke of luck or by a gift . . . but he got his by his own wisdom and care. . . . and . . . he brought up our Anytos well, and educated him well, as the public opinion is—at least, they choose him for the highest offices.
>
> *Meno* 90 a and b, trans. W. H. D. Rouse

As the conversation proceeds, Anytus' shallow self-confidence and ignorance become ever clearer, as does his superficial and ill-informed horror of the sophists. Though, as he later admits, he is quite unacquainted with them, he is confident that they are pernicious. When Socrates mentions them as possible teachers of political excellence, Anytus is shocked: "Oh Heracles! Hush my dear Socrates! May none of my relations or friends, here or abroad, fall into such madness as to

---

II 326 n. 1, contended that this dialogue was influenced by Old Comedy and should be dated in the third century B.C. More recent scholarship has been willing to date it to the fourth century, and sometimes even to defend its authenticity. For the recent bibliography see H. Cherniss, *Lustrum* 4 (1959) 71-72.

[53] Anytus, like Cleon, derived his wealth from leatherworking, scholia to Plato, *Apology* 18 b. He was a general in 410/9 and again in the revolution at the end of the war, Lysias 13.78,82. See *PA* 1324. After the expulsion of The Thirty he was one of the most powerful men in the city, Isocrates 18.23.

go to these persons and be tainted! These men are the manifest canker and destruction of all they have to do with" (*Meno* 91 c, trans. Rouse). In this short passage of the *Meno* Plato has sketched a paradeigmatic anti-intellectual politician, a man of great self-confidence who is quite sure of what is true and false, useful or harmful, without troubling to acquaint himself with facts or reasons.[54] He is the sort of man who would, as Xenophon tells us, neglect the education of his own son (*Apology* 30-31) and feel he was doing a public service when he prosecuted Socrates.

The convergence of the Socratic dialogues with Old Comedy is a striking argument that some of the politicians of the late fifth century were ill-educated and uncultured. Meidias and Anytus, to be sure, may not have been typical of the rest. Nicias was neither pretentious nor arrogant and it seems harsh to call him uncultured. Yet there is something very

[54] Anytus' attitude toward the sophists is, I believe, typical of most democratic politicians. It is sometimes argued that, since Cleon and Hyperbolus and other politicians were unquestionably effective speakers, they must have studied under the sophists. The evidence in fact points in quite the opposite direction. We do not find these politicians in the circle of listeners around the sophists reported by Plato and Xenophon. Apart from Alcibiades, only two of the politicians of the 420's and 410's are ever said to have studied under the sophists. Euathlus (Diogenes Laertius 9.56) is a possible case; Hyperbolus is a very dubious one. The evidence in his case is a joke in Aristophanes, *Clouds* 876, that Socrates received a talent for teaching Hyperbolus to speak effectively. We are rightly skeptical of what the line implies about Socrates; similar caution must be applied to its implications about Hyperbolus, especially in the light of Eupolis fr. 193. Note also K. J. Dover's note on *Clouds* 553. In the absence of confirming evidence, the argument that the politicians studied under the sophists cannot be considered a strong one. The fact of their eloquence is no proof. There were brilliant speakers long before the sophists; even distinctively sophistic traits in the speech of a fifth century orator would not prove that he studied under a sophist, for the sophistic techniques of oratory could not long be kept secret, and any observant and clever speaker might pick up a few.

There is, moreover, one strong argument that few politicians of the period were associated with the sophists: Comedy found both the politicians and the sophists worthy targets for its attacks. (For its treatment of the sophists see V. Ehrenberg, *People of Aristophanes* [Oxford 1951] 275-280.) The slightest hint of association between the two would have provided a perfect opportunity for jokes and satire—yet Comedy normally attacks each group separately. In this case the *argumentum e silentio* is a telling one.

rigid and unsophisticated in his intellectual makeup. It is hard to picture him associating with the other leading think-ers of the day, as Pericles had with Protagoras and Anaxag-oras. He was a profoundly conventional and pious man, so much so that in the midst of one of his city's greatest military disasters, when a quick and decisive retreat was all that could save a remnant of his force, he decided that an eclipse of the moon required him to wait on the spot for thrice nine days (Thucydides 7.50.4ff.). His actions are those of a man who had not been much affected by the growth of learning and rational thought in the past few generations in Greece. Nicias' case, to be sure another extreme, is the best example of super-stition among Greek politicians but it is basically not rad-ically different from that of his great rival and enemy Cleon —whose words, as reported by Thucydides, are monumental in their distrust of the intellect:

> . . . lack of learning combined with sound common sense is more helpful than the kind of cleverness that gets out of hand . . . as a general rule states are better governed by the man in the street than by intellectuals. These are the sort of people who want to appear wiser than the laws, who want to get their own way in every general discussion, be-cause they feel that they cannot show off their intelligence in matters of greater importance, and who, as a result, very often bring ruin on their country.

> Thucydides 3.37.3 and 4, trans. Rex Warner

Lack of training of the intellect and distrust of the intellect, two companions through the ages, are found together in Cleon and Nicias and, we might suspect, in many of their friends and rivals. The anti-intellectualism of these men is consistent with all we hear of them. We have suspected that many of the politicians of this period were newly rich or the sons of newly rich fathers. Many were successful business-men. And like their modern equivalent, the "self-made" man, they often regarded the training of the intellect as superfluous, or at best as an elegant and superficial polish. That they were often bright and capable men need not be doubted; that they were better educated than Comedy would admit is extremely probable; but that they were the sophisticated and fully-trained products of the newest and most controversial techniques of education is most unlikely.

Old Comedy and the New Politicians

Throughout our inquiry we have observed the attitude of Old Comedy to Cleon, Hyperbolus, and many other politicians of the late fifth century. They are mocked with regularity not only by Aristophanes but also by Eupolis, Plato the Comic poet, and, it would seem, by most of their colleagues. The jokes, moreover, betray something other than light-hearted amusement, often political venom. There is heat and hostility in Old Comedy and nowhere is it more obvious than in the treatment of Cleon and his successors. This intensity of feeling makes it difficult to use these plays as a historical source for the period, but at the same time it makes these works all the more valuable as indicators of the emotional climate in Athens, and as guides to some of the reactions which these politicians evoked. It would be as rash to dismiss Comedy entirely from consideration as it would be to accept its jokes as literal truth.

When one studies these plays, their unanimity is most striking. Cleon and Aristophanes had quarreled and had good reason for disliking each other.[55] If the attacks in Old Comedy came only from Aristophanes or were directed only against Cleon, we could conclude that we were dealing with a personal feud, and perhaps nothing more. But the unanim-

---

[55] Aristophanes attacked Cleon in the *Babylonians* (426 B.C.) and was brought into court by Cleon as a result. The feud continued in the *Acharnians*, *Knights*, and *Wasps*. Edmonds' testimonia on the *Babylonians* provides a convenient collection of the principal ancient sources.

ity of Comedy refutes this notion. Aristophanes was not the only comic poet to attack Cleon; nor is Cleon the only target.[56] Hyperbolus is treated in much the same way by several poets. He regularly appears as a lampmaker, a foreigner; his father and mother are slandered, his paternity doubted.[57] Cleophon is another example. His father had been a general and was probably too well known to be the object of the facile invective used against Hyperbolus' father, but the effect was simply that more scorn was heaped on Cleophon's mother. In the play *Cleophon*, by the comic poet Plato, she was represented as speaking like a barbarian. And Cleophon, like Cleon and Hyperbolus, was said to be a foreigner.[58] With variations, similar attacks are brought against many, though by no means all, politicians of the period.[59]

The unanimity of the comic poets, not only in the choice of target but also in the means of attack, indicates the nature of the problem. Surely their attitude cannot be explained as personal pique or dislike—it arises from something more than a private feud between Cleon and Aristophanes, or a few other individuals. A different type of explanation is demanded.

Foreign Birth

The very unanimity which makes it clear that the problem is more than a personal feud may also contain the clue to its solution. For, as we have already begun to see, there is a common pattern to the treatment of these politicians in Comedy.

---

[56] The comic poets squabble among themselves, each claiming to have been the first to attack him: Plato Comicus fr. 107; Eupolis frs. 308 and 456.

[57] Note especially Plato Comicus fr. 166, 170; Eupolis fr. 190; Polyzelus fr. 5; Cratinus fr. 196.

[58] See the play *Cleophon* by Plato Comicus, esp. fr. 60, Aristophanes, *Frogs* 679-681 and the scholia on these lines, and the scholia to *Frogs* 1504 and 1532.

[59] Some politicians escaped quite lightly. If, for example, we look at the treatment of the three men the *AthPol* praises in 28.5, Theramenes, Nicias, and Thucydides son of Melesias, we find that Comedy is relatively mild in its treatment of them. Note however Eupolis fr. 237 on Theramenes. Thucydides perhaps comes off the best of all, if indeed Aristophanes, *Wasps* 907 and *Acharnians* 708ff., refer to him.

Consider for example the charge of foreign birth, one of the most frequently used weapons of the comic poets. The intention behind its use is clear: it disqualifies the man from political leadership; it denies that he is a real Athenian. Old Comedy is not content to present the politician as silly, incompetent, or ludicrous; rather it insists that he is unqualified for the career to which he aspires. The political intent of the attack is clear.

For that intent to become effective the comic poet must operate within the attitudes of politically-qualified citizens. To succeed in his attack on a politician, he must persuade the Athenian voter to repudiate such a leader. It will not do to appeal to an elite, a disgruntled group of stray aristocrats, an old-fashioned minority of agricultural conservatives. Old Comedy must have a mass appeal: it must be heeded by precisely the same citizens who listened to and supported Cleon and the others in the assembly.

This is no very surprising assertion. Indeed, all our evidence suggests, that whatever the purely personal views of its writers, Old Comedy was a truly popular art form, one that appealed to the Athenian citizenry. It operates within conventional democratic attitudes. There is very little within it that could be called anti-democratic; there is essentially no oligarchic ideology, nor any call for reaction to nondemocratic forms. There is, to be sure, social criticism and escapism, but nothing to offend the fundamental tenets of a democratic *polis*. In private, it must be admitted, the writers of comedy may have been embittered oligarchic revolutionaries, but, if so, their plays do not express their politics. Instead their works have a broad appeal and their criticisms are normally made from popular viewpoints. Consider one example: the criticism that Cleophon's mother was a barbarian. This charge has force under democratic law, and, we can infer, in democratic attitudes. Pericles, in 451/0, introduced a measure which required both parents of a child to be Athenian if he was to qualify as a citizen.[60] The measure was apparently a popular one, and not likely to harm the typical Athenian. But the old aristocratic families had long been accustomed to marry abroad, choosing other Greeks or even, like Miltiades, a Thracian princess.[61] Thus Comedy in attacking Cleophon's ancestry was appealing to a democratic, not an aristocratic attitude.

Class Prejudice

But if it is granted that Old Comedy operates within democratic attitudes, our original problem still remains. Why is Comedy so vehement about the new politicians? One explanation readily suggests itself. Since we have already seen (above, The Wealth of Other Politicians) that there was some feeling against *nouveaux riches*, is it not likely that class prejudice motivated Old Comedy? Can we not assume that animosity against the newly acquired wealth of many of these politicians, who were often well-to-do manufacturers and entrepreneurs, was wide and strong in the society and that the Comic poets shared it?

This explanation will not, I believe, prove fully adequate. What it fails to explain is the peculiar form of Comedy's attack. If class feeling were so strong, we could expect a wealthy, haughty, but vulgar Cleon on the comic stage. Comic poets have after all often found the newly rich a perfect target. But Old Comedy operates in quite a different way. It chooses to lower the social position of Cleon and Hyperbolus so that "they are placed on the same level as retailers and hucksters. Even the cattle dealer Lysikles, Perikles' friend who after his death married Aspasia, was called a 'cattle-retailer,' a vocation that surely did not exist."[62]

Whatever prejudice there was against the prosperous

---

[60] *AthPol* 26.3.

[61] On Miltiades' marriage see Herodotus 6.39 and 40 and the genealogical chart in *PA* 10212.

[62] V. Ehrenberg, *People of Aristophanes*, 120.

manufacturer or entrepreneur, Comedy neglects. Instead it adopts a bolder course. It caricatures much more freely in order to exploit the very clear prejudice against the *kapelos*, the retailer, a man who "was on the whole looked down on. Dishonesty was the characteristic feature of the 'mind of the *kapelos*,' and . . . this phrase . . . simply meant the desire and ability to cheat. The women who sold bread were . . . typical . . . of the profession, notorious for their powers of invective and abuse; like all hucksters, they were low people who might easily receive harsh treatment."[63]

The technique that Comedy uses in its attacks on Cleon and others strongly suggests that the prejudice against successful manufacturers was not a general one within Athenian society. To be sure, old aristocrats were likely to be contemptuous of upstarts, and any man who was too pretentious, too aggressive, too much of a *nouveau riche* might be despised. But if the prejudice against men like Cleon were as strong and widespread as is sometimes suggested, Comedy would not have metamorphosed them into peddlers. It would have been sufficient, and probably more effective, to point out, in lurid colors of course, what was in fact the truth: that these men had recently acquired their wealth by means other than agriculture.

Furthermore, there is some reason to suspect that Nicias, who receives relatively favorable treatment in Comedy, was also not of an old landed family, but derived his wealth from mining.[64] If the attitude of the comic poets was determined by class prejudice, why is Nicias spared? Was his social standing so much better than Cleon's?

The conclusion we must draw, I believe, is that class preju-

---

[63] V. Ehrenberg, *People of Aristophanes*, 114f. Compare A. W. Gomme, *Essays* (Oxford 1937) Chapter III esp. 42-66, and M. I. Finley *CP* 30 (1935) 320-336.

[64] Nicias' genealogy cannot be traced back before his father. The silence of Plutarch about his ancestry is a strong *argumentum e silentio* that it was not especially distinguished. On his wealth see above n. 37.

dice against these men was neither widespread within the society nor the basis for the apparent dislike of the comic poets. We must search for some other explanation.

Cleon's Offense

Let us continue to concentrate on our best-documented example, Cleon. He was a wealthy manufacturer and Old Comedy denied it. And despite all Comedy says it is evident that he had sufficient wealth to win himself a very respectable position in Athenian civic life. We have seen that there was no automatic snobbery likely to disqualify him from public life. Although he could not boast a very distinguished family, he did have money and a crafty intelligence. By judicious cultivation of his friends, by care in arranging good marriages for himself and for his children, by attending the right symposia, by performing various liturgies with liberality and éclat, by an occasional judicious speech in the assembly, hand tucked firmly in cloak, he might eventually win himself—if not fame—at least respect and prestige. And he might look forward to greater advancement for his children. He was in a position, in other words, to follow the path whereby many a wealthy Athenian had attained respectability and standing in the city—to become a *chrestos*.

The central fact about Cleon is that he chose not to follow this path. His exact reasons cannot be known, but it is clear that his decision was not wholly foolish. It brought him power and success, more rapidly and unreservedly than he could have hoped for if he had held to a more traditional course. It brought him a kind of standing in the city as well, but standing without full respectability. Until his coup at Pylos Cleon lacked both family prestige and the record of military accomplishment which then and now can often compensate for the absence of prestige. And the way he won the success at Pylos —shouting his way to command, madly promising a success within an impossibly short period—seemed again unorthodox

173

and unacceptable to many. Moreover he had repudiated his old friends, and thus lacked the connections that might otherwise have excused and justified his conduct. To Athenians of traditional temperament Cleon would seem surprising and shocking—even a deliberate affront to an established system of values. He seemed to defy all the rules: he dismissed his friends, violated all decorous behavior on the public platform, sought a political career without prior family or military accomplishment, claimed no distinguished genealogy, and, as far as we can tell, placed no great reliance on his wealth.

And therein his offense. A politician who pretended to a good genealogy but really lacked it, who was a social climber, who wished the friendship of the mighty in order to attain a share of their power, who exaggerated his own wealth, might appear ludicrous and might bring down on his own head public laughter and contempt. He might, if he were incompetent or vicious, prove a danger to the city, but he represented no immediate threat to the values of society. Indeed his actions in a bizarre way affirmed the validity of those standards. The laughter directed against him might be devastating, but it would contain more ridicule than venom.

Cleon was the antithesis of such a person. He was not just a man in a hurry seeking a short-cut to power. He offended not because he was contemptible, but because he showed contempt for a system that others had accepted. His style and gestures were open vaunting insults to the careers of others and to the established mores of the city. He was a danger to the system of values that many Athenians had taken for granted; hence, the more competent he was, the more dangerous he became.

Comedy's response was to take him at his word. It adopts a kind of dogged literal-mindedness in transforming real life into fantasy. It pretends to accept everything Cleon says, and then to discover to everyone's surprise that the words are ambiguous or absurd. If Cleon emphasizes that he claims neither a distinguished genealogy nor great family connections, then Comedy brings on an outlandish Paphlagon, a man quite without Attic descent. If Cleon does not play the politics of largess, displaying his wealth and using it to win support and honor, then perhaps he has no wealth and is after all not a wealthy manufacturer but a poor tanner. If he repudiates his friends, let him appear on stage without *philoi*, though of course with flatterers. If he professes to love the *demos*, then in a wink a lusty Cleon appears as the suitor of a shaggy old man, Demos. Comic literalism, combined with the inevitable exaggeration of his voice and his manners, and the usual slapstick and ribaldry, produce the model caricature of Cleon, perfected in the *Knights,* and used with variations for other politicians throughout Old Comedy.[65]

Withdrawal from Politics

The feigned literal-mindedness with which Comedy proceeded against Cleon was extended in another direction. It observed his success and drew the logical and unavoidable conclusion: success in politics no longer belonged to the well-bred scions of wealthy and cultured families, but to the vulgar and boorish: "The *demagogia* is not for a cultured or well-behaved man, but for the ignorant and the obnoxious" (Aristophanes, *Knights* 191-193).

Thus in the logic of Comedy the traditional qualifications for politics are reversed. All the orthodox sources of power become hindrances; the old obstacles have now become the road to the summit. As the Sausage-seller is told, "You have the qualifications for leader of the *demos*: a foul voice, bad

---

[65] Eupolis' attack on Hyperbolus in the *Maricas* seems quite similar to Aristophanes' treatment of Cleon in the *Knights*. Hermippus' *Artopolides* and Theopompus' *Teisamenus* as well as Plato's political comedies, *Peisander* and *Cleophon*, are perhaps further examples of a sub-type of comedy modeled on the *Knights*. This view is supported by Aristophanes' comments in the revised parabasis of the *Clouds* 553ff.

birth, connections—in the agora. You've got everything it takes for politics" (Aristophanes, *Knights* 217-219). To defeat Paphlagon a hyper-Paphlagon is required. The well-born, well-educated, well-mannered cannot do it. What is needed is someone like the Sausage-seller, who can succeed, as someone tells him, "because you're low class, you're from the agora, and you've got guts."[66]

The animosity of Comedy against Cleon and many other politicians of the time, and the notion that politics has become a calling in which only the most vulgar can succeed, are signs of a process very significant for the history of the last years of the century, but comparatively neglected in modern study. These years were for Athens a time of revolution, counter-revolution, and the threat of revolution. If the fifth century as a whole was one of those rare times of political stability and order, the last dozen years were a relapse into the chaotic political strife which had so often been seen in Archaic Greece. When the historian comes to explain the disorder of these years, he naturally turns to the external affairs of the city—military defeat and the loss of empire—for causes. If he seeks more widely, he will perhaps, as Thucydides did, emphasize mistakes by the leaders and the citizenry of Athens, the excessive rivalry, confidence, and arrogance which led the city toward disaster. With all this I have no quarrel. But there is, I believe, another factor which deserves consideration as well—the withdrawal of a significant part of the Athenian citizenry from participation in politics. The signs of this process are sometimes ambiguous; its extent is not easy to measure. But traces of a pattern of withdrawal can be detected suggesting that it was a serious problem in Athenian politics, and one that merits our close attention.

That Comedy can instruct us about the nature and extent of this problem I hope later to show, but a different source

[66] Aristophanes, *Knights* 181. The pun is in the translation, not the original: ὁτιὴ πονηρὸς κἀξ ἀγορᾶς εἶ καὶ θρασύς.

can give us the best introduction. Luck, or the good sense of some ancient compiler, has preserved a valuable political pamphlet from the early years of the Peloponnesian war.[67] It has been transmitted among the works of Xenophon, but the one thing we know for certain about its origin is that the historian and companion of Socrates named Xenophon was *not* its author. It was written too early for that. Whoever wrote it did not share Comedy's habit of laughing at politics. He is deadly serious, and his wit is bitter:

> Now I say that the *demos* at Athens knows which citizens are *chrestoi* (useful/good) and which are *poneroi* (low class/bad). And since they know, they love the ones who are well disposed and beneficial to themselves, even if they are *poneroi*. But even more they hate the *chrestoi*. For they do not consider that the competence of the *chrestoi* exists for their good, but rather for their harm. Self-interest is always excusable. But whoever is not himself a member of the *demos* and chooses to live in a democratic city rather than in an oligarchically ruled one, has planned injustice and knows that it is easier for a bad man to get away with it in a democratic city than in an oligarchic one.
>
> pseudo-Xenophon, *Constitution of Athens* 2.19-20.

This is perhaps nothing more than an individual reaction. It does not show that significant numbers of Athenians were disaffected from the life of their city, nor that many citizens felt as intensely as this writer about the course events had taken.[68] But, whatever the limitations of the pamphlet, it does help us understand the situation in which an Athenian gentle-

---

[67] On the date of the pamphlet see Appendix II.

[68] It is, however, possible to reconstruct some more conventional contemporary criticisms of the democracy. The first nine sections of pseudo-Xenophon are especially valuable in this regard, for the writer in adopting an independent stance for the criticism of the democracy indicates what some of the more ordinary criticisms were. In sum these objections are that the poor and the *poneroi* are given greater power than the better classes, and that it takes good

man who was interested in politics in the last third of the century might find himself.

Once the new pattern of politics which we have described was established, many Athenians of traditional views would find themselves in awkward positions. They wanted, even expected, a political career. But the lesson which the success of Cleon taught seemed to be that success went to the vulgar and sensational. What was a respectable Athenian gentleman to do? He could follow the recommendation in this passage of the so-called *Constitution of Athens* to leave the city for an oligarchy. But this would entail immense personal and financial loss. Or he might try to adapt to new ways—cultivate the *demos*, adopt an extravagant style of speech, perhaps make some spectacular gesture to show that he was truly *philo-demos*. Or if this was too much for him, he could maintain his old ways, and try his luck at politics, while muttering and complaining as Axiochus is said to have done in a conversation with Socrates:

> SOCRATES: Who could be happy putting his life at the disposal of the masses, bridled and spurred like some pet of the *demos*, driven out, hissed at, punished, killed or "mercifully pardoned." Tell me, my political Axiochus, where did Miltiades die? Where did Themistocles die? Where did Ephialtes die? ...
>
> AXIOCHUS: You're right, Socrates. I've had enough of the public platform, and nothing I've ever seen is harder than a public career. That's quite clear to us who are in it. You babble on about it, but you know it only from a distance.

men to know what's good for the city. These complaints call to mind the comments of a Georgia congressman about the American House of Representatives in the 1850's, "[The present Congress] . . . furnishes the worst specimens of legislators I have ever seen. . . . There is a large infusion of successful jobbers, lucky serving men, parishless persons and itinerant lecturers among them who are not only without wisdom or knowledge but have bad manners, and therefore we can have but little hope of good legislation" (Robert Toombs, M.C., quoted in R. Hofstadter, *Anti-intellectualism in American Life*, 167).

We who have been through it have first hand experience. The *demos*, Socrates, is ungrateful, fickle, vicious, jealous, uncultured, a buffet of buffoons and of overpowering rubbish. The man who makes the *demos* his *hetairos* is more miserable by far.[69]

Axiochus' indictment, though exaggerated, has some substance to it. Politics was a hazardous career. Even the most famous and successful leaders could suffer the most miserable treatment—Miltiades died in chains, Themistocles fled the city, Ephialtes was assassinated, Cimon was ostracized, Pericles was fined and deposed. Politics in ancient Athens could lead to the pinnacles of power, but one slip could mean a precipitous and disastrous fall. Old man Demos was craftier and more fickle than some of his admirers suspected. He might seem dependent on a single adviser, but he knew the not so gentle art of dispensing with the indispensable: "There are no brains under your long hair if you don't think I know what I'm doing. My folly is deliberate. I lead a merry life nursed like a baby all day. I'm perfectly happy to fatten a single *prostates* even if he's a crook. When he's fattened up, I'll knock him out and butcher him" (Aristophanes, *Knights* 1121-1130).

In these circumstances a traditional Athenian gentleman might conclude that politics was unappealing. Instead of following any of the courses just mentioned he might stay in the city but refuse all part in her civic life. That there were Athenians who tried each of these courses we need not doubt. Each group would repay careful study, but for the moment it is only the last, those who withdrew from politics, that concerns us. These men were called by various names. They

[69] Pseudo-Plato, *Axiochus* 368 d-369 b. A. E. Taylor, *Plato* (reprint of sixth edition, New York 1957) 550-552, discusses the dialogue and accepts a late fourth century date for its authorship. Since the dramatic date of the dialogue is close after the battle of Arginusae (405 B.C.), we must presume Axiochus has returned from the exile mentioned in Andocides 1.16, if we wish to regard the dialogue as historically accurate.

might refer to themselves as *apragmones* (non-meddlers); others might call them *aspoudoi* (unenthusiasts) or *achreioi* (useless ones).[70] It does not matter a great deal what term we use, but it is extremely important to know how many and how strongly motivated these men were, and to watch for any sign that their disaffection from the city was undermining the stability of the democracy.

Comedy

We return once again to Comedy. We know we must be cautious of its testimony, but nowhere else are we likely to get such an immediate and intimate look at the life of the city. Thus when we find in it maxims such as "The man who doesn't care for office is worse than the man who cares too much" (Eupolis fr. 234 as emended), we are tempted to regard them as further evidence that the disaffection of some parts of the citizenry was becoming a problem for Athens.

This inference is perhaps correct, but it is on another level that Comedy gives the most significant testimony about the withdrawal of some citizens from politics. Many of the finest plays of Old Comedy are fantasies of escape from the *polis*, or at least from the contemporary city of the Athenians. The characters in these plays escape, or try to escape, into some remote world where a purely private existence is possible. Dicaeopolis' search for a private treaty with the Spartans in the *Acharnians*, Pisthetaerus' and Euelpides' quest for Cloudcuckoo land in the *Birds*, and Trygaeus' flight on the giant dung beetle in the *Peace* are all variations on this theme. The fantasy behind them is consciously absurd—the characters seek as individuals what can properly come only

[70] There is an indication in the Periclean funeral oration, Thucydides 2.40.2, that the *apragmon* was already a recognizable type in Pericles' last years. See also J. de Romilly, *Thucydides and Athenian Imperialism*, trans. P. Thody (Oxford 1963) 78, and V. Ehrenberg, "Polypragmosyne," *JHS* 67 (1947) 46-67. On *aspoudoi* see Eupolis fr. 234.

to the city—but that very absurdity emphasizes the strength of their desire for the imagined goal. Each wishes for a world of peace and happy tranquility, and each tries to find it by leaving or forgetting about the city.

These plays are all, at least in part, plays of disengagement, though the kinds of disengagement vary greatly. Sometimes the emphasis is on avoiding the more obnoxious types of the city, the sycophants, oracle-mongers, bad poets and the like. At other times a more intense and positive yearning appears, and the vision of that world of peace and tranquility turns the plays into short-lived comic Utopias.

This fantasy of escape from the city seems at first the very antithesis of the "political" plays such as the *Knights*. Yet the two fantasies are perhaps closely related. In the *Knights* Aristophanes addresses himself to a political problem—freeing the *polis* from Cleon's influence. The play is fantastic, based on the fantasy of a hyper-Cleon, a rival who exaggerates all the features not only of Cleon but of his comic equivalent, Paphlagon. The Sausage-seller is to Paphlagon as Paphlagon is to Cleon—more vulgar, more illiterate, more absurd, more laughable. To be sure the laughter that we direct toward the Sausage-seller has little bitterness in it. Perhaps, we tell ourselves, for all his *poneria* he will really serve old Demos well. Comedy ends as Comedy must, with a promise of happiness, even if the basis for that promise is vague and the hope for its fulfillment insubstantial. The audience laughs, applauds, and withdraws. But a doubt persists. Suppose Aristophanes is right, that only a hyper-Cleon can stop a Cleon. Where does this leave the intelligent citizen with a sense of dignity? Where does it leave the old pattern of civic order and prestige? Must each citizen become worse than Cleon in order to stand against him? If that is the case does a man of self-respect have any alternative but to escape in one way or another from the city? The *Knights* inevitably generates ques-

181

tions of this sort, and its fantasy generates another: the success of hyper-Cleon compels us to imagine escaping from the city altogether.

But one can suppress the doubt and deny that it takes crassness to put down crassness. "It was only a play." But the striking thing about this period is that the experience of the assembly seems to confirm the implications of Comedy. Comedy brings on the Sausage-seller; history reports Diodotus. He is the only politician we know of who inflicted a defeat on Cleon. Thucydides does not give us a full account of the debate, and we must not presume that Diodotus was the only speaker to oppose Cleon's demand for the execution of the Mytilenians. But Thucydides' decision to report Diodotus' speech was a penetrating one. The antilogy is sharp, the argument incisive and revealing. The exchange between the two men is perhaps one of the most surprising in all of Thucydides' history. The issue we recognize is one of humanity: should all Mytilenians suffer for the offenses of a few? We anticipate the arguments from justice, reasonableness, and mercy. But Diodotus knows that these terms have been preempted by Cleon for his own ends, and adopts the only strategy that can succeed: to out-Cleon Cleon, to feign, perhaps even to accept, a tough-mindedness that banishes all sentimental and humanitarian arguments and admits only considerations of self-interest (3.44).

Diodotus and those of similar views carry the day, by a small margin, and the Mytilenians are spared. Cleon is defeated, though not permanently. Of Diodotus nothing more is heard. And yet he is the really interesting participant in the debate. We wish to burst through the bonds of history and interrogate him, ask him what he really thought, and why he spoke as he did. We wish to listen to him again and to observe him. If we could, we would not find, surely, the vulgarity and *poneria* of the Sausage-seller, but we might be struck by one telling similarity between the two. When ranged against

182

Cleon each of them must use Cleon's weapons in the fight, and defeat him only by surpassing him.

Other ages, too, have found that to maintain the values they esteem most highly men of integrity must play at similar games and must master the art of dissimulation. The method can be made to work, but the risks are high. Humanity and self-interest are not always as immediately reconcilable as they were in this affair. More important, the men most needed in politics are often precisely the ones most outraged at deceptions of this sort, and least willing to demean themselves with the poses of tough-mindedness. They may prefer to become aesthetes, utopians, scholars, or dreamers, rather than turn their energies to the struggle for political success. In the long run this loss may count for more than any other.

Tragedy

In Aeschylus and in the earliest datable plays of Sophocles there is little expression of the feeling that political power is undesirable. That it is awesome, that it can lead to *hybris* or *atē* are common themes, but the idea of a man deliberately repudiating a political career is infrequent and exceptional.[71] It is no easier to find in Pindar.[72] By the 420's, however, a conspicuous change has taken place. Greek audiences were hearing lines like those which Sophocles gave to Creon in the *Oedipus Tyrannos*:

> Would any sane man prefer
> Power, with all king's anxieties,
> To that same power and the grace of sleep?
> Certainly not I.
> I have never longed for the king's power—
> only for his rights,

[71] The idea does, however, find expression in the earliest play of Euripides, the *Peliades* fr. 605 (*TGF*) which was produced in 455 B.C.

[72] Pindar, *Paean IV* fr. 52 d (Snell), perhaps around 458 B.C., refers to the reluctance of Melampus to leave his fatherland and become a ruler, but the point is that he was unwilling to leave home, not that he didn't like the idea of becoming a ruler.

Would any wise man differ from me in this?
As matters stand, I have my way in everything
With your consent, and no responsibilities.[73]

This change may, to be sure, be a mere accident of preservation, and it would in any event be rash to draw any sweeping
conclusions from speeches that are admirably appropriate to
their own dramatic context. But at roughly the same time that
Sophocles was at work on the *Oedipus,* Euripides was writing the following speech:

> I am
> no man to speak with vapid, precious skill
> before a mob, although among my equals
> and in a narrow circle I am held
> not unaccomplished in the eloquent art.
> That is as it should be. The demagogue
> who charms a crowd is scorned by cultured
> experts.[74]

In the *Hippolytus* the argument takes a distinctive and, I believe, a contemporary turn. Like Creon's speech in the
Oedipus the lines succeed fully in their dramatic purpose;
they characterize Hippolytus and make the audience realize
what sort of young man stands before them. But the technique whereby they achieve their goal differs from that in the
Oedipus. As Grene's translation brings out, or even exaggerates, the words chosen remind us of fifth century Athens

---

[73] Sophocles, *Oedipus Tyrannos* 584-590, trans. D. Fitts and R. Fitzgerald.
The exact date of the play is uncertain, but I find Bernard Knox's arguments
for 425 (*AJP* 77 [1956] 133-147) attractive.

[74] Euripides, *Hippolytus* 986-989, trans. D. Grene. I have chosen this translation not for literal accuracy but because it brings out extraordinarily well
the technique of the passage. The Greek reads:

ἐγὼ δ' ἄκομψος εἰς ὄχλον δοῦναι λόγον,
εἰς ἥλικας δὲ κὠλίγους σοφώτερος·
ἔχει δὲ μοῖραν καὶ τόδ', οἱ γὰρ ἐν σοφοῖς
φαῦλοι παρ' ὄχλῳ μουσικώτεροι λέγειν.

The date of the *Hippolytus*, 428, is attested by the hypothesis to the play.

and her assemblies. The mythic times of King Theseus are made to sound, as so often in Euripides, surprisingly like the contemptorary world of democratic Athens. Thus these lines can quite properly be called "anachronistic": not that they are mistakes in the time-scheme of the play, rather they are timeless and make their point by implicitly linking Hippolytus to the world the audience knows so well. The same technique makes Hippolytus seem real and credible later in the play, when he defends himself against the charge which Phaedra contrives against him. Theseus, his father and the ruler of Athens, has believed the story that Hippolytus attempted to seduce her. In his defense, Hippolytus says,

> Was rule so sweet? Never, I tell you, Theseus,
> for the wise. A man whom power has so enchanted
> must be demented. I would wish to be
> first in the contests of the Greeks,
> but in the city I'd take second place
> and an enduring happy life among
> the best society who are my friends.[75]

In these lines Hippolytus appears as a recognizable contemporary type, a young man proud of his accomplishments, relaxed among his friends, and yet quite unwilling to plunge into the sordid world of politics. Remove him from his mythic setting and he is not far different from the young man Charmides, whom Socrates once attempted to convince that he should follow a political career:

> He noticed that Charmides the son of Glaucon was an exceptional man, far more able than contemporary politicians, but one who hesitated to address the assembly and to tend to public affairs. He said to him:
> SOCRATES: Tell me, Charmides, what would you think of a

---

[75] Euripides, *Hippolytus* 1012-1018, trans. D. Grene. The lines contain one serious textual problem, discussed by W. S. Barrett in his commentary on lines 1014-1015. But the last part of the passage at least is secure.

man who was good enough to win a crown in the competitions and in this way to bring honor on himself and make his city more famous throughout Greece, but who didn't want to compete? What sort of a man would you think he was?

CHARMIDES: That's clear, soft and spineless (*deilos*).

SOCRATES: But if a man was capable of strengthening his city by tending to public affairs and in this way to win himself honor, but hesitated to do so, wouldn't he too be considered spineless?

CHARMIDES: Perhaps, but why ask me?

SOCRATES: Because I think you are capable and that you hesitate to attend to exactly those affairs which you as a citizen ought to participate in.

Xenophon, *Memorabilia* 3.7.1-2.

When Charmides asks Socrates what basis he has for that judgment, Socrates points out that in conversation about public matters Charmides acquits himself quite well. "It's not the same thing to speak in private and to compete in a crowd," Charmides protests.[76] The parallel between Charmides and Hippolytus is quite precise, and perhaps quite deliberate. Not that Euripides was modeling his character on one contemporary young Athenian, Charmides or someone like him, but one can detect in the *Hippolytus* and in some other Euripidean plays a contemporization of myth by which figures from traditional Greek mythology come to resemble types that could be found in the fifth century city. In these plays the myth moves unobtrusively from past to present, or more precisely, it incorporates small but recognizable bits of the present into itself. The effect is an involvement and an immediacy that few dramatists have been able to equal.

[76] *Memorabilia* 3.7.4. Socrates' conversation does not seem to have had much effect. Charmides is not known to have taken part in public life except under the Thirty, when he became one of the Ten in charge of the Piraeus, Xenophon, *Hellenica* 2.4.19. There is a useful discussion of Charmides in J. Davis, *Athenian Propertied Families* 8792 ix.

The technique in the *Ion* is in some respects similar. Once again a young man who, like Hippolytus, has the royal blood of Athens in his veins, chooses to avoid any attempt at prominence in the city. He thinks himself, quite incorrectly, a foreigner, and he believes that he will be despised in Athens. But he has a further objection, and this one is from our point of view more interesting:

> But if I make an effort to be in the first rank of the city and to be somebody, we'll be hated by those of no ability. For superiority always rankles. But all the better sort (*chrestoi*) and those who are capable of being wise (*sophoi*), who keep quiet and do not hasten into public life, will treat me as a laughing stock and as a fool if I don't mind my own business in a city filled with fear. And if I do arrive at some reputation, I'll find myself hemmed in by the votes of politicians and those active in the city. That's the way things are, father. Those who have civic power and prestige are always hated by their rivals.
>
> Euripides, *Ion* 595-606

The lines admirably serve Euripides' dramatic purposes at this point in the drama, but they are at the same time extravagant and surprising. We want to pause over them, and ask ourselves why there should be "politicians" of such power in a monarchy of the mythic type. And why does Ion speak of a city "filled with fear"? Once again we suspect that Euripides is deliberately using anachronism to involve us in the situation.[77]

Both the *Hippolytus* and the *Ion* picture a city in which those who are, or fancy themselves, the better citizens turn their backs on the quest for political power and advancement.

[77] The exact date cannot be ascertained but sometime between 412 and 408 seems highly probable; see A. Lesky, *Tragische Dichtung der Hellenen* (Göttingen 1956) 186, and T. B. L. Webster *The Tragedies of Euripides* (London 1967) 5. At this time the description of Athens as a city filled with fear was perhaps uncomfortably contemporary.

Even their language is similar. Those who withdraw are called *sophoi*, wise ones, and laugh at or despise the more involved citizens.[78] In a slightly later play of Euripides we see the effects of one form of this self-imposed withdrawal. The setting is the mythical period of Atreid Argos, but it is apparent that the political system has a powerful assembly, like a modern democracy. In the midst of the *Orestes* a messenger comes on stage to tell Electra of the assembly's deliberation over the punishment to be imposed on her and on Orestes for the slaying of their mother. The messenger is sympathetic, but he makes it clear that few in the assembly were equally well-disposed toward Electra and her brother.

> But at last
> someone stood up to take the other side.
> Nothing much to look at, but a real man;
> not the sort one sees loafing in the market
> or public places, ma'am, but a small farmer,
> part of that class on which our country depends;
> an honest, decent, god-fearing man,
> and anxious, in the name of common sense,
> to say his bit.
>
> Euripides, *Orestes* 917-922, trans. W. Arrowsmith

The spokesman is an *autourgos*, a man whose farm is small enough for him to work himself, someone quite without prestige, wealth or famous genealogy. This "honest, decent, god-fearing man" comes up with the proposals that the matricides ought to be awarded a crown and treated as public benefactors, an idea which understandably wins few converts in the assembly, but which seems eminently just to the messenger. Euripides then has the messenger add a further detail:

[78] In the *Hippolytus* note especially 987-989 and in *Ion* 598-599. In the latter passage they are also called *chrestoi*; compare *Orestes* 930. Herwerden's emendation in *Ion* 598 is attractive and would allow *dynamenoi* to take on a political sense, "those capable of exercising political power" (i.e. wealthy and well-born), cf. pseudo-Xenophon, *Constitution of Athens* 2.18.

> . . . He seemed to convince the better sort (the
> *chrestoi*),
> but no one spoke.
> *Orestes* 930-931, trans. W. Arrowsmith

One would expect, of course, that the better sort, the *chrestoi*, would in normal times have been the ones to lead the discussion. But neither mythic Argos nor contemporary Athens was enjoying normal times. Instead a repudiation of politics similar to that mentioned in the *Hippolytus* and the *Ion* helps shape the action of the play. The *chrestoi* are, to be sure, in the assembly, but they leave the speaking to others, and when someone finally comes up with a proposal to their liking they fail effectively to back it. As a political force they appear immobilized, unwilling to take the initiative, incapable even of rendering support.[79]

It was surely not Euripides' intent to depict, through his plays, the political situation of contemporary Athens. But if we are correct in suspecting that he might from time to time have used elements from contemporary life to strengthen and develop his plays, then it is likely, I believe, that in the *Hippolytus*, the *Ion*, and the *Orestes* we have signs of a process at work in the city in the late fifth century. We should like, of course, to test our suspicion by a detailed study of the biographies of a significant cross-section of the Athenian citizenry. Only such a test could provide definitive proof. The data is lacking for such an investigation, but what we have detected in the tragic drama of the period is consistent with the tone of the pamphlet on the constitution of Athens which we investigated earlier, with the exchange between Socrates and Charmides, and with other scattered bits of evidence as well.[80] Finally, some such presumption as we have made is

---

[79] If I understand this play correctly, they are also represented as depraved in their political and moral judgment. As we come to see, the *autourgos'* proposal is senseless, and in the context of the play it is reprehensible to approve it.

[80] The politician Theogenes (*PA* 6703) name his son "Idiotes," "private citizen." Was he an embittered politician turning his back on public life?

necessary, I believe, if we are properly to understand one other important comment on the politics of the late fifth century.

Aristophanes' Way Out

We have already observed that Old Comedy recognized and responded to this withdrawal from civic life. It does not directly describe the disaffection that many *chrestoi* seem to have felt, but its slanders and exaggerations provide some measure of the intensity of feeling against many of the new politicians. And we have come to suspect that the fantasy of escape from the city is in part a response to the success of Cleon and others. Even short fragments, torn from context, are sometimes helpful in letting us understand the feelings of some citizens. There is, for example, the complaint in Eupolis that service does not win the honor it deserves: "And if a runner takes first place, he wins a prize; but when some really fine and useful citizen (*chresimos*) beats everyone else in being valuable, he gets no reward" (Eupolis fr. 104). Old Comedy is constantly and sometimes surprisingly revealing about the society which gave it birth. We have no right to expect more than it willingly provides. We cannot demand from it a full and balanced diagnosis of the city's ailments, still less a curing prescription.

But at one point, late in the century, Aristophanes took advantage of the traditional opportunity which his form gave him to speak out on the plight of his city. In the *parabasis* of the *Frogs* it is the poet himself who speaks and his words are ones of deep concern:

> We've been thinking much of late about the way the city
> treats
> all the choicest souls among its citizens: it seems to be
> like the recent coinage as compared with the old
> currency.

190

We still have the ancient money; finest coins, I think, in
    Greece.
better than the coins of Asia, clink them and they ring
    the bell,
truly fashioned, never phony, round and honest every
    piece.
Do we ever use it? We do not. We use this wretched
    brass,
last week's issue, badly minted, light and cheap and looks
    like hell.
Now compare the citizens. We have some stately
    gentlemen,
modest, anciently descended, proud and educated well
on the wrestling ground, men of distinction who have
    been to school.
These we outrage and reject, preferring any foreign fool,
redhead slave, or brassy clown or shyster. This is what
    we choose
to direct out city—immigrants. Once our city would not
    use
one of these as public scapegoat. That was in the former
    days.
Now we love them. Think, you idiots. Turn about and
    change your ways.
Use our useful men. That will look best, in case of
    victory.
Hang we must, if we must hang; but let's hang from a
    handsome tree.
Cultured gentlemen should bear their sufferings with
    dignity.[81]

---

[81] Aristophanes, *Frogs* 718-737, trans. Richmond Lattimore. On the coinage
of late fifth century Athens see E. S. G. Robinson, "Some Problems in the Later
Fifth Century Coinage of Athens," *Museum Notes* 9 (1960) 1-16, and W. E.
Thompson, "Functions of the Emergency Coinage of the Peloponnesian War,"
Mnemosyne Ser. IV, 19 (1966) 337-343.

Aristophanes, in other words, detects a kind of Gresham's law in operation in the city of his day. Given a choice between good and bad coinage, the citizens will choose the bad; in politics the *poneroi* will drive the *chrestoi* out of circulation.

From this diagnosis follows the prescription, "use the useful men"—χρῆσθε τοῖς χρηστοῖσιν αὖθις. Bring the better classes back into politics. Aristophanes, in short, seems to be concerned with precisely the problem with which we have been dealing in this section: the separation of the *chrestoi* from full political participation. To be sure, his diagnosis is an oversimplification of the malady. The problem was not just that the Athenians had refused to use the *chrestoi*, as Aristophanes implies; rather, in some cases at least, the *chrestoi* refused to participate. They felt sickened by the spectacles they saw and the vulgarity they deplored: "There's a sickness that afflicts the better classes (*hoi ameinones*) when a *poneros* gets prestige, dominating the *demos* with his discourse, somebody who was nothing before" (Euripides, *Suppliants* 423-425). Or again, "Whenever some base sort (*kakos*) succeeds in the city, he provides the better people with a demonstration of the power of the base, and infects their minds" (Euripides fr. 645 [*TGF*]).

The result of this infection was, as we have seen, the withdrawal of many *chrestoi* from politics. One may doubt, then, that Aristophanes' prescription could be entirely effective, at least immediately. But there are two things to be said in his favor. He recognizes the gravity of the problem and does not retreat into clichés about the vitality of the Athenian democracy; second he avoids the doctrinaire remedies that were much praised in his day—restriction of the franchise or some other form of oligarchic reaction. Aristophanes says nothing about changing the democratic machinery of government. He is concerned here, as in the earliest plays, not with the democratic machinery but with those who operate it. Throughout his career he never repudiated democracy, but recognized the crucial importance of getting the right people to take part in it.

Otanes' Withdrawal

Earlier in this study some similarities began to appear between a debate which Herodotus says took place in sixth century Persia and the situation of Athens in Herodotus' own day. The comments allegedly made by Darius in that debate called to mind fifth century Athens. When he spoke of the transition from a democratic state where friendship groups exercised great power to one in which the people chose a single protector, he used the language of Athenian politics in Herodotus' day, and he propounded ideas that were highly relevant to the fifth century political situation. Now another similarity emerges. In Herodotus' story of the debate, Darius carries the day. He demonstrates the tendency that all political arrangements have to turn into monarchies of one sort or another. Having set forth this "iron law" of monarchy, he goes on to convince all his companions—save one—that one of them must rule. The exception is Otanes, the spokesman for democracy in the debate, who demurs, and proposes a pact. He will not compete with the others for the position of supreme ruler, if the others will agree that they will not rule him. "I give up all claim to rule, on this condition, that neither I nor any of my descendants will ever be ruled by any of you" (Herodotus 3.83.2). The bargain is struck. His household becomes the only free one in Persia, and "is ruled only in so far as it is willing. . . ."

Otanes' repudiation of the quest for power and his acceptance of a purely private life, quite unaffected by the meddling, the *polypragmosyne*, of a public existence, resembles the tendency toward withdrawal from politics that we have been investigating. Otanes, to be sure, turns away not from a democracy, but from a state ruled by a true monarch. Yet, granted this difference, Otanes seeks for himself a domestic autonomy similar to that which Euelpides and Peisthetairus sought in the *Birds*, or that which Dicaeopolis won for himself in the *Acharnians*. Whatever the historical facts about Otanes may be, the story that Herodotus made of them touched on matters of great concern to Athenians of the last third of the century. Otanes embodies the fantasy of a truly autonomous existence, one quite outside the state. Herodotus insists the story is factual. Perhaps he is correct. But the appeal and power of the story is not in its historicity but in its contemporaneity. In the Herodotean world where history *lives*, Otanes is a man of the present as well as of the past, and one that many an Athenian *chrestos* would understand.[82]

Toward Revolution

Our study has concentrated on a single phenomenon in Athenian history—a change in the pattern of politics that came about in the lifetime of Cleon, perhaps largely because of him. We have observed the gradual breakdown of an old form of politics built on an elaborate complex of friendship ties, and we have seen a new pattern emerge which emphasized mass alliances and direct appeals to many citizens who formerly had little say in the affairs of the city. We have seen how clever Cleon and others were in exploiting the weakness of the old form, and in presenting themselves as the truly devoted servants of the whole city.

These changes had something fresh and exciting about them, a sense of healthy innovation. And, as we have noted, they were badly needed modifications, for the formal constitutional structure of Athens was not well suited to carry out the complex and continuing business of the imperial city. Expert leadership was needed—the new politicians promised it, and sometimes provided it. Moreover, their statements and gestures of devotion to the city must have seemed a step for-

[82] For the implications of this discussion for the dating of Herodotus 3.80-83, see Appendix I.

ward, toward a higher and clearer ethical standard. They asserted more clearly than ever before that the first duty of a politician was to the city, not to some small clique within it. They professed civic virtues and civic concerns, and moved beyond the provinciality of family and faction that had so often characterized Greek politics in the past. They seemed to foretoken a new era in which the interests of all citizens would be equitably represented, in which ever closer ties would bind the citizen to the *polis* and in which, as Pericles put it, "No one, so long as he has it in him to be of service to the state, is kept in political obscurity because of his poverty" (Thucydides 2.37.1, trans. R. Warner).

It is perhaps in the nature of history that hopes such as these should never fully be realized. Since the new pattern of politics, as well as its traditional Athenian structure, placed great demands on the judgment of both politician and citizen, one might almost expect failure. More surprising than the fact that some were corrupt, some deficient, is the long endurance which Athens showed in a war that overturned all expectations. Even after her defeat many features of this new type of politics survived and were incorporated into the restored democracy of the fourth century.

Yet as we study the politics of Athens in the last decades of the century, it is the sense of disappointment which predominates. It is as if the first green growth of spring had been frozen and killed: disaster abroad, growing severity in the handling of the empire, increasing bitterness at home. In 412 began an era of plot and counterplot that lasted almost to the end of the century:

> They held the assembly in a narrow space at Colonus, about a mile out of the city, on ground sacred to Poseidon. Here the committee brought forward one proposal and one only, which was that any Athenian should be allowed to make whatever suggestions he liked with impunity; heavy

penalties were laid down for anyone who should bring a case against such a speaker for violating the laws or who should damage him in any other way. Now was the time for plain speaking, and it was at once proposed that the holding of office and drawing of salaries under the present constitution should now end; that five men should be elected as presidents; that these should choose 100 men, and each of the 100 should choose three men; that this body of 400 should enter the Council chamber with full powers to govern as they thought best, and should call meetings of the 5,000 [best qualified, i.e. wealthiest citizens] whenever they chose. . . . It was no easy matter about 100 years after the expulsion of the tyrants to deprive the Athenian people of its liberty—a people not only unused to subjection itself, but for more than half of this time, accustomed to exercise power over others.

Thucydides 8.67.2 and 3, and 68.4, trans. R. Warner

It would be false to ascribe this revolution, the treason of oligarchs, and the other troubles of the last years of the century to the politicians of Athens. The city had long been tortured by war, plague, the difficulties of administering an empire and fighting the greatest land power of Greece. She had been confronted with problems of a magnitude rarely seen before in the world of the Greek cities. And if some of these difficulties had been increased or compounded by the advice of her political leaders, the blame cannot be placed exclusively on them.

Yet one problem, growing out of the style developed by Cleon and others, contributed to the deterioration of Athens' public life. One result of the flamboyance of the new style was animosity and annoyance among the Athenian *chrestoi*. In some cases this feeling, intensified by reports and rumors of scandals and corruption by the leaders of the city, led to a strong reaction—which took two main forms. For some the best course seemed to be to withdraw from politics into private circles of like-minded friends, small informal gatherings such as the group Charmides felt at ease with, or the "narrow circle" of cultured comrades of which Hippolytus speaks. This form of reaction was essentially apolitical; the other, however, aimed at a new kind of political arrangement in which the "better" people would again be dominant.

The ironic result of both these responses was a recrudescence of *philia*. And in the second case *philia* again became political, no longer as the open and visible tie between groups of citizens but as the quiet bond that made conspirators out of disaffected *chrestoi*. Athenians had long gathered in symposia and small groups to drink, to joke, to dine, to talk. Many of these *hetaireiai* were innocent enough, but as the end of the century approaches they become increasingly the refuge of those who repudiated, or had been repudiated by, democratic politics. Conspiracy is in the air, and the *hetaireiai* become in some cases *synomosiai*, bands of sworn revolutionaries, determined to overthrow the democracy.[83] Political friendship takes on a new and more virulent form.

The significance of these groups of plotters is plain. They formed the "cells" in which a revolution could be developed, and Thucydides' narrative makes their importance clear.[84]

[83] It is in the 420's that we begin to hear regularly of *synomosiai*, though writers as early as Aeschylus (*Agamemnon* 650, *Eumenides* 127, *Choephoroi* 978) speak of "swearing together" and of "conspirators," *synomnymi* and *synomotai*. Cf. also Herodotus 1.176.2, 7.235.4, 7.148.1, Sophocles, *Philoctetes* 1367. The word is common in Aristophanes, especially in the *Knights* and *Wasps*, as an accusation made by Cleon and his followers. Thucydides' narrative, e.g. 8.49, makes clear the significance of these groups at least in the period ca. 412. Thucydides is more skeptical about the presence of a *synomosia* behind the affairs of 415 (note especially 6.28.3 and 6.60).

There may, I readily admit, have been *synomosiai* much earlier in Athenian history. I would be surprised if there were none. But it seems likely that the events of the last two or three decades of the century gave their members grounds to hope for success and increased their numbers and importance. On the *synomosiai* see F. Sartori, *Le eterie nella vita politica ateniese del VI e V secolo a.c.* (Rome 1957), and the review of Sartori by A. E. Raubitschek in *AJP* 80 (1959) 81-88.

[84] Note especially Thucydides 8.48-49, and 65.

But there were equally great dangers in the other type of response. The most pernicious effect of the temptation to withdraw from politics altogether could be that many Athenians who did not actively support the overthrow of the democracy were nevertheless immobilized, rendered incapable of working either for the preservation or for the reformation of the city's government. Their withdrawal could open the way for revolutionaries.[85]

Repelled, annoyed, disaffected, the *chrestoi* of Athens withdrew from politics and denied the city the wisdom and ability of which they so often boasted. Their response was intelligible and natural, as were the attempts of the new politicians to win political power. Neither group can easily be condemned. But if we are reluctant to judge, we must not be reluctant to learn. The withdrawal from politics of intelligent, well-educated, and capable citizens was a symptom of a serious malaise in Athens and a prelude to revolution. Other ages, other continents, may recognize that the same symptoms betoken the same illness.

[85] Cf. Aristotle, *Politics* 5.1302 b 11-13, "It is also clear how honour (*timē*) may serve as an occasion [for *stasis* and revolution]; what influence it may exert; and how it may lead to sedition. Men turn seditious when they suffer dishonour themselves and when they see others honoured . . . " (trans. Barker).

The Debate in Herodotus 3.80-83

THROUGHOUT the preceding pages reference has frequently been made to a debate in book 3 of Herodotus in which Darius, Megabyxos, and Otanes, Persians of the sixth century B.C., debate about the best form of government. I have been repeatedly impressed by similarities between this passage and the developments in Athenian politics in the late 430's and 420's, and have concluded that the debate must reflect Greek political thought of this period. Hence it seems to me that it was probably written quite late in Herodotus' lifetime. This notion is consistent with the views of at least some students of the chronology of Herodotus' composition. See, for example, J. E. Powell, *History of Herodotus* (Cambridge 1939) viii. (The tediously iterated charge that Powell's views have been misrepresented is for once correct: Podlecki's claim, *TAPA* 97 [1966] 367 n. 31, cf. Morrison, *CQ* 35 [1941] 12, that Powell supports a date between 448 and 442 for the debate is unwarranted, cf. Powell in *CQ* 29 [1935] 153-154.) There is, however, no consensus on the date of the passage and some further discussion seems in order, especially since two recent articles advocate an earlier date.

I will restrict myself to these two articles and not attempt a general discussion of all the problems involved. Let me specifically disclaim any intention of dealing with a perennial question: was there really such a debate in sixth century Persia? Did three sixth century Persian gentlemen get together and debate the relative merits of democracy, aristocracy, and monarchy? To many scholars it has seemed improbable, but Herodotus (6.43) seems quite sure of himself and I see no good way either to confirm or to refute his belief. (There is a useful discussion of the point in P. T. Brannan, S.J., "Herodotus and History," *Traditio* 19 [1963] 427-438.) The problem with which I am concerned is much narrower and is essentially philological: since the form, the argumentation, the language of the debate are all Greek, what is the most likely setting for the debate within the development of Greek thought and the Greek language? This question inevitably involves comparing the debate to other more readily datable documents. This is the approach taken by A. J. Podlecki in the first of the two articles I would like to discuss ("Creon and Herodotus," *TAPA* 97 [1966] 359-371). Podlecki points out parallels between the debate and Sophocles' *Antigone* and dates the debate near the play, i.e. in the 440's. Cf. Morrison, *CQ* 35 (1941) 12-13. The parallels adduced, however, are unimpressive: a similar image (the rushing torrent) used in each work (though for rather different purposes), a common concern with *philia* and with traditional laws, emphasis on the unlimited power of the tyrant and on the apparent attractiveness of his position, etc. Whether these similarities are anything more than reflections of a common cultural situation and a widespread notion of what tyranny was like seems to me very dubious. Other more revealing features of the debate —Darius' ideas of the progression of constitutional forms, the criticism of the role of *philia* in a democracy, the appearance of the *prostates tou demou* and the development of that position into a monarchy—are not to be found in the *Antigone* and seem to me to point to a later date.

There is, moreover, a further difficulty in Podlecki's view. His criticism of the view that Protagoras was the source for many ideas in this debate has merit, but his alternative suggestion, that Hippias was the source for Sophocles and "perhaps then, too, for certain details in Herodotus' Debate" (p. 370), leads to an awkward chronological problem. Hippias' activity is likely to have been after the 440's, as Podlecki's own discussion reveals (*n.b.* p. 370, and notes 48-50, and cf. Zeller, *Philosophie d. Griech.*, I⁶ 1317). Against the view that he was already influential around 443 many arguments can be brought, none decisive, but cumulatively strong: Plato, *Apology* 19 e, implies he was still alive and active in 399 B.C.; the presentation of him in the *Protagoras* and the explicit statement in *Hippias maior* 282 e suggest that he was a good deal younger than Protagoras; while the testimony about Aphareus is contradictory (see *VS* 86 A 3), it is likely that Kirchner (*PA* 2769, cf. the stemma in *PA* 7716) is correct in thinking him the son (not grandson) of Hippias; hence his activity in the 350's implies a late date for Hippias. Indeed nothing apart from Podlecki's speculations represents Hippias as active in the 440's. If then the suggestion that Hippias' influence was behind the debate in Herodotus is correct, a later date is preferable.

A second suggestion about the date of the debate in Herodotus 3.80-83 is contained in a stimulating article by G. T. Griffith, "*Isegoria* in the Assembly at Athens," *Ancient Society and Institutions* (Studies presented to V. Ehrenberg, Oxford 1966) 115-138. Griffith restates an old observation, that the word *demokratia* is absent from the debate, and uses this to date its ultimate origin:

> Its absence from the celebrated debate . . . is certainly very striking, as Vlastos remarks . . . and it seems best explained by assuming (what seems likely anyway) an early written source used by Herodotus for his account of the debate. . . . I suggest that the place and time most likely to produce such a source was Ionia in the years before the Ionian revolt. There monarchy was still a live proposition as a form of government. . . . An intellectual justification of monarchy applied to a situation at the court of Persia seems less a waste of time coming from an Ionian aristocrat in those circumstances than from any other Greek living elsewhere . . . (132 n. 4).

It is easy to raise petulant objections against this argument: Is this an adequate statement of the function of the debate? Is the debate essentially an "intellectual justification of monarchy"? Were later discussions of Persian monarchy, e.g. the *Cyropaedeia*, "a waste of time"? Is it likely that theoretical discussions of the forms of government were being written before the Ionian revolt? But these questions should not distract us from the central question to which Griffith has once again called our attention. Why does the word *demokratia* not occur in a passage where it would be fully appropriate? This is a difficult question, a bit like being asked why mermaids do not exist, but I feel an answer can be given to it. Indeed, two answers:

First, the word is not common anywhere in Herodotus. The noun occurs in 6.43.3 and 6.131.1; the related verb in 4.137.2 and 6.43.3: four instances. The occurrences in 6.43.3 refer back to this debate in book 3 without embarrassment or any sign that Herodotus is now, belatedly, modernizing his terminology. The reason for the comparative rarity of the word throughout Herodotus is not, I believe, that Herodotus failed to modernize sources written before the word came into common use, but rather that Greek provided a wide field of words of roughly similar meaning and that Herodotus had a large range of alternatives.

The choice of words within this field was not, however, purely random; hence a second explanation for the absence of *demokratia* from the debate. As Vlastos points out, "*Demokratia* is a utility word. It would be hard to imagine a simpler, more exact, and more serviceable label for the Greek form of popular government. *Isonomia* belongs to a totally different sort of linguistic genre. It is far more a banner than a label." (I quote from Vlastos' second essay on *isonomia*, published in *Isonomia*, edited by J. Mau and G. Schmidt [Berlin 1964] 8.) This illuminating statement, it seems to me, has important implications for the study of the debate, not least for the question of its dating. It makes it perfectly clear why, when popular government is first alluded to by its advocate Otanes in 3.80.6, the word *isonomia*, not *demokratia*, is chosen. Otanes naturally wants the "banner" word, the *onoma panton kalliston*, the "finest name of all," as he himself says. In the same section other expressions denoting democratic government are used, *plethos archon* and *to plethos aexein*. Here again, I submit, the choice is not random but deliberate. The reiterated word, *plethos*, emphasizes the quantitative appeal of such a government and prepares us for the *sententia* with which the speech closes: ἐν γὰρ τῷ πολλῷ ἔνι τὰ πάντα, "for in the many all things are contained."

In the next speech, Megabyxos' argument for oligarchy, the speaker begins, perhaps quite unconsciously, by picking up the terminology just used. Once again *plethos* is used where we might have expected *demokratia*. But Megabyxos, like Otanes, is eager to find emotionally charged words; he too has no need for "*demokratia*." Instead he quickly begins to speak in ways that will put popular government in the most unfavorable light. For example, ὁμίλου γὰρ ἀχρηίου οὐδέν ἐστι ἀξυνετώτερον οὐδὲ ὑβριστότερον, "nothing is more irrational or presumptuous than a useless crowd" (3.81.1). It is the connotation of the words he is interested in, not their denotation. A phrase like *demou akolastou*, "ill-disciplined *demos*" (3.81.2), is exactly what he wants.

Darius' critique of his predecessors' arguments begins by reverting to use of the word *plethos*. But soon his language becomes more original and interesting. In 3.82.1 he uses the odd collocation *demou aristou*. Here again, I think, the word choice is significant, for it underlines a weakness in Megabyxos' position, namely that he argued from the worst abuses in a democracy rather than by considering the typical or best examples of each form of government. Moreover, this phrase implicitly prepares the ground for Darius' own ingenious case, in which he will argue that monarchy is inevitable and, in fact, best for the mass of citizens.

Finally when Herodotus summarizes Otanes' position in 3.83.1 he uses Otanes' own description, *isonomia*. Thus there are very few instances in the entire debate where *demokratia* could have been as appropriately used as the alternative expressions actually adopted. Perhaps the only example is *demou archontos* in 3.82.4, a perfectly normal Greek expression. It would be very difficult, I believe, to construct a sound statistical argument based on the absence of *demokratia* on four pages of Oxford text. Nor does it seem plausible that Herodotus, of all writers, should so slavishly have followed some early written source that he failed to introduce here a word which he elsewhere used. Herodotus is enough of a verbal craftsman to have had better reasons than *that* for the choice of his language. A recognition that speakers in a debate would be concerned with the emotional effects of their language is, I believe, precisely that reason.

There are further objections to the view put forth by Griffith. The threefold division of constitutions may itself be later than the date Griffith suggests for the source; cf. Walbank on Polybius 6.3.5; Pindar, *Pythian II* 86-88, is perhaps the earliest example. Moreover, there is a trace of a sixfold theory in Herodotus, as H. Ryffel, *Metabole Politeion* (Bern 1949) 65 n. 196, indicates. This classification seems decidedly later than Griffith's theory would allow. Further, if one wishes to argue from the absence of *demokratia*, what will one make of the presence of *oligarchia*, a word elsewhere attested only well after the Ionian revolt? Neither argument is decisive, and we cannot insist on an early origin for this debate on the basis of vocabulary studies of one or two words.

Is there then, it may be asked, any secure basis for assigning an absolute date to the debate? Until a clearer consensus is reached on the problem of the composition of Herodotus' history should we not simply say that he was writing some time between the 450's and the 420's and let it go at that? Perhaps, but several considerations point to the later rather than the earlier end of the range for the final form of the debate. In setting forth three of those reasons let me emphasize that I am concerned with the debate as Herodotus finally composed it; that some form of it might have been found in an earlier writer is a possibility on which I prefer not to speculate. The three considerations are:

1. The debate shows signs of relatively advanced political theorizing, not only in the classification of constitutions, but also, in Darius' speech, a sense of dynamic which converts one form into another. Moreover there are some signs, especially in Darius' speech, of sophistic influence; cf. H. Appfel, *Die Verfassungsdebatte bei Herodot* (Erlangen 1957) 94-95, and A. W. H. Adkins, *Merit and Responsibility*, 178.

2. The view that democracy turns into monarchy by the dominance of a single man who puts down those cabals of friends which in a democracy manipulate public business is, as I have suggested in the main body of this work, most likely to have been developed only after the tendency to concentrate leadership in a single man was observed and criticized, hence during Pericles' career, probably the latter part of it, or even later. (Old Comedy's criticism that Pericles acted like a tyrant or divinity is not found before Pericles' last ten years or so: Cratinus, *Cheirons* [note esp. frs. 240, 241, 241 B, 242 A, and cf. Adespota fr. 99] is probably 436-431; the attack is less clear elsewhere in Cratinus, but see *Thrattai* fr. 71, whose date, as Geissler saw, is probably later than Edmonds' conjecture of 442. The *Nemesis* [fr. 113] is probably 432/1, see F. R. B. Godolphin *CP* 26 [1931] 423-426. Telecleides' dates are difficult to determine but the late 430's seem best for frs. 17, 42, and 44 A, B. The mention of Cleon in Hermippus fr. 46 points to a late date for it, and no one, I think, would wish to put Eupolis fr. 403 much before 430. Adespota fragments 60 and 99 are undatable.)

The allusion in 3.82.4 to the leader as *prostas tis tou demou* also points to a relatively late date; cf. Chapter 3 above, *Prostates tou demou*.

3. The motif of Otanes' withdrawal from competition for

supreme power is, as I have tried to point out in Chapter 4 above, Otanes' Withdrawal, an important one and integral to the whole development of the debate. It is most likely to have been emphasized when Athenian *chrestoi*, many who once held views that were probably much like Otanes', were becoming increasingly disaffected from the life of the city. This too points, I believe, to the late 430's or the 420's.

On the Date of pseudo-Xenophon's
Constitution of Athens

UNQUESTIONABLY one of the most important works for the study of Athenian domestic politics is the short pamphlet preserved with Xenophon's works, often called the *Constitution of Athens*, or less justifiably, the *Old Oligarch*. But since it is difficult to date the work precisely, its exact significance remains in dispute. Useful discussions and bibliography can be found in Hartvig Frisch's edition (Copenhagen 1942) esp. 47-62, and in G. Bowersock, *HSCP* 71 (1966) 33-38, both of whom maintain dates before the outbreak of the Peloponnesian war, and in A. W. Gomme, *HSCP* Suppl. Vol. 1 (1940) 211-245, reprinted in *More Essays* 38-69, who dates it between 420 and 415. Kirchoff's position (*Abhandlungen* Berlin Ph.-Hist. Klasse 1878, 1-27) is between these two groups, and his termini, 432/1-414/3 seem to me to be sound, even if his exact date (first half of 424) claims excessive precision. With a dating within his termini the work fits neatly into the pattern which has been sketched in this work. To some, however, above all to the advocates of a date before the war, my treatment of the pamphlet will seem controversial. Since the most recent article on the subject, Bowersock's 1966 *Harvard Studies* essay (cf. his contribution to the Loeb Xenophon *Scripta Minora* [London 1968]), maintains an early date (443), some justification of my treatment is perhaps necessary. (See, however, D. M. Lewis' telling review of the Loeb Xenophon *Scripta Minora, CR* N.S. 19 [1969] 45-47.)

The echoes of speeches which Thucydides ascribes to Pericles in the last years of his life (*n.b.* pseudo-Xenophon 2.14 and Thucydides 1.143.5), the phrase *peri tou polemou* in 3.2 so brusquely dismissed by Bowersock (p. 35), and sentences such as this: ". . . they now manage in the following manner: their property they place about the islands relying on their command of the sea, but the Attic soil they suffer being laid waste, because they know that if they take pity on this, they will lose other and greater advantages" (2.16, trans. H. Frisch, cf. Thucydides 2.14), all seem to me to speak strongly for a date early in the Archidamian war. That the author should say that the *demos* under these circumstances *adeos zei* (2.14 *ad fin.*) is more revealing, *pace* Bowersock p. 34, about the narrowness of perspective and arrogance of view in this work than of the historical circumstances of its composition. Nor does Bowersock's explication of 3.11, for all its utility, compel an early dating. I will not dispute that the three historical precedents cited refer to a period no later than 446, for this is not the central issue. The real question is whether the author could have found in the next twenty years of Attic history better examples to support his case. To this I think we must give a firm No. Bowersock alleges the case of Samos, but with obvious and justified caution. He concedes that "there is certainly no reason to think that the Athenians themselves either installed or actively supported the oligarchs on Samos" (pp. 37-38), but insists that the fact that "an oligarchic rule was tolerated" would have been sufficient to provide the author with a strong clear example. Indeed he contends "It is inconceivable that anyone who had lived through the time of the Samian revolt would not have mentioned it in an account of the ruinous incompatibility of democracy and oligarchy."

But this misstates the treatise's position. Its author is not arguing a generalized statement that democracy and oligarchy cannot coexist, but something much more specific, ὁποσάκις δ' ἐπεχείρησαν αἱρεῖσθαι τοὺς βελτίστους, οὐ συνήνεγκεν αὐτοῖς—"every time when they have tried to side with the aristocracy they have been unfortunate" (trans. Frisch). Thus what is needed for illustration are instances of clear choice, where Athens turned its back on the *demos* and supported the upper classes. The emphasis in the passage is quite strong: the author uses forms of *haireo* six times in the two sections under consideration and begins with an explicit statement that he is concerned with cities in *stasis*. Examples of Athenians preferring the upper classes to the *demos* are not likely to have been numerous, and Samos was not a satisfactory one.

Furthermore, to adduce Samos as an example would have overburdened the argument. It would have implied a further proposition, the "incompatibility of democracy and oligarchy," the desirability of eliminating nondemocratic regimes whenever they occur. The author is too cautious for this. He wisely contents himself with the much securer position that Athens is sensible in supporting the *demos* when *stasis* breaks out. The Athenians learned this lesson in the 440's; hence there were few possible examples afterwards. The tenses too emphasize the difference between past and present policy. Thus I am unpersuaded by Bowersock's attempts to revive the early dating of this treatise.

Bibliography

In CONSTRUCTING this bibliography I have attempted to list only those works which seem to me truly fundamental. As a result many works important for the understanding of individual points or problems are mentioned only in the footnotes. I have also excluded from this list some very important and often cited works listed under "Abbreviations" above.

A.W.H. Adkins, *Merit and Responsibility* (Oxford 1960).

G. M. Calhoun, *Athenian Clubs in Politics and Litigation* (Bulletin of the University of Texas, no. 262, Austin, Texas 1913).

K. J. Dover, ΔΕΚΑΤΟΣ ΑΥΤΟΣ, *Journal of Hellenic Studies* 80 (1960) 61-77.

V. Ehrenberg, *The People of Aristophanes* (Oxford 1951).

W. S. Ferguson, "The Salaminioi of Heptaphylai and Sounion," *Hesperia* 7 (1938) 1-74.

M. I. Finley, "The Athenian Demagogues," *Past and Present* 21 (1962) 3-24.

C. Hignett, *A History of the Athenian Constitution* (Oxford 1952).

A.H.M. Jones, *Athenian Democracy* (Oxford 1957).

N. M. Pusey, "Alcibiades and *to philopoli*," *Harvard Studies in Classical Philology* 51 (1940) 215-231.

O. Reverdin, "Remarques sur la vie politique d'Athènes au Ve siècle," *Museum Helveticum* 2 (1945) 201-212.

J. Toeppfer, *Attische Genealogie* (Berlin 1889).

Index

Italic numbers (followed by a colon) give line or section references in the ancient work.

Acestor, 130
Adams, John Quincy, 164
Adkins, A.W.H., 42n14, 106n27, 205
Aelian, *Varia Historia, 11.9*: 38, 56; *12.43*: 158
Aelius Aristeides, scholia to, *Dindorf III 446*: 6n4
Aeschines, *1.25*: 133n86; *39*: 63n54
Aeschines, associate of Cleon, 29n47, 130
Aeschylus, *Suppliants 963*: 111n38, 113n45
agathos polites, 48
agoraioi, 154f
Aischron, 156n40
Alcibiades, 70ff, 147, 158, 164; and Hyperbolus, 27, 79-84, 135; and Nicias, 140f, 162; speech in Thucydides, 21, 102
Alcmaeon of Croton, *VS 24 B 5*: 56
Alcmaeonidae, 12-14, 19.
See also genē
alliances, *see* coalitions
amicitia, 64n58, 65n59
Anaxagoras, 69, 96n13
Andocides, 102, 161f; *1, 13 and 15*: 28n43; *4*: 79, 136n88; *4.4*: 27; *4.8*: 102; *4.33*: 75n67; fragment concerning Hyperbolus, 81
Andrewes, A., 95n12, 125
Androcles, 143, 155n40
Anthemion, 165
Antiphanes, 158f
Anytus, 165f
Aphareus, 201
Appfel, H., 205
apragmones, 180n70
Aristogeiton, 161
Archedemus, 35, 139n3
Archidamus, King of Sparta, 49, 127

Areopagus, Council of, 9, 38
aretē, 42
Aristides, 16f, 27, 55f, 76
Aristophanes, 108, 133, 192; *Acharnians*, 180, *38*: 116; *134-74*: 130n76; *Babylonians*, 168n55; *Birds*, 180; *Clouds 399ff*: 130n76; *876*: 166n54; *1187*: 101; *Frogs 718-37*: 190f; *Knights*, 96, 176, 181; *75*: 126n68; *178-89*: 90n4, 176; *188-92*: 163; *191-93*: 110, 175; *217-19*: 175f; *732*: 97; *748*: 103n24; *786f*: 101; *852-57*: 129; *875-78*: 98n15; *1103*: 131; *1121-30*: 113n46, 179; *1128*: 111; *1256*: 130; *1340-44*: 97, 107, 142n9; *Lysistrata 545-48*: 102f; *Peace*, 180; *680f*: 113n46; *756*: 129; *Wasps*, 119n56; *42ff*: 130; *410-13*: 103; *418*: 130n77; *474*: 102; *599ff*: 130; *1220-21*: 129f; *1232*: 92n9; *1238*: 29n47; *1244*: 130; *fr. 108*: 102n21
Aristophanes, scholia to, *Clouds 624*: 114n46; *Frogs 679*: 145n15; *Knights 129 and 132*: 106n28; *225*: 152n32; *627*: 152n32; *1304*: 145n15; *Peace 681*: 142n7; *Wasps 42*: 130n76
Aristotle, *Nicomachean Ethics 1156 a 6ff*: 46n20; *1169 b 6*: 39n10; *Politics 1284 a 21*: 40n11; *1287 a 35-38*: 44; *1302 b 11-13*: 198n85; *1305 a 11ff*: 144; *1320 a 6ff*: 142n9; *Rhetoric 1359 a 30ff*: 125; *1387 a*: 155; *1408 b 25*: 127n68, *See also Athenaion Politeia*
Arrowsmith, W., 50n28
Aspasia, 69

213